To: _____

From: _____

Date: _____

STAND FIRM

DAY BY DAY

Let Nothing Move You

A Men's Devotional from Walk Thru the Bible

Matt Erickson and Tammy Drolsum, *editors*

PUBLISHING GROUP

www.BHPublishingGroup.com

NASHVILLE, TENNESSEE

Dedication

To our dear friend Walt Wiley, who is making a lasting impact for God's kingdom through the art of biblical encouragement. Walk Thru the Bible will be forever grateful for his fifteen years of service with us—he simply made us better.

Introduction

Our hope and prayer is that Stand Firm: Let Nothing Move You will help you to do just that—stand firm in a continually shifting world. We live in tumultuous, trying times. Life has always been difficult, but it's hard to deny that the world is moving faster and faster these days. Change seems to be the only constant.

And yet God's Word is an unchanging rock, suitable for all times and places and people. The Scriptures are ancient and contemporary, having been breathed out by the "Ancient of Days" (Dan. 7:22), who is "a helper who is always found in times of trouble" (Ps. 46:1). Our God and Father, "the One who is, who was, and who is coming" (Rev. 1:4) is able to guide us safely through this life and into the next as we learn to trust Him. He loves us (John 3:16) and has promised to do so (Prov. 3:5–6).

A good devotional book reminds us of these things, in big and small ways. It helps us keep the big picture in mind—God's grace—as we go about our daily life, facing inevitable challenges at work and in relationships, as well as temptations, weakness, and pain, but also great joy and blessing. Our hope is that as you read these devotionals, you will read them through the lens of your Savior's love for you, and His Spirit's empowering you for joyful obedience. And we pray that they will increase your hunger for His unchanging Word of hope. Stand Firm, dear brothers, and let nothing move you.

Matt Erickson

Prepare for Takeoff

Be strengthened by the Lord and by His vast strength.
(Eph. 6:10)

Launching Out

By the time a space mission takes place, astronauts have gone through hundreds of simulated launches and landings and virtually everything else in between. Ron Garan, who flew into space on the shuttle *Discovery*, says that because so many things can go wrong during launch, most of their training—as much as 90 percent—is focused around that one phase of the flight.

That's an interesting ratio, especially when it appears on the first page of a new devotional book, whether you're starting out on New Year's Day or at any new beginning point during any season on the calendar of your life. Starting right is way more than half the battle.

Gearing Up

So as you prepare for the 365 days that stretch out ahead of you, take this opportunity to look at more than just your quiet-time habits. Do you need to forgive anybody? Is your schedule set up to allow some space for both necessary rest and unexpected intrusions? Are you withholding anything from God's reach—a particular habit or attitude or some other treasured entitlement?

Is your heart as open and ready as it can possibly be, expecting this to be the most positive, most powerful year of change and spiritual growth you've experienced in a long time?

Ephesians 6:13 says to "take up the full armor of God, so that you may be able to resist in the evil day, and having prepared everything, to take your stand." If you're serious about starting right, there's a good chance you're going places.

Bottom Line

This is more than just a new day. It's the start of something special in your life.

Responding to Hurt

As the One who called you is holy, you also are to be holy in all your conduct. (1 Pet. 1:15)

A Worldly Response

Have you ever been hurt? A friend betrays you. A coach cuts you. A company fires you. A girlfriend rejects you. Your wife walks out on you. Those closest to us can hurt us the deepest.

What is your typical response to these kinds of rejections? Do you want to hurt them back? Physically attack them? Seek revenge? See them in court? If no one could possibly know you were behind it, would you key their car? Slash their tires? Send incriminating letters to their boss and friends? Take measures to reveal their sins publicly? The prevailing thought in the world system around us is to get even, to hit back, to make those pay who hurt us.

A Christian's Response

The Christians living in ancient Rome knew hurt. They were enduring the wrath of Emperor Nero, who accused the Christian community of starting a fire in Rome that they didn't start. They were on the receiving end of some extremely painful abuse, and they likely wanted to attack their attackers, persecute their persecutors, and hurt the ones hurting them.

But the apostle Peter told them (and us) that Christians don't respond that way. He says we are "to be holy in all [our] conduct." The word *holy* means "distinct, separate, not the same, out of the ordinary, unusual."

When the hurts come, and they will, a Christian responds with love, grace, humility, and forgiveness. In this way we reflect the nature of Jesus. In this way we are different.

Bottom Line

Believers in Christ have been commanded to live lives of holiness even when people hurt us. Is your response different?

Snow Days

A Sabbath rest remains for God's people.
For the person who has entered His rest has rested
from his own works, just as God did from His. (Heb. 4:9–10)

The Consequences

Several catastrophic accidents in recent century—Three Mile Island, the fatal navigational error of Korean Air Lines 007, Chernobyl, Exxon Valdez—each occurred in the middle of the night with fatigue-stressed operators. That's probably not just a coincidence.

When we ignore our need for rest, we do so at the peril of others and ourselves. When we don't rest, we lose our way. We miss the compass points that show us where to go. We make faulty judgments. We miss the solitude that gives us wisdom. Consequently, our lives become endangered. Failure to take time to rest can be costly.

The Benefits

Rest is not optional. Rest was never meant to be a luxury but rather a necessity for growth, maturity, and health. We don't rest because our work is done; we rest because God created our physical, emotional, and spiritual components with a need for breaks.

When you were a child and woke up to a large, overnight snowfall, you probably hopped out of bed and immediately turned on the radio or TV to see if school was called off. When it was canceled, you rejoiced. You had a free day, completely unplanned, in which you could do anything you wanted. It was a gift. The gift of rest.

Determine to plan your own snow days, a weekly time off from your responsibilities, to rest your body and to recharge your soul.

Bottom Line

Rest is not optional. God graciously commands it.

Tight Turns

If you respond to my warning, then I will pour out my spirit on you and teach you my words. (Prov. 1:23)

Turning From

Have you ever been challenged by the sharp turn of an unexpected curve in the highway? Were you daydreaming or driving a little above the speed limit? Were you on your cell phone or taking a sip of coffee? Was it a close call? Did your reflexes jerk the steering wheel too far? Whatever the circumstances, we've all been shocked by the hairpin curves of country highways or the sharp curves that life can throw at us sometimes.

Pete Seeger's number-one hit song of the 1960s was "Turn, Turn, Turn," based on the opening verses of Ecclesiastes 3. Turning is a common biblical principle. We usually think of it as turning *from* something—from sin, from temptation, from selfishness, from idolatry, from laziness. This turning away is what Jesus means when He tells sinners they must repent (see Luke 13:3).

Turning To

We might first think of turning as a *turning away* from something, but we also need to focus on the positive side of turning. When we turn away from one thing, we're always turning *toward* another. So when we turn away from sin (when we repent), we're also turning toward Jesus. When we turn away from selfishness, we turn and start serving others. God wants us to replace the old way of sin and self with the new way of righteousness and love. This is always a turning away, as well as a turning *to*.

Bottom Line

See if there's something you need to turn away from, then concentrate on the positive side of what you're turning toward.

Can You Be Bothered?

When I heard these words, I sat down and wept.
I mourned for a number of days, fasting and praying
before the God of heaven. (Neh. 1:4)

The Reaction to the Problem

Nobody likes to hear bad news, but it often comes rushing in like an unexpected downpour. Nehemiah experienced that. In short order he was told that the walls of Jerusalem were crumbling, the holy city was a wreck, and the people were suffering from a severe lack of leadership.

When he heard this dismal report, Nehemiah had two choices. One, he could toss up his hands in despair and say, "What can I do? I'm only one guy!" Or two, he could allow the news to move him to action. As we know, Nehemiah chose option two and led the people to rebuild the walls. The fact that countless books have been written and numerous sermons preached lauding Nehemiah's leadership skills suggests he made the right choice.

The Response to the Problem

Nehemiah's choice is our choice, too. We can choose to ignore problems and harden our hearts to the things of most importance to God, or we can choose to make ourselves available for whatever role He would have us play in making things better. It's all about our hearts. A calloused heart builds up an immunity to suffering and avoids inconvenient problems. A tender heart, on the other hand, not only sees the need but surrenders with compassion to the will of God, becoming an active solution to the problem. Which kind of heart do you have?

Bottom Line

God has put you in a position to help meet some of the needs of our world. Are you making yourself available to Him?

Singing Her Praises

Let her works praise her at the city gates. (Prov. 31:31)

Just Say It

The final chapter of Proverbs extols the virtues of a wife and mother who is a woman of character and whose truest and deepest beauty lasts. Her deeds are to be praised "at the city gates"—that is, people will openly talk about what a blessing she is to her husband and family.

Well, let the praise start with you. Take time today to mentally enumerate the many things your wife does that are worthy of praise. Then *speak* of those things often. Point them out to your kids within earshot of your wife. Verbalize that you appreciate who she is and what she does. Don't just assume she knows it. Even if she does, she needs to keep hearing it from you.

Words Have Power

Ongoing affirmation is vital to the health of your marriage. Even if you don't consider yourself the verbal type, your wife really needs to hear words of praise coming from you. Sometimes guys feel the feelings but forget to say the words. Make it a point to tell your wife, out of the blue, something you appreciate about her. Say it in terms of who she is as well as what she does. And brag on her to others. One big way guys can honor their wives is by speaking to others of her qualities.

Honest praise enriches marriage. When a man publicly and sincerely tells others, "I have the most incredible wife," he is touching her heart and bolstering the strength of his marriage.

Bottom Line

Words of praise should water your marriage like the rain regularly waters the earth.

Full Body Workout

*I want their hearts to be encouraged and joined together in love,
so that they may have all the riches of assured understanding, and
have the knowledge of God's mystery—Christ. (Col. 2:2)*

Personal Training

Ever try to lose weight or get yourself in better shape? Dumb question. Most guys want a fitter physique. Many of us have even purchased some sort of workout equipment. Sales for the home fitness industry total more than $4 billion every year. But most of those treadmills and weight machines end up gathering dust, catching our laundry, or cluttering up the garage.

While a majority of guys fail to follow through on their good intentions, some do accomplish their goal of body transformation. Their not-so-secret tip for success? *Get a workout partner*—somebody committed to giving encouragement and getting stronger together.

Part of a Group

The same principle works in building spiritual muscle. Many men want to become more Christlike. We join a church, but we slip into the service on Sunday morning and slip out the minute it's over—then wonder why nothing changes inside. What we need is a spiritual workout partner. Even better might be a whole group of Christians with similar goals and interests. Paul writes in Colossians 2:2 about the encouragement that comes from being "joined together." He says that we "fulfill the law of Christ" when we commit to "carry one another's burdens" (Gal. 6:2).

Believers have always grown stronger in groups, not when left to ourselves and our easy excuses. Small groups provide a quality place to firm up our faith—where we can ask questions, share our struggles, build friendships, and help one another through life's journey.

Bottom Line

Small groups can help you grow into a spiritual muscleman.

A Critical Spirit

Who are you to criticize another's household slave?
Before his own Lord he stands or falls. And he will stand.
For the Lord is able to make him stand. (Rom. 14:4)

Legalism and a Critical Tongue

The Pharisees saw themselves as morality police. They assumed the duty of correcting public and private morals. They judged others by their own rigorous standards—even stricter than the Bible's. Jesus called them "blind guides" (Matt. 23:16). They were super-attuned to the tiniest faults in others—mere "specks" of sin—but couldn't see the colossal errors in themselves—huge, vision-blocking "logs" (see Matt. 7:3–6).

The irony is that the Pharisees didn't see themselves as legalistic, judgmental, or hypocritical. In their own eyes they were sincere followers of a righteous God. But to Jesus they were afflicted with terminal legalism. Legalism is invisible to the legalist, but there is one way to tell if you've got it.

Who Are You to Criticize?

A critical tongue is a sure sign of a legalistic heart. Paul asks, "Who are you to criticize?" (Rom. 14:4). Your true master is Jesus. You answer to *Him*, as do all your neighbors, friends, family, and even your enemies. They do not answer to you; they do not live to please you. So when you indulge the sins of the tongue—when you criticize, judge, backbite, or gossip—you usurp Jesus' rightful place. You judge one of His servants, and you reinforce your own self-righteous pride. Every Christian ultimately answers to God alone. It's time for us to bite our tongues and remember that "love covers a multitude of sins" (1 Pet. 4:8).

Bottom Line

We need to remember that God is the righteous judge, and we're not.

Self-justification

They are justified freely by His grace through the redemption that is in Christ Jesus. (Rom. 3:24)

Who Are You?

From childhood we are programmed to seek approval. Kids and youth glance nervously at parents and peers, eager for affirmation. Children whose worth is not affirmed in childhood often suffer emotional and spiritual problems in adulthood. The search for approval is part of a larger quest for identity. *Who are you? Why are you here? What is your worth?* Countless people work hard all their lives to answer these questions but never find satisfactory answers. The follower of Jesus, however, need not perpetually struggle with these questions. There is an answer.

Whose Are You?

As a child of God, you derive your identity from Christ. You are united to Him by faith (see Rom. 6:1–10, for example). You share Christ's nature, His status, His history, His destiny, His possessions, and even His name. You are the man God says you are, no matter what the people around you say. Your Father in heaven loves you just as He loves His Son (see John 17:23). Therefore, His affirmation is all the affirmation you'll ever need. To esteem Him is to esteem yourself (see 1 Cor. 1:30–31).

So don't let other people define you. Don't let them send you on a futile quest to prove your worth. It's not only exhausting; it doesn't work. Find your worth in Jesus instead. In Him you have nothing left to prove.

Bottom Line

You can't impress God, and—guess what?—you don't need to. You already have all the affirmation from Him that you need. Let this truth define you.

Presents from Heaven

*Sons are indeed a heritage from the LORD,
children, a reward. (Ps. 127:3)*

The Gift That Takes

The Bible makes clear that our children are a gift from God. When things are going great, when our young kids draw pictures of us to put on the refrigerator, they feel like a gift. When they hit their teens, however, they may not feel so much like a present. But unlike a gift from a store, your children are nonreturnable and nonrefundable. God will eventually want them back from you but not until He achieves His aims for both parent and child.

The Gift That Gives

Most of us Christian dads are pretty clear on the idea that God is using us to mold and shape the character and heart of our kids. But we are often less clear on the fact that God is using our kids to mold and shape *us*. To be a good dad is to live a sacrificial life. It comes with the job description. We invest our time, energy, money, emotions, blood, sweat, and tears into the lives of our kids. And we keep on doing it over the long haul.

It's not easy. But when we love our kids even during the times they break our hearts, we gain deeper insight into the heart of our Father in heaven who relentlessly loves and gives to us. God is using our kids to make us more noble, more mature, and more like Jesus. And like every worthwhile thing in life, the challenges only make the rewards sweeter.

Bottom Line

Identify five ways God is using your children to shape your heart. Then pray that you'll learn each lesson well.

Our Forgiving God

Tear your hearts, not just your clothes, and return to the LORD your God. For He is gracious and compassionate, slow to anger, rich in faithful love, and He relents from sending disaster. (Joel 2:13)

Great Compassion

It's easy for us to feel magnanimous when we show a little compassion. Our children mess up, and we cut them a little slack. A coworker drops the ball, and we cover for him. Our wife says something hurtful, and we let it roll off our back.

But our efforts to show compassion will always pale compared to what Almighty God demonstrates toward His people. In the Old Testament they were always turning their backs on Him, marrying people they were told not to marry, worshipping false gods, and committing countless wicked acts in direct, deliberate violation of His commands. While God did judge the Israelites for their sins, He remained ready to forgive when the people turned back to Him.

Ultimate Forgiveness

Our culture and even our churches tend to judge people and write them off. Many states have enacted "three strikes and you're out" laws that keep people in jail without hope of release. Although such measures are often necessary for the safety of society, God never throws us out of the game spiritually. He remains gracious and loving, even when we ignore Him or break His laws. God always forgives when we turn our hearts toward Him and return to following His ways.

We deserve destruction, and yet we receive Jesus. We should be made to eat our words and work off our debt, but we receive freedom and grace instead.

Bottom Line

Look for ways to live out God's example of forgiveness and compassion—at home, in your past, over all your internal objections.

Under Construction

Give my son Solomon a whole heart to keep and to carry out all Your commands, Your decrees, and Your statutes, and to build the temple for which I have made provision. (1 Chron. 29:19)

House Building

Have you ever watched a house being built? After the foundation is laid, the walls and roof seem to spring up in a few days. But then it takes months before the house is in move-in condition. A six-thousand-square-foot custom home averages about seven months to build. Of that time just over three weeks is needed to frame the house and put on the roof. A bulk of the time is used on finer carpentry and finishing items. While the outside of the house looks good rather quickly, the intricate work that makes the inside of the house structurally sound and livable takes months to complete.

Heart Building

As Christians we need to maintain that same "building" mind-set in our personal lives. Instead of concentrating on our external appearance, we need to focus the vast majority of our efforts on the inside. God is more concerned with the state of our heart than with our looks. King David knew this and asked God to "give my son Solomon a whole heart to keep and to carry out all Your commands" (1 Chron. 29:19). The heart is what matters most.

Building a heart for God doesn't happen overnight. It requires discipline and effort, consistency in reading and applying God's Word, learning to serve others joyfully, and praying throughout the day. It takes time, but the work of creating a godly heart will build for you an incredible life.

Bottom Line

Think of one thing you can do to build your heart for God. Then do it.

Nonstop Praying

Pray constantly. (1 Thess. 5:17)

Like Breathing

Focused prayer is good. Time set aside to be with our heavenly Father is essential, pouring out our hearts to Him and hearing from Him. But prayer is not meant to be limited to particular times or locations. It's meant to be as constant as breathing. It's meant to occur throughout our day. It's meant to be an ongoing conversation where we ask for His assistance and look and listen for His help and leading.

Our relationship with God runs on prayer. It's the way we communicate with a God who is so close to us He has even taken up residence inside of us: "But the Counselor, the Holy Spirit—the Father will send Him in My name—will teach you all things and remind you of everything I have told you" (John 14:26). Prayer is at the center of our Christian experience. It is spiritual breathing for us.

Our Greatest Privilege

Whenever we think of prayer primarily as something we must do, as an obligation, as a religious duty, we err. We miss the whole point. We fail to see that communion with God is not only our purpose but also our greatest pleasure and privilege. The reality is, we are dependent creatures who are constantly in need, and prayer is the way God meets our needs. A lot of things won't happen in your life or in your relationship with Him apart from prayer. So learn to pray constantly.

Bottom Line

Is prayer always happening in your life? It should be a constant throughout your day. There's no better way to live.

A Sacred Workday

*Whatever you do, do it enthusiastically, as something done
for the Lord and not for men. (Col. 3:23)*

A Sudden Step Down

In the 1940s film *The Great McGinty*, the main character
cleans a table in his tiny restaurant while telling a patron, "I used
to be the governor of New York." In a flashback the movie then
explains how he tumbled from that high office to a humble job.

Many men today can relate somewhat to that story. Hard
economic times and a changing workplace have cost large numbers
of men both prestige and earning power. Some have been
forced to take entry-level jobs outside their chosen fields. And
the temptation, when life delivers a sudden demotion like that, is
to work halfheartedly, bogging down in bitterness and self-pity.

Consecrating Our Work

We sometimes forget the hard, tedious work done by some
of the Bible's greatest heroes. Paul was a bivocational minister,
earning his keep as a preacher by being a tentmaker, the equivalent
to today's leather worker. Before God could fully use Moses,
He let him tend sheep in the desert for forty years. Even Jesus
Himself spent more of His earthly years sanding and shaping
wood than He did teaching and healing.

The job itself, whether heralded or humble, is not what's
most important. It's our love relationship with God. The attitude
we bring to our work reflects what we believe about Him and
the degree of our love for Him. He is worthy of receiving our
best.

Bottom Line

We may feel we've been handed a job that's beneath us. But
when we consecrate our work to God, doing it wholeheartedly,
He can bear fruit through us.

That's Funny

Abraham fell facedown. Then he laughed and said to himself, "Can a child be born to a hundred-year-old man?" (Gen. 17:17)

Are You Kidding Me?

Does God speak to Joan Rivers? We'll probably never know, but He did speak to another elderly Jewish woman with a sly sense of humor: Sarah. Actually, she overheard what God had told Abraham, and the first response of both husband and wife was to laugh. When God revealed that He was about to bless this elderly couple with a son, they chuckled. God was a bit offended by Sarah's lack of faith but not her sense of humor. He even shared in the family joke by choosing the name Isaac for the child (which literally means "he laughed").

The Bond of Humor

Perhaps Abraham and Sarah had many other humorous exchanges that didn't find their way into the Bible. Other biblical couples were also placed in situations that no doubt prompted laughter. Just imagine what the jailer's wife said when her husband walked in the door with Paul and Silas. We can almost hear her say, "Should I set the table for two felons or four?"

Through good times and bad, humor permeates a marriage just like leaven works its way through a loaf. Laughter shared by a husband and wife ripples through an entire home, and it's a precious gift to pass on to our children. So don't let life's troubles cause you to lose your sense of perspective or your sense of humor. Actually, maintaining a sense of humor can give you a whole new perspective on your troubles.

Bottom Line

A marriage grows stronger when a husband and wife share lighthearted laughter that doesn't mock or tear down the other person.

A Good Example

Let your light shine before men, so that they may see your good works and give glory to your Father in heaven. (Matt. 5:16)

Rodney and Ginger

While explaining to his kids why he tries to be a good role model to them, Rick made the comment that he might be the only "Jesus" they ever see. The kids thought about it for a second, then one of them replied, "We see Jesus in Rodney and Ginger too."

Rodney and Ginger could not possibly have received a more sincere compliment. They had become close friends of the family through Little League baseball, and the way they lived their lives had left a lasting impression on Rick's kids. We need to remember that people are always watching us. We're always representing Christ. That ought to turn us back toward Him instead of relying on ourselves to try making a good impression.

Seeing Jesus

Letting Christ's light shine through you doesn't mean you're out to impress anybody. It's actually just the opposite. The good works you do are for the benefit of others and for the glory of God without regard for your own reputation. That doesn't mean you and your reputation don't benefit from the good things you do, but this shouldn't be your primary motivation.

Take a moment to do a quick evaluation of how things are going in your own walk with Christ. Are you letting your light shine? Are you seeking to glorify God? That's your calling, and Christ will enable you to do it.

Bottom Line

Let your light shine. And know that God will provide everything you need for this to happen.

Return of the King

This Jesus, who has been taken from you into heaven, will come in the same way that you have seen Him going into heaven. (Acts 1:11)

A Promise Made

Jesus promised to come back. Angels testified that He will return. The apostles and prophets repeatedly underscored that our King will return on a date known only to God. Therefore the only uncertainty is the timing, not the event itself.

We can easily get complacent about this—investing our time and attention in the here and now, conducting our daily lives as though the possibility of Jesus' soon return is so remote we essentially discount it—an attitude that would have been shocking to believers of earlier eras.

The Event Looms Large

How do we keep a sense of longing for His return? How do we shake off the complacency that creeps in? Perhaps it would help if we upped the "ouch factor." Sometimes we don't long for His presence because, frankly, life can be pretty good down here sometimes. Praying for the return of Jesus may come more naturally if you are persecuted, impoverished, imprisoned, sick, or sad. It may rarely cross your mind, however, if you're sporting a fat bank account and a bass boat.

One way to increase your expectation and focus is by deliberately investing in the kingdom of God to the point that it hurts a little bit—that it costs you—pouring more of yourself and your money into the things that matter to Jesus. After all, He could actually come this week.

Bottom Line

Does your support for the work of God reflect a belief that Jesus could come back at any moment?

Grounded in History

After He had suffered, He also presented Himself alive to them by many convincing proofs, appearing to them during 40 days and speaking about the kingdom of God. (Acts 1:3)

Eyes Wide Open

Becoming a Christian requires a leap of faith but not a blind leap. Anyone who receives Jesus does so by faith, but this faith rests on a mountain of evidence.

We were not there to see the resurrection with our own eyes, but the New Testament records many compelling accounts from those who were, not to mention repeated passages from the Old Testament (such as Isa. 53 and Ps. 22, written centuries beforehand) that so precisely detail the crucifixion and resurrection that it's hard to explain them away. Many of the early disciples suffered brutal deaths rather than deny their assertion that Jesus had risen from the grave and had spoken with them repeatedly. And how do we explain the conversion of the once rabidly anti-Christian Saul of Tarsus, who repeatedly stated that the resurrected Jesus had personally appointed him an apostle?

A Rational Leap

No one alive today ever saw George Washington take the oath of office, but we all believe he was the first United States president. Why? Because the history is so compelling. The faith to believe it is reasonable and rational. And the more you dig into the Bible, the more you'll find the same thing. You will discover the story of Jesus so powerful that you are willing to stake your life on it. And the more you stake your life on it, the stronger your faith will grow.

Bottom Line

You can stand firm on the evidence that Jesus was crucified to pay for our sins and rose on the third day.

Come Clean

*Confess your sins to one another and pray for one another,
so that you may be healed. The urgent request of a righteous
person is very powerful. (James 5:16)*

The Fatal Flaw

When New York's Citicorp tower was completed in 1977, many structural engineers hailed the tower for its technical elegance and singular grace. But a year after the building opened, the structural engineer, William J. LeMessurier, came to a frightening realization: some of the joints that should have been welded were bolted. Under severe winds, the building could buckle.

LeMessurier weighed his options. He confessed the mistake and corrected the problem. And though the repairs cost millions of dollars, his career and reputation were not destroyed but rather enhanced. One engineer commended his courage for admitting the problem and fixing it.

The Vital Fix

You may be at that point where you realize your life is like this flawed building. Although by all appearances you are strong, successful, and together, you know you have points of weakness that make you vulnerable to collapse. Sin is corroding the foundation of your life. What do you do? You come clean, get help, and fix it.

Confession is good for the soul. When we hide sin, we hide ourselves from others, and the darkness continues to grow. Today's verse suggests that we confess our sin first to God and then to those who have been affected by our sin. We need to come clean.

Bottom Line

Confess your sin. Get it out of your heart. Make it right. And move on.

Don't Give Up

You need endurance, so that after you have done God's will, you may receive what was promised. (Heb. 10:36)

The Easy Out

Often the easiest thing to do is to quit. Just give up. Return to the comfort and convenience of mediocrity. Forget about your dream, your passion, or your goal. Give in to the words of the critics, give up to the opposition, and give way to the obstacles. Simply tuck tail and run away.

But effective people are able to accomplish seemingly impossible tasks because they never give up. They never buckle under. Despite mounting criticism, intense opposition, and overwhelming obstacles, they persevere with determined resolve. They refuse to throw in the towel.

The Fight Within

Great power is embodied in persistence. The race is not always won by the fastest; the game is not always won by the strongest. Instead, the one who keeps on keeping on will receive "what was promised." Consider the postage stamp. Its usefulness consists in the ability to stick to one thing until it gets there.

When you are tempted to quit, resist. Endure in the battle until the evil day is over. Press on in the face of every reason to withdraw. Until the war is over, fight to the end. Until the race is finished, keep running. Until the wall is built, keep stacking bricks. Never give up. Never. The promises of God are always at the end. So don't quit. Don't give up.

Bottom Line

It is always too soon to quit. Keep persevering. Keep fighting.

Repeated Rescues

I sank to the foundations of the mountains;
the earth with its prison bars closed behind me forever!
But You raised my life from the Pit, LORD my God! (Jon. 2:6)

Jaws of Death

In the highlands of Scotland, sheep often wander off into precarious places looking for grass to eat. Often the sheep will jump down ten or twelve feet to a ledge with a patch of grass, and then they can't jump back up again. But the shepherd, hearing them bleating in distress, will not rescue them until they have eaten all the grass and are so faint they cannot stand. Why doesn't the shepherd attempt a rescue when the sheep first get into the predicament? Because the sheep are so focused on eating, they would dash away from the shepherd, tumble over the precipice, and destroy themselves.

Such was the case with Jonah. When he finally gave up all hope of surviving, God intervened and saved him. Jonah had to die to his own desires before he could live.

Jaws of Life

Sometimes we must experience the feeling of death before we can know the freedom of life. In a spiritual sense we must give up before we can be raised up. When we realize there's nothing more we can do, that's usually when God intervenes and saves us—the moment we have given up trying and cry out to Him for help, when we realize we can't liberate ourselves. In fact, this seems to be one of His specialties—delivering us from self-inflicted predicaments that leave us helpless. The truth is, we need a Savior from start to finish.

Bottom Line

We need to let go of our selfish, silly pursuits so God can give us the gift of grace and mercy.

Why Is This Happening?

We do not focus on what is seen, but on what is unseen. For what is seen is temporary, but what is unseen is eternal. (2 Cor. 4:18)

When You're Down

Some of life's challenges are completely out of our control, like an illness, accident, or job loss. Others are the result of bad decisions, like debt or marital strain. Over time these kinds of things can cause stress, impacting our health, relationships, productivity, and self-esteem. We become more impatient and quick to anger, prone to temptation by things that help us feel better, at least temporarily.

This happens because our focus has shifted. We're looking at the situation and its impact on us rather than focusing on God. If we're even praying at all (and that's a big "if"), our prayers tend to be complaints or pleas for deliverance. Our grateful, trusting hearts have gone into hiding.

Look In, Reach Up

So how should we respond when we find ourselves in a place of discouragement? A good place to start is a personal assessment: (1) Do I have sin in my life that I need to stop? (2) Do I harbor unforgiveness, bitterness, or resentment that has gone unchecked? (3) Have I been putting off doing something God has directed me to do?

If the answer to any of these questions is yes, God may be using your circumstances to get your focus back on Him. Spend time with Him in prayer. Meditate on His promises. And welcome the opportunity to grow in faith and perseverance.

Bottom Line

God can always be trusted to use your circumstances for your good and His glory. Continue to trust and obey.

Marriage Workout

The training of the body has a limited benefit,
but godliness is beneficial in every way, since it holds promise
for the present life and also for the life to come. (1 Tim. 4:8)

Turning Pain . . .

When we work out, we expect the soreness that comes from torn and strained muscles. We know that some pain and discomfort are necessary in order to build new muscle and get us into the shape we want to be in. The same is true in marriage. Since marriage is the union of two imperfect people, struggles and dissatisfaction are inherent. But clashes in marital relationships—painful and exasperating though they be—can make us stronger, develop godly character in us, and strengthen our faith for the long run.

Unfortunately, not all marital struggle results in spiritual maturity. We must first deal with two of the most persistent and damaging aspects of our sin nature: selfishness and pride. Our selfish nature tells us we deserve better, we should get even, or we should avoid further pain and just run. Meanwhile, pride keeps us from seeking and/or offering forgiveness. The result is further division, resentment, and regret. This is injury, not growth.

. . . into Gain

Spiritual muscle is developed when we acknowledge and confess our selfish, prideful ways and ask God to help us. Instead of focusing on the emotional toll that marriage sometimes takes, we must recognize the opportunity it presents us to love our wives the way Christ loved the church—selflessly and unconditionally, showing honor instead of contempt.

Bottom Line

Jesus calls us to abandon our self-defenses, bring our problems to Him, and learn to love. Pray and persevere in your marriage!

Risk and Reward

Faith Required

While his father cowered in fear, the courageous Jonathan took matters into his own hands. Flanked only by an armor bearer, he launched a surprise attack on an entire garrison of Philistines. It was a risky move that could have left him dead. But Jonathan was not going to sit back and do nothing.

Listen again to what he said: "Perhaps the LORD will help us." Is there a lesson here? Too often we wait for a perfect sign before we act. We suffer paralysis by analysis. Real, godly leaders, however, are willing to take risks. Without risk, where is faith?

Calculated Risk

We suffer today from a crisis of passivity, a failure to take decisive action when it is called for. What this really amounts to is a crisis of faith. Fear of disapproval or fear of failure often leads men to adopt a defensive posture, hiding behind vague claims of searching for "God's will" or "waiting on the Lord." Both of those are things we should do, of course, but God rarely serves up a burning-bush or wet-fleece experience. Instead, He expects us to prayerfully weigh our options, seek appropriate counsel, and then act. So ask God for wisdom, and trust that He's willing and able to guide you. Then act in faith.

Bottom Line

Following God is not a risk-free proposition. If we're not risking, we're not living by faith.

Get on the Mountain

The LORD said to Moses, "Come up to Me on the mountain and stay there so that I may give you the stone tablets with the law and commandments I have written for their instruction." (Exod. 24:12)

Moses' Ministry Objectives

In Exodus 24:1, God told Moses to come up to Him. But interestingly, Moses didn't immediately go up to see God. Instead, he went about doing God's work, speaking to the people, writing down God's laws, arranging an altar of worship. All good stuff, but what God really desired was face-to-face time with Moses. So God came back to Moses a second time and commanded, "Come up to Me on the mountain." Then God added a little tweak, "and stay there."

Like Moses we can easily allow ministry to get in the way of actual intimacy with God. And then when we do spend time with God, it can be rushed and superficial if we're not patient enough to stay in His presence long enough for our hearts and minds to quiet down and listen.

Good Versus Great

Perhaps Moses thought he was too busy for the mountain. Maybe he thought his calendar was too full of important activities to spend time with God. But that's wrong thinking. Ministry is important to God, but time with Him is crucial. Like Moses we can get this backward, forsaking the great in pursuit of the good. What we don't realize is that time on the mountain fuels ministry. Time in the Word and prayer fills up our empty hearts so that we have something to give to others.

Bottom Line

Being busy for God is a cheap substitute for time with God.

Reacting to Upheaval

Those who were scattered went on their way preaching the message of good news. (Acts 8:4)

Suffering Is Inevitable

Jesus told His friends, "You will have suffering in this world" (John 16:33). His words were quickly fulfilled. The early church suffered severe persecution to the point that all the believers except the apostles had to flee Jerusalem.

Put yourself in their sandals. You embrace the message of salvation, you are filled with joy, you feel courage rising within you, and then suddenly you're facing incredible opposition. Dark forces foment violence against your family. Your world is turned upside down as you hit the road, looking for a new place to live and work. Scary. Bewildering. Painful.

Misery Is Optional

And yet the early Christians did not sink into bitterness about their plight. On the contrary, today's passage says they "went on their way preaching the message of good news." There is a huge lesson here.

God in His providence sometimes lets upheaval, dislocation, and trauma become part of our life for His broader purposes. Just as the scattered Christians did not grow self-absorbed, let us grow so deep in God that we can bow to what He allows in our life and keep proclaiming Jesus even in persecution, job loss, deployment, illness, or tragedy. Indeed, our faith truly captures the minds and hearts of others when they see us trusting God even when life gets hard. Let the words of Jesus ring in our ears: "Be courageous! I have conquered the world" (John 16:33).

Bottom Line

Life is not about our comforts and convenience. We are soldiers in a spiritual battle. Hard times are expected—even promised! But God is with us.

Fruit Happens

"I am the vine; you are the branches. The one who remains in Me and I in him produces much fruit, because you can do nothing without Me." (John 15:5)

Jesus, the Vine

Jesus called Himself "the vine" and called His people "the branches." In calling Himself the vine, Jesus meant He is the true source of life. His life originates in Himself (see John 5:26). Our life, however—like that of a branch—is dependent on and derived from Jesus, as are any of the good works we do.

Unfortunately, many Christians burn themselves out striving to produce their own version of the fruit of the Spirit, not realizing what a misguided waste of time this is, since true fruit is always and only the by-product of connection to the vine. Any branch that remains in Him, constantly cultivating relationship with Christ, is sure to produce "much fruit."

Branch Openings

Jesus warned us that we can do nothing of spiritual value without Him. Human effort can never produce a fruitful life. Only Jesus can live the victorious Christian life. But because He lives in intimate connection with you, He can reproduce His life and character through you.

The secret of Christlikeness is not imitation but rather habitation. It is Christ in you. He indwells you to make you what He says you should be. Your prime directive is to remain in Him. Abide in Christ. Nurture your connection to the Vine. Continually turn from self to Christ, and you will produce much fruit.

Bottom Line

Stay close to Christ and your life will be fruitful. He is the Vine, and you are a branch.

By Itself

*"The kingdom of God is like this," He said.
"A man scatters seed on the ground;
he sleeps and rises—night and day,
and the seed sprouts and grows—he doesn't know how.
The soil produces a crop by itself." (Mark 4:26–28)*

A Crop by Itself

In this parable Jesus said the "soil produces a crop by itself." The Greek word translated "by itself" is *automatos*, which gives us our English word *automatic*. The seed carries life and power within itself. Given the right environment the seed will germinate. It will create a living, reproducing organism—a replica of the original.

The seed sower cannot create life. The seed contains its own life, with its own characteristics. The sower can't make the seed grow. He doesn't even know how it works, Jesus said. The sower can only supply the right conditions. But when he does, life happens seemingly automatically.

Life Happens

The "seed" in Jesus' parable represents God's Word: "The sower sows the word" (Mark 4:14). The "soil" represents the human heart. And the growth represents the maturing expression of the kingdom of God within you.

It is a mistake to try creating God's kingdom in the world around you before you've begun to let God create it within you. As you mature in God through His Word, the qualities of the kingdom—like "righteousness, peace, and joy" (Rom. 14:17)—will increasingly express themselves through you. This process happens by God's own life, God's own power, and God's own energy. It is not your effort that creates life but God's grace.

Bottom Line

When you nurture the seed of God's Word in you, life happens in you and then through you.

Great Expectations

*My son, don't forget my teaching, but let
your heart keep my commands; for they will bring
you many days, a full life, and well-being. (Prov. 3:1–2)*

Big Dreams

As fathers we have big dreams for our children: first female president, scientist who cures cancer, astronaut who colonizes Mars. It's our job to push our kids to shoot for the moon (but not fall apart if they end up in Iowa).

Often the world fights our efforts to create lofty goals. Reports about the economy can make kids cynical. Even toys can be a downer. Popular children's brand Little Tikes sells a Young Explorer workstation—a preschool cubicle, complete with double mouse pads. So instead of raising Susie Scientist, we're rearing Olivia Office Worker.

Live Long and Prosper

When giving our kids dreams, we need to shoot beyond the sky to heaven. By encouraging our children to live God-honoring lives, they'll benefit society and the people around them.

Before Spock ever uttered his famous words on *Star Trek*, King Solomon wrote the words of today's verse, assuring his son that by keeping God's wise commands, they would grow to experience "many days, a full life, and well-being." If your kids are going to live long and prosper, they must know and remember God's teaching. Encourage your children to memorize the Bible. Help them understand that His commands are for their benefit, not to take away their fun. Then watch your kids fly.

Bottom Line

Instead of solely pushing your kids to achieve earthly goals, encourage them to keep God's commands.

For Richer or Poorer

This is why a man leaves his father and mother and bonds with his wife, and they become one flesh. (Gen. 2:24)

Financial Foundation

If you want to stay richer, stay married. That's the finding from a fifteen-year study of more than nine thousand people by Ohio State University's Center for Human Resource Research. The best way to build wealth, the project determined, isn't through savvy investments—it's through marriage.

"If you really want to increase your wealth, get married and stay married," research scientist Jay Zagorsky said. "On the other hand, divorce can devastate your wealth."

Married people actually saw their wealth increase in greater ways than simply adding together the assets of two single people. Similarly, divorce caused a larger decrease of wealth than just splitting a couple's assets in half.

Work That Really Pays

God designed marriage for a man to bond with his wife, enabling them to become "one flesh." Staying together is part of God's plan. It benefits each spouse physically, emotionally, spiritually, as well as financially. So working on your marriage is a great investment in multiple ways.

If you find it hard to be romantic with your wife but can be motivated by money, remember that these two things are more connected than you may think. Hold on to your wife. Put effort in making her feel loved. Be as conscientious at home as you are at the office. That's good advice. And good financial sense too.

Bottom Line

All good things come from God—including your wealth and your wife.

Christian Report Cards

Each of us will give an account of himself to God. (Rom. 14:12)

The Right Stuff

The flight crew was jostled this way and that in the ultra high-tech training simulator. The pilots in the front two seats wrestled with the controls until they were finally "on the ground," safe and sound. Then after a couple of hours, they stopped by the test conductor's office to pick up the results of their session.

The printout was a complicated jumble of numbers. There were categories to rate how hard the left and right main landing gears had touched down and how much steering had been used to keep the craft on the runway. Most would not understand the pilots' report card, but the indicators it revealed were all positive. It proved the pilots did indeed have the "right stuff."

Peer Review

What would it be like if we received report cards rating our lives as Christians? What if our wife, kids, and friends were responsible for the grading? How would they say we're doing in our walk with Christ? How would members of our church say we're doing?

A peer review can be a nerve-racking experience. You're not perfect, and no one expects you to be. What's important, however, is that you do your best to "walk the walk" and not just "talk the talk." Hold yourself accountable for your actions, and seek input from those closest to you. Above all, ask the Spirit to empower all your efforts. After all, God is the One to whom we are ultimately accountable.

Bottom Line

Do you have the "right stuff" when it comes to living life as a follower of Christ? Producing the right stuff takes effort, but it is God-empowered effort.

Integrity at Work

Finding Work

Looking for work is a challenge at any age—whether you've just graduated from school, gotten fired, or resigned a position based on principle. If your plant has shut down or your position phased out, it's scary to be on the job hunt. A man likes to be "worthy of his wages," but when he has no income to begin with, or the income disappears unexpectedly, the future can look pretty bleak.

When you're without a job, it's a good time to think about the things that go into making a good employee. Actually, when you've got steady work, it's good to think about them too.

Fulfilling Work

What qualities make you valuable in your workplace? The word *integrity* usually comes up first when we talk about men and work. But what does integrity look like in a man's behavior?

You'll see it in a man who gets to work on time, a man who does his job without complaining. You'll see it in a man who respects others and his boss. You'll see it in a man who doesn't cut corners in performing his job, a man who doesn't take company property for personal use. You'll see it in a man who is a team player, a man who is satisfied at the end of the day because he's given his best.

Are you doing your job with integrity? Work can be tough, and doing the right thing isn't always easy, but it's always worth it in the long run.

Bottom Line

Take a look at your work ethic, and see how you stack up in the things that add up to integrity.

Communication Bombs

Do nothing out of rivalry or conceit, but in humility consider others as more important than yourselves. (Phil. 2:3)

Communication Casualties

A major cause of explosions in marital communication is selfishness. We think our points are sound and hers are nonsense. We assume the more she disagrees, the stronger we need to argue. We conclude that we must win the argument. Yet these stances accomplish nothing more than raising blood pressure, ruining the evening, and creating marital strife.

When voices are raised and tempers are lost, what do we hope to accomplish? That she'll calmly concede and say, "Your arguments are profound, my liege. Would his majesty care for some steak?" You may like that, but it isn't going to happen. Why? Because in hurtful marital arguments, everyone loses.

Averting the War

Paul says we are to do nothing out of rivalry or conceit, which amounts to an overappraisal of our own worth. Rather, we are to consider others—including our wives—as more important than we are.

If you and your wife are in a disagreement, and you truly consider her more important than you, it will be impossible to disrespect her viewpoint, raise your voice, and determine to win at all costs. Yes, she should follow that Scripture too, but you each answer individually to the Lord. Furthermore, you are the leader in the marriage. What better way to lead than to follow the example of the Lord: take up the towel, humble yourself, and serve.

Bottom Line

As the leader in your marriage, it is up to you to keep disagreements from becoming hurtful arguments.

A Father's True Aim

*"What can we do to perform the works of God?" they asked.
Jesus replied, "This is the work of God—that you believe
in the One He has sent." (John 6:28–29)*

Measuring Success

A father's definitions of his children's success has a profound impact on his kids. These definitions guide how he spends time with them, the criteria for his encouragement, and the basis for his rebukes.

How do you measure success in your children? Do you focus on GPA, social adjustment, or proper manners? Do you emphasize your kids' sports accomplishments, college aspirations, and future career? What matters most?

Through Jesus, our heavenly Father both simplified and clearly communicated His priority for us. When Christ's followers asked about God's priorities for them, they showed an expectation of multiple answers by using the word "works": "What can we do to perform the works of God?" Jesus, however—the same Savior who summed up all of the Law and the Prophets into two easily remembered commands (see Matt. 22:37–40)—responded simply: believe in Me.

God's Scorecard

Is God's priority for His children really that simple? Yes! The Lord desires for us to have a straightforward, wholehearted, and childlike faith. And though His priority for us is simple, its impact is profound. Followers of Christ are called to love Him with everything they are and to love their neighbors as themselves. That's the primary way success should be measured for us and for our children.

Bottom Line

God's priority for your children does not involve report cards, accomplishments, or stat sheets. His priority for your kids is that they believe in His Son.

Stay Connected

*Build yourselves up in your most holy faith and pray
in the Holy Spirit. (Jude 20)*

Total Communication

Ever wish you could talk to your wife, update your Facebook page, and text your children—all while you're driving? Okay, that would be dangerous. But with technological advances it's possible. Today's society puts a premium on being connected. We want to be able to communicate with who we want, when we want, for as long as we want.

Although wireless technology is a relatively new advancement in the scope of history, we've actually had the ability to communicate with God in this manner for thousands of years. The Bible tells us that anywhere we are is a good place to pray.

Solid Connection

As the world becomes more interconnected, we shouldn't lose sight of the importance of our all-access pass to the Creator of the universe. God gives us unlimited minutes and perfect WiFi reception to talk with Him at any time and about anything that concerns us. When we ask God to watch over us, when we pray to Him for wisdom, when we thank Him for His blessings, it takes some of the burden from our shoulders and helps us grow closer to Him. And as we see God answer those prayers, He becomes even more real in our lives.

Committing to communicate frequently with the important people in your life is critical to maintaining strong relationships. It's no different with God. Keep the communication lines open through constant prayer.

Bottom Line

Take advantage of God's invitation to pray constantly. Start at five minutes a day and strive for a continuous conversation.

Playing Catch

He would speak the word to them with many parables like these, as they were able to understand. (Mark 4:33)

Bible Baseball

The word "parable" comes from a Greek word made up of two roots—*para*, which means "alongside of," and *ballein*, which means "to throw." When Jesus wanted to teach a principle about the kingdom of God, He would throw out a story and see who would "catch" it. "A certain man had two sons. . . . A shepherd lost a sheep. . . . A man planted a vineyard." He was, in effect, playing a spiritual game of catch with those who would listen to Him.

Perhaps this also gives us some direction for parenting. Is your primary method of teaching your kids that of rules and regulations? Do you constantly nag or criticize them when they fail?

Internalizing the Truth

Jesus taught His followers by telling stories and asking questions. This forced them not merely to obey His orders but to learn what the truth was and how blessed they would be when they followed it. His disciples learned to love God from the inside out instead of being motivated by a big stick.

You'll find many resources for teaching your children. Another option is simply to listen to your kids. When they ask a question, ask it right back to them. Help them process truth in their minds and hearts. They may even "pop your glove" with a surprise answer or two. That's great. It shows that they're thinking. Remember, your job is to nurture faith, not enforce it.

Bottom Line

Listening and asking questions takes more time than simply quoting rules and laws, but it teaches your kids to uncover truth for themselves.

Know Love

The one who does not love does not know God,
because God is love. (1 John 4:8)

No Love

Romantic love is a big deal in our culture. It's glamorized in the continual stream of romantic comedies in the theaters and the number of love songs in all genres of music. Unfortunately, an alarming number of men are looking for love in all the wrong places. According to numerous statistics available today, roughly half of Christian men have a problem with pornography.

Unlike what we were taught as boys, the opposite of love is not hate. The opposite of love is lust. Love is selfless, but lust is selfish. Love gives; lust takes. Love honors; lust degrades. By going down a path of pornography, many men are ruining their love lives.

The Greatest Love

God is serious about love. He wants us to know it, live it, and give it. As 1 John 4:8 says, "The one who does not love does not know God, because God is love." That really puts things in perspective.

Since God is love, He can't stand the opposite. We show love when we fight against lust. Lust is a powerful force, but the Bible is clear that love is greater. Instead of following a path of no love, we must know love and follow God. Through the power of God's love, we can break free of the trap of false love—which is really just sinful lust—and then give and receive the true love we were made to experience. So with God's help go for the real thing.

Bottom Line

If you have a problem with pornography, find help. Talk to someone. Do whatever you can to break the habit.

First Love

"You have abandoned the love you had at first." (Rev. 2:4)

Slipping into Neutral

Creating a relationship is intentional, and so is preserving it. When you first began dating the woman in your life, you made decisions to foster the bond. You carved out time for her. You made her a priority. You thought of places to go and things to do together, and you made it happen. But unless you continue to invest the time, energy, and creativity it took to win her, you can find the emotional bond ebbing away. Without intending to, you can let your relationship slip into neutral. We so easily do this with our wife and even with our God.

Putting It Back into Drive

In today's passage Jesus reminds one of His churches that it had emotionally checked out on the love it used to have for Him. His call to the church is a truth that speaks to our relationship with Him but also with any important relationship, beginning with marriage.

If your relationship with your wife has lost much of its strength and closeness, do what you used to do when things were at their best, and the feelings will follow. It works that way for so many things that are good for us, things we know we should do—working out, eating right, getting enough rest, reading the Bible, and so forth. Right actions produce right feelings. Try it in your marriage and see if it isn't true.

Bottom Line

You can rekindle the relationship with your spouse, your God, and your family. Do the kinds of things that build the bond, and then watch love bloom again. Reinvest in the relationships that matter most to you.

Search Me

Search me, God, and know my heart; test me and know my concerns. (Ps. 139:23)

Gaping Holes

Have you ever been studying something you thought you knew pretty well, and then realized after listening to an expert that your knowledge is full of gaping holes? A lot of times we don't know what we don't know until it's too late.

Nowhere is this phenomenon more true, and potentially more harmful, than in the area of our own self-knowledge. The truth is, we all have major blind spots—gaping holes in our self-understanding. And this ignorance about ourselves affects everything about us: our attitudes, our hopes and dreams, and especially our relationships. We need help from the outside or we'll continue to make the same mistakes over and over again.

God's Searching Love

If we're willing to let people in, they can help us see ourselves more clearly, and we should be thankful for that. It's a wonderful gift from God. At the same time no one can show us ourselves the way God can when we seek Him in prayer. The amazing thing is, He knows absolutely everything about us and still loves us and accepts us just as we are. His kind of love encourages us to open ourselves up to Him completely, holding nothing back. And when we do, His Spirit is able to gently point out areas that need to change. When we know we're loved and accepted even with our flaws, we're so much more willing to listen to correction.

Bottom Line

Asking God to search and test you takes courage. And yet it's something we all need to do if we expect to grow in self-understanding and godliness.

Perfectly True

He has reconciled you by His physical body through His death, to present you holy, faultless, and blameless before Him. (Col. 1:22)

No More Guilt

When God says you're "holy, faultless, and blameless," He really means it. Of course, that's not the same thing as saying you're sinless, perfect, and awesome in terms of your everyday performance right now. Obviously each of us has some work to do before reaching a state of sinless perfection. (That will come in heaven.) But by gospel miracle, right this very minute, you are completely holy, faultless, and blameless in God's eyes if you have received His forgiveness through faith in Christ.

God gives us Christ's perfect record. He was holy, faultless, and blameless, and therefore so are we. You've heard that before. But don't let this fact cause you to overlook the unbelievable blessing of the great exchange—our sin for Christ's righteousness. It is the theological rock upon which a sturdy faith is built. If you're going to *stand firm*, it will be because you understand the cross.

Feel This Truth in Your Bones

There is a huge difference between knowing a truth and really knowing it experientially. Our justification, our right standing with God, is meant to move us emotionally. Like Pilgrim in *Pilgrim's Progress*, we can cast off any guilt and shame we've been carrying around and run free in God's love and grace. That's what God wants for us. We just need to believe it.

Bottom Line

Carrying around guilt and shame doesn't make us more spiritual. It's actually unbelief in God's truth. Embrace what God says about you, and live free by the power of the gospel.

Get in the Game

"If you ask Me anything in My name, I will do it." (John 14:14)

No Holding Back

God wants us to pray like little children. Kids just say what's on their mind, and they're not afraid to ask for what they want . . . and then to keep asking. Far from being disrespectful, this kind of faithful persistence in prayer delights our heavenly Father. He longs to give His children good gifts (see Matt. 7:11). He is not put off by our neediness. After all, He knows perfectly well that we are completely dependent on Him for everything. In providing what we need, and often what we want, He shows Himself to be the ultimate giver. He is never reluctant to bless us.

In fact, His generosity is an expression of His glory, and our thankfulness for His good gifts reverberates back to Him in the form of more glory. But we've got to ask if we're going to receive. We've got to get in the game unashamedly.

In Jesus' Name

Obviously God doesn't give us everything we want. We can be thankful for that because our prayers are sometimes unwise and selfish. But just because we're imperfect and our motives are imperfect doesn't mean we shouldn't ask for what we want or pretend we're more spiritually mature than we are. God wants to interact with the real us. When we spend time with Him, He has a way of changing our perspective so that our requests become more in line with His will. And when that's the case, we can be sure He will answer.

Bottom Line

Understand that God doesn't get tired of hearing from you. Ask, ask, and keep asking!

The End of Ourselves

*"The poor in spirit are blessed,
for the kingdom of heaven is theirs." (Matt. 5:3)*

You Can't Do It

Something in us hates feeling insufficient. We want to be able to handle whatever life throws at us. But if we're not careful, we can adopt this inaccurate mind-set even in our relationship with God.

It's usually pretty subtle. We easily slip into the "God is my copilot" way of living where we're still the one behind the wheel of our life, and God is just there in the passenger seat to keep us company and occasionally hold up the map for us.

All the while, we can actually believe we're pleasing God in attempting to bring about our own moral reformation. Nothing, however, could be further from the truth. This kind of striving will always result in painful failure. But this failure is actually one of the best things that could ever happen to us. When we reach the end of ourselves, God is free to work powerfully in us and through us.

Who's Really Blessed?

According to Jesus, the "poor in spirit" are blessed. To be poor in spirit means to declare oneself spiritually bankrupt, to admit our utter powerlessness to please God in our own strength. It's not so much a condition to be sought as a reality to be understood and lived from. And what a great relief it is to be spiritually poor! What a great relief to give up futile self-effort and breathe in the fresh air of grace.

Bottom Line

"Poor in spirit" is an accurate description of our true spiritual condition. We ought to embrace this. There's freedom in being who we are—dependent.

Put on Kindness

*Put on heartfelt compassion, kindness,
humility, gentleness, and patience. (Col. 3:12)*

Plenty of Opportunities

In this rough-and-tumble world of ours, kindness can be in short supply. People are so busy and frazzled that their concern for other people—basic kindness—can get left in the dust.

And yet the all-too-common coarseness in our society actually presents a great opportunity for Christians—for you—to be different. As the Roman philosopher Seneca once said, "Wherever there is a human being, there is an opportunity for kindness." Jesus told His followers to "let your light shine before men, so that they may see your good works and give glory to your Father in heaven" (Matt. 5:16). Be assured, kind people shine brightly for God.

Be a Blessing

Adopt the mind-set that everyone around you needs and deserves your kindness. Believe that you possess the God-given power to bless other people through your kindness, and then look for ways to do it. Again the opportunities are endless. Take the grocery store cashier. That's a person who could use your smile and your kindness. After all, he or she has likely been dealing with a lot of cranky (or at least preoccupied) people all day. Your kindness can make a difference. The same goes for your coworkers. Yes, you're busy, but take the time to be kind.

Everyone wins with kindness. It brings joy to both the giver and receiver, and it tends to have a cumulative effect. One kind deed inspires another.

Bottom Line

Kindness never goes out of style. God wants His people to represent Him well by showing kindness to others. Look for opportunities to be kind.

God's Help

Do not fear, for I am with you; do not be afraid,
for I am your God. I will strengthen you; I will help you;
I will hold on to you with My righteous right hand. (Isa. 41:10)

The Cost of Fear

Fear is a terrible foe. It robs us of life and energy. It limits our thinking and steals our hope. It is the antithesis of faith, which increases courage, vitality, and optimism about the future. Unlike faith's life-expanding influence, fear shrinks our ambitions; worse, it shrinks the size of our God down to nothing. He becomes almost irrelevant.

If we live in fear, we won't even begin to tap into our God-given potential. Instead we'll act like the unfaithful servant in Matthew 25:14–30 who decided that burying his talents was a safer course of action than investing them for the benefit of his master. According to Jesus, taking this approach to life is not just being cautious, it's being evil and lazy.

The Illogic of Fear

Despite its terrible payoff, fear is actually a natural default. So many things out of our control could go wrong. But fear leaves God out of the equation—and if you're one of God's children, then God is never out of the equation. On the contrary, He is the answer to every challenge and perplexity life can throw at you. When God tells us not to fear, He also reminds us that He is with us to strengthen us and help us. So we need not fear. God is enough.

Bottom Line

Fear can ruin your life if you let it. Remind yourself that God is with you to strengthen you and help you. Fight fear with faith.

Shedding Weight

Since we also have such a large cloud of witnesses surrounding us, let us lay aside every weight and the sin that so easily ensnares us. Let us run with endurance the race that lies before us. (Heb. 12:1)

Every Weight Must Go

Hebrews 12:1 is not the only place in the New Testament that likens the Christian life to a race. "Don't you know that the runners in a stadium all race, but only one receives the prize? Run in such a way to win the prize" (1 Cor. 9:24). And in 2 Timothy 4:7, Paul says, "I have fought the good fight, I have finished the race, I have kept the faith." The race is on, guys.

If you've ever watched the Boston Marathon or the Tour de France, you notice that the guys out front are pretty lean and mean. They're not carrying around any extra pounds or gear. It's all about going as fast as possible, and anything that gets in the way of the goal must go. You don't just luck out and win a race. You prepare well and then stay laser focused throughout.

Brutal Honesty Required

It's usually easier to recognize the sins that slow us down than to recognize some of the other "weights" that prevent us from running our best. That's because these weights usually aren't inherently sinful; they're just not particularly helpful. They tend to be diversions or distractions that, when kept within proper limits, can serve as helpful rest breaks. The problem is, we often have trouble disciplining ourselves to get back on track. Do you need to shed some weight?

Bottom Line

Running the race well requires intentionality and focus. Be honest with yourself. Are there some things in your life that need to go?

Hoping and Coping

*According to His great mercy, He has given us
a new birth into a living hope through the resurrection
of Jesus Christ from the dead. (1 Pet. 1:3)*

The Certainty of Eternity

When we use the word *hope*, we generally mean a wish or a desire. We say, "I hope it doesn't rain," meaning "I wish it wouldn't rain." But in 1 Peter 1:3, hope refers to a certainty or reality. The word literally means "to expect with confidence." In other words, because of the resurrection of Jesus Christ from the dead and our corresponding trust in His work, eternal life is assured, guaranteed, a certainty.

Nobody can take eternal life away from you. God's permanent will has been made with indelible ink, and it can't be canceled or changed. Your place cannot be destroyed or ruined. Your status in God's family is beyond the reach of change and decay. Your position cannot be altered by time or by performance. Your place in heaven is guarded by the power of God, like an army of troops securely guarding a beachhead.

The Reality of the Present

Our present problems diminish when the future reality is secure. It has been said that if you can hope, you can cope. If you know the future is going to be better, the present is better already. Without hope, though, life can seem pretty bleak sometimes. Hope is the great perspective-giver. When our primary focus is on the end of the journey and how gloriously happy we will be, it makes the sometimes painful walk of today much more bearable.

Bottom Line

Where is your focus? God has given you the ability to focus your thoughts on unshakable, eternal realities. That's where hope is found.

Proof and Faith

. . . so that the genuineness of your faith—more valuable than gold, which perishes though refined by fire—may result in praise, glory, and honor at the revelation of Jesus Christ. (1 Pet. 1:7)

The Hard Test

For believers in Christ, one of the benefits of life's difficulties is that they prove the genuineness of our faith. Not in the sense of whether our faith is real or not, but in the sense of its being able to hold up under pressure. Think of a rookie quarterback going through his first NFL training camp. He needs to be tested. He needs to be prepared for what he'll face once the season starts.

The Passing Score

We tend to think of testing as punishment when we need to look at it like a student who goes into the classroom confident because he has studied and prepared. He doesn't dread the exam; he welcomes it. He says, "Go ahead, professor, ask me whatever you want. I know the answers."

Like that student, believers can say, "Go ahead, world, give me your best shot. My God can take it. My faith in Him is strong. My convictions are secure." The tests of life prove that our faith is genuine, pure, and strong. The tests make us stronger.

The circumstances that seem to be keeping you down today may actually be the ladder that will allow you to climb up. The onslaught that comes your way may be the exercise that tones your spiritual muscles. How you come out on the other side will determine your grade, indicating what you really know.

Bottom Line

Are you passing the test? What will your score be on your test of faith?

Proper Perspective

*You rejoice in this, though now for a short time you
have had to struggle in various trials. (1 Pet. 1:6)*

Short-term Pain

Peter seems to have gone off the deep end. How can we be
glad and rejoice when we are facing difficulties and frustrations
and trials? The answer is found in four words—"for a short time."
Peter is suggesting that we can praise God because our tribulations are short in duration. But we respond, "Not so, Peter! My
trials are lasting a very long time!"

Yes, our trials seem long. But in comparison to eternity,
they are short. The attitude we bring to our battles depends on
the perspective we have. To get the right perspective, we need
to understand that the proper standard of comparison for the
length of our trials is the length of eternity.

Long-term Benefit

We're told that childbirth is one of the greatest physical
pains a human being can experience. The birthing mother often
undergoes a tremendous amount of pain in bringing her child
into the world. But when the helpless, tiny baby—the new little
life—is placed for the first time in the arms of the mother, at that
point the memory of the pain begins to fade away.

So it is with our pain, our suffering, our trials. Those discouraging battles may from time to time seem intense. But one
day the difficulties of life in this world will be forgotten because
we will be caught up in the ecstasy of the moment when we
enter into the presence of God for all eternity.

Bottom Line

Identify a battle in your life and compare it to the joy you'll
experience in your heavenly home.

No Way

The Jebusites had said to David: "You will never get in here. Even the blind and lame can repel you." (2 Sam. 5:6)

Naysayers Are Loud

Jerusalem was intended to be a center of worship for God's people. But even as Joshua led the Israelites to take the promised land, the city went unconquered. Years later David had a vision of unifying his kingdom, and he believed Jerusalem would be a good capital city.

A big vision always attracts people who are against it, and at this time David was surrounded by them. Author Gordon MacDonald calls these people "VDPs," or "Very Draining People." Their last seven words are typically, "We never did it that way before." The Jebusites were like that. They tried to get inside David's head, saying "even the blind and lame can repel you."

Nevertheless

"Yet David did capture the stronghold of Zion" (2 Sam. 5:7). Despite the fact that it had never been done, that he was surrounded by VDPs, that his strength was lacking, David did what no Israelite had ever done before: he conquered the city of Jerusalem.

What vision has God given you that has attracted criticism? God never trusts His work to those who can do it apart from Him. He gives His greatest assignments to those who are weak so that He may show His strength through them.

They say it's never been done before? Maybe God is waiting for you to be the person to do it! Don't take your cues from the critics!

Bottom Line

Focus not on the greatness of your task but on the greatness of your God.

Hey There, Young Man

*Let no one despise your youth; instead,
you should be an example to the believers in speech,
in conduct, in love, in faith, in purity. (1 Tim. 4:12)*

Seeking a Position?

You attended the men's retreat, but everybody was your dad's age or older. You're too young to be considered as a Sunday school teacher, you feel out of place in the choir, and the last thing you want to do is serve on a committee. Should you leave and attend a church with more people your own age? Not necessarily.

Many churches find it challenging to plug young adults into ministry. But just because you can't seem to find a way to serve doesn't mean you should hop to another church full of young singles. God can still do great things in your life while you patiently wait on Him.

Seeking God Himself

Don't seek position but God Himself. It's easy to throw stones and criticize the church. Instead of doing that, try to listen twice as much as you speak—and when you speak, make sure what you're saying is constructive. Learn to view everyone you meet as someone God wants to use to teach you something. Be a quiet example of Christ to others.

Adopting this approach may lead you to begin working with preschoolers or taking out the trash after a church fellowship. But volunteer for the job no one wants, and shine for Christ through it. Perform your labor of love as to the Lord. He may not give you position, but you'll have the satisfaction of knowing you served Him alone, whether you received recognition or not.

Bottom Line

Live as an example of Christ, no matter what your age.

The Righteous Sinner

If He rescued righteous Lot, distressed by the unrestrained behavior of the immoral (for as he lived among them, that righteous man tormented himself day by day with the lawless deeds he saw and heard). (2 Pet. 2:7–8)

Evil Twin

Second Peter 2:7–8 tells us that Lot was a "righteous man." But the historical record of Lot in Genesis 13, 14, and 19 show little in the way of behavioral righteousness. In fact, the story of Lot is about as close to an R-rated story as you can find in the Bible. Lot was far from perfect.

Here's a short list of what we learn about Lot in the book of Genesis: he is greedy and materialistic; he compromises with evil; he is unwilling to protect the virtue of his daughters; he gets drunk to the point that he doesn't even realize his own complicity in incestuous behavior.

Righteous? Really?

Lot's willingness to receive the angels in Genesis 19 and his willingness to leave Sodom show his faith. But his behavior leaves much to be desired in terms of righteousness. This means his righteousness had to come from somewhere else—and that "somewhere else" is the graciousness of God—the same "somewhere else" that our own righteousness comes from.

This is about the best news we can possibly receive, but it is also difficult to understand. Our natural tendency is to revert to looking at our own performance as the basis for God's blessing. But grace alone is our only security.

Bottom Line

On your best day you are never good enough to be considered righteous; on your worst day you are never so sinful as to be beyond the reach of grace and the imputed righteousness of Christ.

What Is Faith?

*Abram believed the LORD, and He credited
it to him as righteousness. (Gen. 15:6)*

Walking by Sight

In Genesis 12 and Genesis 15:1, God promised Abraham
that He would bless him. And one of those blessings would be
that Abraham would have many children, becoming the father
of a great nation. In Genesis 15:2–3, Abraham expresses his own
doubts about God's promises. The main reason he doubted was
that he was walking by sight. His "sight" told him that he was
too old to father children, that his heir would not—could not—
come from his own body, as God promised.

Walking by Faith

In Genesis 15:4–5, God told Abraham that what he saw
with his human "sight" did not correspond to God's reality. God
would intervene and enable Abraham to father a child despite
Sarah and Abraham's advanced age—a promise Abraham ultimately chose to believe despite what his eyes were telling him.
Faith always involves accepting God's version of reality over our
own.

This happens initially in salvation where our human "sight"
tells us we have to earn God's favor. At that point we must accept
God's version of reality: salvation is by grace through faith, not
works.

The walk of faith continues in like manner. All the days of
our lives we must trust God's view of reality over what our sight
tells us. Yes, it can be a little scary sometimes, but the alternative—relying on our own wisdom—is far more dangerous.

Bottom Line

Faith always involves a question of trust, and it is a day-
to-day walk. Are you trusting in what your sight tells you is real
today or in what God's Word tells you is real?

A Good Thing

A man who finds a wife finds a good thing and obtains favor from the LORD. (Prov. 18:22)

Marital Monotony

You walked the aisle. You said the vows. You exchanged the rings. You kissed. Now it's smooth sailing through wedded bliss. Or is it? Many marriages encounter stormy seas as spouses get busy in the details and responsibilities of everyday life.

Maybe you can relate to this scenario. One evening you're talking with your wife and she mentions that you haven't brought her flowers lately. You respond by: (a) reminding her about all the stuff you have given her; (b) telling her she ruined the surprise because you were planning to bring her flowers but now you're not; or (c) surprising her with a huge bouquet the next morning in bed. Hopefully, you went with the last option.

Revving Up Romance

Obviously the issue isn't a lack of flowers; it's a lack of romance. Dating doesn't end at "I do." Spending consistent, meaningful, private time together—whether once a week or once a month—will remind you why you tied the knot in the first place. And the benefits of better communication, increased romance, and feeling connected aren't too bad either. As Proverbs 18:22 says, finding your wife was "a good thing"—one of the best things that ever happened to you. So don't take God's gift of your spouse for granted. Honor your wife with little gifts, notes, and loving words—and most important, with a heart that truly beats to love and cherish her. That will go a long way toward reigniting your relationship.

Bottom Line

Take the lead in keeping the spark alive in your marriage. Be romantic!

Leadership Training

I didn't think it was a good idea to know anything among you except Jesus Christ and Him crucified. (1 Cor. 2:2)

Jesus and Our Bootstraps

Many of us want to grow in our personal and professional lives. It's why bookstore shelves are bulging with volumes on leadership and other self-help themes. Some even claim to distill Jesus' teaching into a set of neutral "best practices" anyone (Christian or not) could adopt.

The irony here is that Jesus didn't intend to create a newer, better set of do's and don'ts. He came to blow a hole in sin's domination of our soul. He came to purchase redemption for men, to birth in us a radically new life that would change the whole of our being.

Jesus Alone

Books and activities are fine, of course, as far as they go. But it's easy to expend our time and energy seeking lesser knowledge and in so doing lose our first love. Paul reminds us of the heart of the matter: not "to know anything . . . except Jesus Christ and Him crucified."

The clutter and noise of a thousand things are pressing against us at all times, tempting us to follow many rabbit trails in life and faith. Yet true fruitfulness will manifest itself in our lives only as we remain focused on the simplicity of the gospel. God has done everything; we are complete in Him. When we put on "the mind of Christ" (see 1 Cor. 2:16), we will find ourselves inwardly thriving instead of striving. Now that's what you might call true leadership training.

Bottom Line

Consider cutting back some activities if that's what it takes to spend time with the Savior through prayer and His Word.

Relationship Realities

*When there are many words, sin is unavoidable,
but the one who controls his lips is wise. (Prov. 10:19)*

Don't Tread on Me

Marriage is wonderful, but it isn't easy. Each couple brings enormous differences to the table: different tastes, hobbies, habits. These differences (even regarding simple things) can cause us to clash, creating friction, bitterness, and conflict. These sparks are then fanned into a roaring fire by a culture that tells us to stridently demand our rights in all situations. The message is, in effect, "Don't tread on me, and heaven help you if you do."

An Alternative

Into such an incendiary environment, the Bible calls us to self-control, wisdom, restraint, and humility. Yes, as men we are the leaders of our home. But remember: our wives are helpmates and companions designed by God, having a whole range of intuition and sensitivity we typically don't possess. Why wouldn't we want to take advantage of those gifts? In fact, as leaders we are commanded to be good stewards of those gifts.

Therefore, whatever the issue, let's resolve to listen. Or to loosely paraphrase Proverbs 10:19, we need to "put a sock in it." Relationships, especially marriage, are prosperous only to the degree that we humble ourselves and restrain quick offense. As we exercise caution and care toward our wives, God will move to bring real unity and understanding.

Bottom Line

When we feel hurt, snubbed, or misunderstood, it seems impossible to be gentle and humble. And it is, on our own. But we're not on our own. Ask God to give you grace and humility.

Closed Doors

"I wish one of you would shut the temple doors, so you would no longer kindle a useless fire on My altar!" (Mal. 1:10)

All or Nothing

God prefers substance over style in worship. We can't simply go through the motions on Sunday morning and think we've pleased God. In Malachi 1, God says He would rather we close the doors to the church and not attend than to worship half-heartedly, with sin in our lives.

As men we tend to compartmentalize our hearts. A piece for our wives and families, a piece for work, a piece for play, a piece for God on Sunday. In our minds it all adds up to 100 percent. But God wants—no, He jealously demands and deserves—100 percent of our heart *first*. He knows that any part of our heart we hold back from Him is a part easily compromised.

Pregame Gut Check

So how can we keep from lighting useless fires in worship? Why not prep for Sunday morning worship the night before? Reflect on your week. Do you have sins to confess? Relationships to restore? Attitudes to adjust? Ask the Holy Spirit to hold you up to His light and show you anything that would keep you from revering His name in worship the next day. You could close by praying for your family members.

Then what? Don't be surprised if you have a fight on the way to church! But keep your cool. God's about to do something great in your family, and He's starting with you. So come to church prepared, bringing all of your heart.

Bottom Line

If you're playing games in worship, God would rather you play them at home.

Set Them Free

"What do you want?" He asked her. "Promise," she said to Him, "that these two sons of mine may sit, one on Your right and the other on Your left, in Your kingdom." (Matt. 20:21)

Is It about You?

Whether we are cheering for them on the field or putting a "Straight-A Student" bumper sticker on our car, we take a degree of pride in the success of our kids. But too often we see it as a direct reflection of our own lives. To push your child toward something so you can bask in their victories is not only wrong; it's unhealthy.

Zebedee's wife is not mentioned by name in Scripture, but her boys James and John were among the closest friends Jesus had on earth. When she approached Jesus and asked that they be co-vice presidents of His coming kingdom, perhaps she saw ultimate gain for herself.

Or Is It about Them?

Did God create your child for your purposes or for His? When we drive our kids to pursue our dreams instead of God's calling, we are not listening to them or observing the talents and gifts God has given them. They can become angry and resentful as a result, struggling to realize who God created them to be or to accomplish all they could.

We love God when we make room for our kids to pursue His calling on their life. Letting your kids be themselves is one of the most difficult jobs a dad can have. But it can also draw you into a closer relationship with your child than you ever dreamed possible.

Bottom Line

Release your child to follow God's vision for his or her life.

Down, Not Out

You, LORD, are a shield around me, my glory, and the One who lifts up my head. (Ps. 3:3)

So Close

Some days it seemed as if the opportunity Jim had been seeking was right there for the taking. The project he'd been working on was finally—finally—going to pay off. He had worked at it for so long and so hard, he felt certain something good was bound to happen eventually, probably soon. That was how he thought on a good day.

Then there were the days when nothing seemed to go right. Thoughts of despair bombarded his mind: *This is never going to work. What was I thinking? How could I have possibly imagined this was going to succeed?* Every defeat left Jim feeling all the more discouraged. With each closed door, he felt absolutely useless.

The Shield

Millions of people face disappointment on an almost daily basis. They have a hard time believing things will ever get better. And yet unshakable hope is available to everyone who believes God is at work and good things are coming.

Take another look at today's Scripture. What images does it stir up? The Lord is your shield—He protects you when you're vulnerable. He is your glory—the One who gives meaning and purpose to your life. He lifts your head, providing comfort and encouragement when you need it most. Don't give in to hopelessness. Continue to look to God for hope and strength.

Bottom Line

No matter how badly things may be going, we always have hope knowing our great and gracious God will help us.

Your Serve

First Serve

John Kennedy's famous inaugural address line is: "Ask not what your country can do for you, ask what you can do for your country." Service is at the heart of greatness. Too many people spend an entire lifetime focusing only on themselves, thinking that significance comes from success. To make a difference, the focus first must be turned outward instead of inward, giving instead of getting, serving rather than being served.

In his letter, the apostle Peter addressed church leaders, a group of people who had given themselves to others. He instructed them to serve enthusiastically and not for monetary gain, providing a model for all to follow. They were simply to follow the example of Jesus, the Servant.

Second Serve

We don't make a lasting impact by what we make. That's secondary. We make a lasting impact by what we give. We tend to equate having money with having influence. Instead of focusing on how much you can get, focus on how much you can give. Instead of counting the number of people who serve you, count how many you are serving. If you want to make a difference in your family, assist them; in your church, volunteer; in your community, give; in your world, help. Ask not what your wife, your children, your neighbor, or your boss can do for you; ask what you can do for them.

Bottom Line

If you want to leave a mark on this world, serve others.

The Way Up Is Down

God resists the proud but gives grace to the humble. Humble yourselves, therefore, under the mighty hand of God, so that He may exalt you at the proper time. (1 Pet. 5:5–6)

What Humility Doesn't Mean

While the world calls for upward mobility, the Bible speaks of *downward* mobility. The world says one ascends into greatness. The Bible reveals that one *descends* into greatness. As odd as it may sound, the way up is down.

Peter communicates this descending movement with the concept of *humility*, a word that comes from *humus* or "soil." Let's be clear about what humility doesn't mean. Humble people are not absorbed with self-hatred or a lack of self-confidence. Neither do they become the proverbial doormat, allowing everyone they encounter to walk all over them. Nor do they look down on themselves or their abilities. Furthermore, humility is not a call to mediocrity and/or a substandard quality of life.

What Humility Does Mean

Humility means thinking true and realistic thoughts about God and about ourselves. It is the habitual quality whereby we live in the truth, acknowledging that we are created beings and not the Creator, that God is God and we are not. Humble people, therefore, reflect the dignity and grace of God by understanding their proper role. Just as God humbled Himself and became a man, so should we humble ourselves.

Humility is perhaps the most countercultural virtue in all of Scripture, especially for people grasping for the top. So instead of promoting yourself or pushing your agenda at the expense of others, humble yourself before God and others.

Bottom Line

The path to greatness flows downward through humility.

Warm Worms

*. . . casting all your care on Him,
because He cares about you. (1 Pet. 5:7)*

Keep 'em Warm

Did you hear about the young boy ice fishing who was catching one fish after another? An old man asked him his secret. The kid bent down and spit something out of his mouth. Wiping off his lips and looking up at the man, he said, "I keep my worms warm."

In like manner some people feel like they have to keep their *worries* warm. Anxieties occupy their mind like the worms occupied the boy's mouth. They're constantly fretting—apprehensive, fearful, and troubled. They lose sleep, lose weight, and lose hope. But there is a better way.

Spit 'em Out

The word *care* or *anxiety* can mean "to strangle." Worry chokes the life out of us. There may be greater sins than anxiety, but few are more disabling and destructive. The word *cast* means to "throw off," like when we cast off a coat or cast a fishing line. It represents a decisive action that is neither passive nor partial. Anxiety is something to get rid of, to throw away, to spit out!

First Peter 5:7 is a directive, a command, not a suggestion: "casting all your care on Him." Give *all* of your cares to God. Let Him carry the weight of worry that has been dragging you down and filling you with fear, rendering you ineffective and miserable. He is willing and able to do that for you. Anxiety is not something to hold on to!

Bottom Line

Worriers don't make much of an impact on this world because they are so busy fighting imaginary dragons that they don't have time to fight the real ones.

The Battleground

*Be serious! Be alert! Your adversary the Devil
is prowling around like a roaring lion,
looking for anyone he can devour.
Resist him. (1 Pet. 5:8–9)*

Satan's Tactic

Lions in Africa prey on weak, unsuspecting animals who have wandered away from the protection of the herd. Likewise, the devil prowls around to deceive and devour unsuspecting, weak Christians who have wandered off from other believers or from God. Believers who refuse accountability with other believers find themselves isolated and defenseless—delicious prey for the crafty deceiver.

The Christian life is not a playground but a battleground. Every day, every hour, every minute we are under attack. We are fighting a real war against an invisible foe who employs highly organized strategies, tactics, and battle plans. If we do not understand these facts, we will lose the battle.

Our Strategy

In order to win the battle, Peter says we need to be sober, be alert, and resist. To be sober—or "serious"—is to be self-controlled, which means letting Christ control us instead of ourselves. To be "alert" is to be on guard and watchful. And to "resist" means being willing to fight. Once Christ is in control of our life and we are alert to Satan's tactics, then we can resist him.

Notice that Peter doesn't say to resist temptation but to resist Satan, the one doing the tempting. The failure to understand and employ this strategy is where many believers stumble and fall. We can only resist Satan by the power and presence of Jesus Christ.

Bottom Line

We don't need to be clever or strong to win each day's battle, but we do need Jesus.

Husband Is a Verb

Husbands, in the same way, live with your wives with an understanding of their weaker nature yet showing them honor as coheirs of the grace of life, so that your prayers will not be hindered. (1 Pet. 3:7)

Weaker Nature

Scripture encourages men to understand their wives' "weaker nature." Most scholars interpret this as referring to relative physical weakness: usually men are physically stronger than their wives. This necessitates a tenderness that might not come naturally.

A husband shouldn't treat his wife "like one of the guys" or manhandle her in any way. Today's Scripture outlaws all bullying, whether physical, emotional, intellectual, or spiritual. By agreeing to marry you, she made herself vulnerable to you. She entrusted herself to you. By agreeing to marry her, you made yourself accountable to God for her well-being and care. When a man fails to husband his wife, God takes it personally.

Greater Honor

The good news is that God's grace can make you the husband you long to be. You and your wife are "coheirs of the grace of life." This means the supernatural, divine power you need to live up to God's standards is available to you. He has supplied "everything required for life and godliness" (2 Pet. 1:3). He has outfitted you with all you need to cherish your wife and show her the honor she deserves.

It only remains for you to do it. Steward your marriage. Love your wife when you feel like it and when you don't. Protect her. Shepherd her. Be the husband God's grace enables you to be.

Bottom Line

Husbanding a wife and family is a huge responsibility, but God stands ready to empower you by His grace.

Introverts

Who is wise and has understanding among you? He should show his works by good conduct with wisdom's gentleness. (James 3:13)

"The Way He Should Go"

God wired each of your children differently, giving them certain temperaments, talents, and proclivities. A wise dad discovers his children's natural bent and nurtures them to be themselves.

If you are an extrovert, fathering an introvert can sometimes feel like fathering an alien. But when dads pressure their introverts to act like extroverts, they produce frustrated, demoralized children. That's one reason God exhorts fathers, "Don't stir up anger" in your kids (Eph. 6:4). Let your child's God-given introversion shine through. Be like Jacob, who blessed each of his children with a custom-tailored, "suitable blessing" (Gen. 49:28).

Blessing an Introverted Child

Here are some guidelines that can help a dad bless his introverted child: (1) Allow your child to observe an activity before pressuring him/her to participate. Don't push your introvert to the front of the line. (2) Celebrate their creative, imaginative world. Ask about their books. Invite conversation over their drawings. Offer one-on-one daddy/child dates. (3) Don't nag about friendships. Introverted kids are happy with one or two close friends. Never label your child as shy, introverted, or a loner. And, of course (4) faithfully pray for your child to use his/her gifts to advance God's kingdom.

Bottom Line

If you have an introverted child, realize that God gave you a great kid, and learn to work with his/her interests and strengths.

Think Inside the Box

I know the One I have believed in. (2 Tim. 1:12)

When the Storm Rolls In

A lot of things confuse us, cause us pain, and leave us reeling for answers. Sometimes life hurts so much that it shakes our confidence in the character of God. We cry out "why?" Why the cancer, the lost job, the broken relationship, the awful situation that seems to have no answer? We are deeply hurt by the realization that our all-powerful God, for reasons we cannot understand, has chosen not to step in and fix things the way we have begged Him to do. Our imagination can take us down dark paths, and we can find ourselves seething at God and walking away from Him. But there is no peace in bailing out on God—only despair.

The Anchor Holds

The apostle Paul, too, found himself in painful circumstances. But when he was bewildered by what he didn't know, he found strength and peace by choosing to focus on what he did know. He knew Jesus took a savage beating and was nailed to a cross for us. He knew Jesus would never abandon him and he would be supplied with the grace he needed when he needed it.

So hang on to what you do know. Stay "inside the box" of revealed truth instead of leaping into the realm of wild speculation. Your pain is real, but your pain does not change the fact of the cross. Run toward God in your pain, not away from Him. He loves you.

Bottom Line

God has not promised to answer all your questions or relieve all your pain in this life. But the cross proves He is deeply committed to you.

Waiting for the Prodigal

His father saw him and was filled with compassion. (Luke 15:20)

When Children Wander

For many dads the experience of parenting is a jumbled mix of great memories and current heartbreak. The child who used to present you with crayon works of art, who could not wait for you to get home from work, is now aloof or flat-out missing. Harsh words were thrown down, doors were slammed, walls went up, and the relationship finally seemed to crash and burn. Emotionally, your son or daughter has moved a million miles away from you and from God. You have lurched between sadness and anger, regret and recrimination. But mostly you hurt and wonder if it will ever end.

You Are Not Alone

Dad, you are hardly alone. The story of the prodigal son has been played out in countless homes for centuries. If you have been waiting, perhaps for years, it can seem like all hope is lost. But it isn't. The parable is not only about a wandering son but also about a waiting father. Keep praying, keep entrusting your kid to God, and keep the door open for a restored relationship.

Even if your child has sinned in a spectacular way, keep your heart soft. Your heavenly Father never closed His heart to you in your own season of wandering. He waited patiently for you to come to your senses. Ask God to work in your heart as well as in the heart of your prodigal. Don't despair. The story isn't over yet.

Bottom Line

Your kid is free to be sinful and rebellious, but God is free to orchestrate circumstances that lead to repentance. Keep asking Him to do His restoring work.

When Nothing's Left

He will not put out a smoldering wick. (Isa. 42:3)

Burned Out?

God knows what we are made of. He understands our frailty, our dark desires, our bleak seasons of grief. He knows what we're dealing with at work; He sees our struggles at home; He fully comprehends the depth of our fears. He knows us better than we know ourselves. He completely gets why we sometimes have crazy, self-destructive impulses to commit awful sins. And no matter how bad you blow it or how weak your faith, He will never wash His hands of you. He won't turn away in disgust. He won't abandon you. He loves you with an unconquerable love that never goes away.

Fanning the Flame

Today's text is about the heart of Jesus. Isaiah says our Savior will not snuff out a smoldering wick. Jesus does not despise weak things; He heals them. He makes them strong. He gives them His own power and grace. If you feel like you have nothing left, you may be exactly where Jesus wants you to be. He wants us to understand that our spiritual life does not come from our own resources. Your faith is not something you drum up on your own. All spiritual vibrancy comes from God. You can't create it, but you can have it. You can ask for it. You can set yourself up to receive it. You can open your Bible and read. You can pray. You can wait expectantly. And He can, and will, fan the flame back to life.

Bottom Line

Keep coming back to God for strength, just as you keep coming back to the fountain to get water. He will revive you.

Down in the Dumps

He brought me up from a desolate pit, out of the muddy clay, and set my feet on a rock, making my steps secure. (Ps. 40:2)

Going Down

Edward Mote, composer of the hymn "The Solid Rock," was neglected by his saloon-keeper parents, and his formative years were spent either in a pub or roaming the streets. But by age eighteen he had become a follower of Christ, as God lifted him from the pit and set his feet upon the Solid Rock of Jesus. He was a simple cabinetmaker for most of his life, but at age fifty-five he entered the ministry and became a pastor.

Sometimes, however, the pit is self-inflicted. Psalm 40 is a prayer of King David, evidently occasioned by sins that had overtaken him (v. 12). Probably all of us have felt that way before. But whether we fell innocently into the pit or dug it on our own, none of us wants to stay there for long. Without trying to give simplistic answers, what can we do when we find ourselves down in the dumps?

Going Up

Among the many things listed in Psalm 40, David waited patiently and cried out to the Lord (v. 1). He sang new songs of praise (v. 3). He made the Lord his trust (v. 4). What God does in us while we wait is probably more important than what we're waiting for. God truly is more concerned with our character than our comfort, and believe it or not, that's something we should be thankful for.

Bottom Line

Wait on the Lord. He will prove Himself to be your help and deliverer (see Ps. 40:17).

Superabundance

His divine power has given us everything required for life and godliness through the knowledge of Him who called us by His own glory and goodness. (2 Pet. 1:3)

What We Lack

The world bombards us with messages of what we lack. Madison Avenue tells us we are not good-looking enough, our bodies not toned enough. The news media constantly tell us of a crumbling economy, political instability, and civil unrest, assuring us that our way of life is in constant danger. The cool, hip people of the world remind us of our social ineptitude. Well-meaning friends discourage us in their attempts to "help" us by recounting our flaws and the things we do wrong. Sadly this message of deprivation can even come from pulpits where preachers turn the Christian message into a self-help program, offering principles and spiritual exercises that place the burden of transformation on our shoulders, thus negating the grace of God.

What We Have

In contrast, God's Word emphasizes all we have in Christ. In Christ, God has given us "everything required for life and godliness" (2 Pet. 1:3). And our sufficiency in Him is sufficient enough to ward off any sense of deprivation in any other area of life. We are not those who lack, who fear the future, or who are overly troubled about the present. The key to our transformation is not in continually ramping up our own efforts but in realizing that God has already done an amazing transforming work in us. We have all we need to change.

Bottom Line

Christ has given us all we need and much more to live a God-honoring life of joy and peace.

Genuine Pleasures

The LORD values those who fear Him,
those who put their hope in His faithful love. (Ps. 147:11)

My Pleasure

What brings you pleasure? Closing the deal? Viewing sunsets with your wife? Seeing your favorite team in a big win? Feeling a smooth golf swing? Driving your car? Admiring a trophy mount from your last hunt? Excelling in your position in the church? Having the corner office? Maintaining your house? Having great sex? Reviewing your portfolio? Lots of guys have many of these and still remain unhappy. Unhappiness and discontentment are epidemic in our society, despite the fact that we have a lot.

His Pleasure

What does God find pleasure in? Owning not only the cattle on a thousand hills, but owning the hills as well (see Ps. 50:10)? No, God finds pleasure not in the "stuff" of life but in our daily attitude toward Him. One translation of Psalm 147:11 describes God as "pleased with" another says "God delights in" those who—what?—"fear Him."

To fear God is to have a deep reverence of all He is and all He does so that it impacts the way you live. It's an ever-present understanding that God hates sin. It means submitting to Him, obeying Him, and worshipping Him acceptably, with reverence and awe (see Heb. 12:28–29). It means acknowledging the ways He is working in your life and praising Him. And the Bible says it is foundational for a happy relationship with Him. Pleasing God brings us the greatest pleasure of all.

Bottom Line

Prioritize your life in terms of what pleases God.

Lean on Me

A man with many friends may be harmed, but there is a friend who stays closer than a brother. (Prov. 18:24)

Artie

Artie is the kind of friend who has your back. He'll rejoice for friends in their successes, and he'll walk with them through life's valleys. Many times he and his wife have met with friends who needed counseling. On one occasion he took off for a weekend road trip with a pal from church who needed him.

And it hasn't always been convenient or easy. Artie once stood in the rain for hours, working on an important project for a friend. He stayed by a sick friend's hospital bedside. It meant the world to a buddy of his when Artie served as a pallbearer at the guy's father's funeral. In each and every instance, Artie was there to help.

Your Best Friend

You can call plenty of people "friends," but who are the one or two guys who would be there for you when you need them the most? Who can you count on, no matter what? Those are the kinds of friends you need. The kind of guy who will help you out in a pinch, even at considerable inconvenience to himself.

A truly good friend won't always agree with you. When you make a mistake, your friend will hold you accountable. But rather than judge or condemn, he will help you find your way through the darkness. That's what a friend does. A friend is a friend in good times and in bad. A faithful friend is a great gift from God.

Bottom Line

Tell or show appreciation for your true friends today.

Passionate Pursuit

Do not lack diligence; be fervent in spirit; serve the Lord.
(Rom. 12:11)

Man's Best Friend

Puppies are a great illustration of passion. When a puppy's master comes home, the puppy doesn't just sit there quietly hoping for a little attention. No, he jumps, yelps, and barks until the man he loves shows him some attention. Every book on dogs is emphatic that canines want to please their masters. A dog is not lukewarm about pleasing the man who cares for him. He is consumed with a passionate love for his master.

What would it look like if men were that passionately in love with Jesus? What if every man's life was defined by passion? A lot of Christian men wonder, but the question is how to get there.

The Path of Passion

You can't wake up at six one day and suddenly decide to run in a marathon later that day, having done absolutely no prior training. And you're not going to turn into a spiritual giant overnight either. But you can and must passionately pursue God right now, right where you are, in your current circumstances, no excuses. What you'll discover is that the more you passionately pursue Him, the more you will want to pursue Him because nothing else is better. And the pursuit is not about earning His favor—you've already been given that through Jesus. God is far more passionate about pursuing you than you will ever be about pursuing Him. Let that knowledge spur you on to greater intimacy with the Master.

Bottom Line

Begin your "passionate pursuit" with small steps. Ask God to stoke the fires of your heart with a passion for His Word and for prayer.

Dealing with Insecurity

The LORD protects you;
the LORD is a shelter right by your side. (Ps. 121:5)

The Need for Security

To feel safe in our homes, we lock the doors and install alarm systems. For job security we toe the company line and do the work of three people. For retirement we invest in 401(k) plans and IRAs, and we trust in Social Security. But as one guy said, "For what they actually send you, you can't afford to be 'social' and really can't feel 'secure.'"

In our desperate hunt for security, we must understand that we will not find ultimate security in government or retirement accounts or the latest technological wizardry.

The Ultimate Protector

God alone gives ultimate security in an insecure world. God protects us because it is His nature to do so. He is like a father (though infinitely more capable) who protects his children from danger. He is like a fortress that protects from invading enemies. He is like a refuge that offers a place of rest and security when threatened. He is like a shelter that protects us from the elements and outside forces that seek to harm us. God is the Ultimate Protector!

We need to abide and reside with God, safe in the security of His love, depending on Him to support and sustain us daily. This is especially true when times are hard or when we feel threatened from things outside of our control. Our reflex reaction should be to turn to God rather than languish in our own strength.

Bottom Line

God's protection plan depends not on us but on Him.

Knowing the Enemy

I have done this so that we may not be taken advantage of by Satan. For we are not ignorant of his schemes. (2 Cor. 2:11)

Read the Book

During World War II, General George C. Patton's troops and tanks were engaged in a counterattack of German forces under General Erwin Rommel. Patton is reported to have shouted in the thick of the battle, "I read your book, Rommel!" In Rommel's book, *Infantry Attacks*, the famed "Desert Fox" had carefully detailed his military strategy. And Patton, having read it and knowing what to expect, planned his moves accordingly.

Satan has authored no book, but God has fully exposed our enemy's tactics in the Bible. Shrouded with a mysterious veil of camouflage, the devil must be unmasked if we are to win the spiritual war. We must first know our enemy if we are to defeat him.

Apply the Strategies

Paul was aware of Satan's tactics, and he reminded the Corinthians to stay alert. Jesus, too, knew who and what He was up against in the desert. We need to recognize that we're in a spiritual war with an enemy bent on our destruction. We need to be vigilant!

When Satan tempts us physically, we are to run away. When he tempts us visually, we are to focus on what is good. When he tempts us spiritually, we are to draw near to God. When he tempts us emotionally, we must recall the truth. Stay alert!

Bottom Line

The effectiveness of Satan's strategy requires ignorance on our part. Wise up and know the enemy's strategy.

Inevitable Change

Abraham and Sarah were old and getting on in years.
Sarah had passed the age of childbearing. (Gen. 18:11)

Reality

At a party, just three months before my daughter was born, I calmly remarked, "Having a baby will not change my life." Momentary silence was followed by an eruption of deep belly laughter. In a few months I came to understand just how wrong I was.

Sarah, Abraham's soon-to-give-birth wife, knew what my friends knew: having a baby does change one's life. She had witnessed others face the challenge. They were much younger. She was old. She knew the challenges and difficulties this life change would create.

Readiness

When a baby is coming, the parents have approximately nine months to prepare a room, to buy the needed essentials, to adjust their lifestyle, to monitor their budget. In a word, change. A failure to adjust and make the needed changes leads only to frustration.

Like having a baby, change is here to stay. We can't always control the circumstances, but we can control our perspective about change. The next time you are faced with any type of change, challenge yourself to think through some different perspectives, then choose one that will help you productively manage the change. To thrive in life, we must be able to deal with change. We must develop an unshakable inner confidence that we can handle anything that comes our way.

Bottom Line

When facing change, acknowledge the past, accept the present, and anticipate the future.

Reconciliation

"If you are offering your gift on the altar, and there you remember that your brother has something against you, leave your gift there in front of the altar. First go and be reconciled with your brother, and then come and offer your gift." (Matt. 5:23–24)

The Title Bout

After the first conflict with his wife, Rick didn't see her for a couple of days. Time to think. Slowly his eyes began to open to what most of us have learned at one time or another: conflict is inevitable. When two or more people come together, the potential for disagreement is always there. Even the best of relationships will have some degree of conflict.

The Tender Meeting

Jesus tells us to take the initiative in seeking reconciliation. Restoring a broken relationship is like mending a broken arm. You take initiative by going to a doctor so it can be set, a cast put on, and healing can take place. Broken relationships, like broken arms, are never mended accidentally. They require purposeful, intentional action.

Jesus prescribes a one-on-one, face-to-face meeting. Letters are wonderful, the phone is a marvelous tool, e-mail is a great invention, texting saves time; but when it comes to approaching someone with the motive of healing a relationship, the biblical practice is face-to-face. And what do we say when we get there? Well, the shortest distance between two people seeking reconciliation is often a straight line like: "I was wrong," or "I haven't been honest with you," or "Your actions hurt me," or "I love you too much to allow our relationship to crumble."

Bottom Line

Reconcile first, then worship. That's the correct order.

First Things First

*"Seek first the kingdom of God and His righteousness,
and all these things will be provided for you. Therefore don't
worry about tomorrow, because tomorrow will worry about itself.
Each day has enough trouble of its own." (Matt. 6:33–34)*

The King on His Throne

No matter the type or magnitude of a problem, the Lord is always completely sovereign. Massive earthquake or monster hurricane? The Lord is in control. Uncontrollable oil spill? The King is on His throne. Ungodly politicians? The Master is unchallenged. Cancer or death? God is forever God. "No wisdom, no understanding, and no counsel will prevail against the LORD" (Prov. 21:30).

Sometimes we need to recognize His sovereignty in an area a little closer to home—our finances. It's pretty easy to fall into worry, thinking that God can't (or won't) help. Regardless of your savings balance, the status of your 401(k), or the real estate market, God is fully in control. He is also fully loving, the perfect model of love, and the definition of love. So whether you have little or much, you could not possibly be in better hands.

A Little Perspective

This life is not about this world, nor is it about earthly kingdom-building. One day Jesus will call you home, and you will shed the burden of this world like a rain-swollen overcoat. The King will remove your worries from you as though they never were, for they will never come to your mind again. Live now in light of that future.

Bottom Line

Seek God first and always. He will provide for your every need. Put your faith in the One who is always faithful.

Your Calling

*Mankind, He has told you what is good and what it is the L*ORD
requires of you: to act justly, to love faithfulness,
and to walk humbly with your God. (Mic. 6:8)

Back to the Basics

In our excitement about a specific ministry calling, we can sometimes lose sight of God's general call to all believers—to glorify Him by serving others. When we forget this, we can easily act like a prima donna wide receiver going for the showy one-handed touchdown catch while forgetting fundamentals of the game like vigorously running your routes every play, blocking for your teammates, and submitting to the coach's leadership. An egotistical player really needs a back-to-the-basics conversation with Coach Lombardi!

Maybe you sense a specific call to pastoring, writing, or speaking. Maybe you envision your own one-handed grab: converting hundreds to the Lord, selling millions of books, or instructing thousands from the stage. But how are you doing on the basics? Are you honest and fair in your personal and business dealings? Are you fighting against lust, anger, and greed in your own life? Do you love people who don't love you back? Do you remember that all of your gifts and all of your strength are from the Lord?

It's Not about You

No matter what ministry the Lord has given you, it should be about His glory. Keep in mind that the Lord doesn't measure by worldly standards: He measures by faithfulness. So let your intent be to glorify Him in all you think, say, and do. This is fundamental to your walk with Christ.

Bottom Line

If you're dreaming of a highlight-worthy ministry, remember that God's Hall of Fame is really more like Hebrews 11—a Hall of Faith.

Before You Quit

Now the LORD had appointed a huge fish to swallow Jonah, and Jonah was in the fish three days and three nights. (Jon. 1:17)

The Predicament

Have you ever thought, *It can't get any worse than this*—and then it does? Just when you've given your last ounce of strength to stay afloat in the midst of insurmountable problems, you're swallowed by a giant catastrophe.

Such was Jonah. Having disobeyed God by sailing away from responsibility, a storm was unleashed because of his rebellion. He was thrown overboard by the ship's sailors, abandoned in the sea, thinking death was imminent. *It can't get any worse than this*, he thought. But it did.

The Reality

Consequently Jonah went down. Down to Tarshish, down into the bottom of a ship, down into the water, and now he was down inside the fish. Jonah had hit bottom. The sea was a place of great fear, a place of chaos and death. Jonah thought he was down and done for, but God was up to something.

When human beings are going down, God is often up to something great. From God's perspective, big fish (like the poor economy, job loss, and illness) are not a problem at all. Even stiff-necked, rebellious, stubborn humans are not a problem. God laughs at insurmountable problems. He is working even when we don't realize it. This is good news. He is far more faithful than we imagine.

Bottom Line

Jonah's story reminds us that God meets us at our lowest place. Just when you think it can't get any worse, God is up to something great. So don't quit.

Parental Influence

*Our fathers sinned; they no longer exist,
but we bear their punishment. (Lam. 5:7)*

The Trickle-down Effect

Have you ever read this verse: "The fathers eat sour grapes, and the children's teeth are set on edge"? (Ezek. 18:2). This verse illustrates the biblical principle that one generation can suffer for the sins of another (see Exod. 20:5). While this was a popular refrain in Ezekiel's time, today we might phrase it: "The fathers have drunk too much beer, and the children wake up with a hangover." Sobering words—"Our fathers sinned but we bear their punishment"—a present generation pays the penalty for the errors of a previous generation.

Parental influence is key. Parents communicate moral and ethical values to their children. Recall that Abraham was deceptive. Well, guess what, so was his son Isaac. And so was Isaac's son Jacob! That's often how it works unless there's recognition of the problem, repentance, and divine intervention.

Examine Your Example

Children listen to and watch their parents for clues about how to live and behave. Paul said, "Imitate me, as I also imitate Christ" (1 Cor. 11:1). Rely on Him to empower you to live an authentically righteous life before your children. When you seek Christ daily through prayer and His Word, you will change and be strengthened. You will be able to set a godly example for your children to follow, no matter your past or your family's past.

Bottom Line

You have been given the privilege and responsibility of shaping your children for Christ. They are looking to you. Make sure you're looking to Christ.

Identity in Christ

This is according to His eternal purpose accomplished in the Messiah, Jesus our Lord. In Him we have boldness and confident access through faith in Him. (Eph. 3:11–12)

Knowing Who You Are

You are so inseparably bound to Christ that you share not only His possessions but His identity too. God sees you just as He sees Jesus. This does not mean you share the divine nature of Jesus; you don't. But everything that is true of Jesus in His humanity is also true of you.

Is He a Son? You share His sonship. Is He a Priest? You are a priest too. Is He the Beloved One? You are beloved in Christ. Is He righteous? So are you. Does He have an all-access pass to the throne room of heaven? You are equally welcome there to find grace and mercy in time of need.

Being Who You Are

Do you *know* your new identity in Christ? When you're tempted to view yourself as the same old person held captive to sin, do you remind yourself of your true identity in Christ, set free from sin's penalty and power? When the world labels you stupid, do you counter with the wisdom of Christ? When the world labels you worthless, do you remind yourself that you are deeply loved by God? The world doesn't define those things for you anymore.

The secret is always to look to Christ for your identity. Abide in Him. Turn to Him. Spend time with Him. Let Him define you.

Bottom Line

No matter what the world may say about you, you are who God says you are, and He says you are complete and perfect in Christ Jesus.

Blown Away

*The LORD's works are great, studied by all
who delight in them. (Ps. 111:2)*

What Has God Done?

God has done a vast array of amazing things, giving to human minds the capacity to delve into His works. Man is uniquely gifted to dig into the treasure troves that are everywhere. If you love the outdoors, there are a million things you could spend a lifetime exploring—glaciers, volcanoes, oceans, rivers, the cosmos. A human biology course will leave you bowled over by the incredible complexity of your own body. At the cellular level the intricate design of the Creator is visible in the bustling activity that keeps you alive. And the Bible, of course, is a history of God interacting with humanity and performing amazing acts of justice, mercy, redemption, and miracles that simply defy what we know as normal.

Dive In!

Today's passage is an open invitation to delve into an unfamiliar subject and discover another aspect of the work of God. Divine fingerprints are everywhere, and God beckons us to find Him in all His works. From astronomy to molecular biology, your mind can be stretched and your faith greatly deepened by the overwhelming proofs for the existence of a spectacularly creative and utterly powerful Creator. The cool stuff you learn can also serve as a bridge to share big thoughts about God with friends and seekers. Many have been initially drawn to faith by the evidence that abounds in the universe.

Bottom Line

Search for something that intrigues you about God's works, and go deeper in your understanding of it to better appreciate our amazing Creator.

The Persecuted Church

They threw him out of the city and began to stone him. (Acts 7:58)

Suffering Is Unavoidable

The church was scarcely born before it was under assault. Stephen was the first recorded martyr, stoned to death by an enraged crowd. And although the severity of persecution has ebbed and flowed with history and geography, the world that tortured and killed Jesus is the world that continues to hate and persecute those whose only crime is naming Jesus as Lord and Savior.

Try inviting people to a Bible study in Syria or Saudi Arabia. Even in nations that pay lip service to freedom of religion, Christians are harassed, imprisoned, ostracized, and even killed. Like it or not, the world is a giant combat zone between the forces of darkness and the forces of light, and humanity is caught up in an intense spiritual conflict that has physical ramifications.

Use Every Opportunity

Our Savior told His followers to expect suffering: "You will have suffering in this world" (John 16:33). So it should be no surprise when we face trials and tribulations. This is the normal Christian life.

Let's pray for our persecuted brothers and sisters and aid them in any way we can. Ministries like Voice of the Martyrs have information and actions we can do to make a difference in the lives of persecuted believers. Many of us are blessed to be living in a time and place in which we are not heavily persecuted, so let's take advantage of every opportunity to share Jesus freely.

Bottom Line

If the world hated Jesus, it will hate those who love Him. Don't let that stop you from faithfully testifying for Him.

The Battle Within

*The flesh desires what is against the Spirit,
and the Spirit desires what is against the flesh;
these are opposed to each other,
so that you don't do what you want. (Gal. 5:17)*

Cage Fighting

The Bible tells us a war rages within us like a cage fight in our soul. The moment you put your faith in Jesus, He breathed His own nature into you. "If anyone is in Christ, he is a new creation; old things have passed away, and look, new things have come" (2 Cor. 5:17). That's the reality. You really are a new man, re-created in Christ Jesus for good works (see Eph. 2:10). That's who you are at your core. Yet the battle against sin is not over. Something "old" remains in us.

Why Is This So Hard?

You have a habit of trying to satisfy your deepest wants in ways that are destructive toward yourself and others and are an affront to God. And that history—that "old man"—is kicking and screaming and lying to you. So you hate sin, but you love it, fighting it and then going back to it. The key question is this: Who will you trust to fulfill the desires God gave you?

We need to get two big ideas into our thick skulls: (1) God really wants to fulfill our deepest yearnings; we can trust Him not to rip us off. (2) Only God can win this battle in our heart, so we need to keep asking Him to empower us.

Bottom Line

The fight against sin is a fight about who you're going to trust. Will you trust your old ways (the old man), or the God who gave you Jesus?

A Lasting Marriage

"They are no longer two, but one flesh. Therefore what God has joined together, man must not separate." (Matt. 19:6)

For Better or Worse

When things get difficult in a marriage, it is not unusual for one or both partners to ask themselves: *Did I marry the right person?* But that's the wrong question, and your emotions will give you the wrong answer. Even if you are not happy in your marriage, and even if you did something that flagrantly violated the Scripture—such as marrying a non-Christian when you were a believer—God has clearly and repeatedly said He considers marriage sacred and binding. He does not want you to bail out. So the real question is: *How do I make this marriage work?*

Limited Options

Start by taking divorce off the table. This may mean working through the tough consequences of making an unwise choice. Instead of thinking up ways to get out, strategize ways to stay in. Once you decide "I am going to make this work," you can get the prayer support, counseling, mentoring—whatever it takes—to equip you to save your marriage. It may seem like a long, uphill battle, but you can make progress if you persevere.

Remember that God is pulling for you. He will give you the grace to make it if you will trust Him on this big issue. Keep in mind that some of the best marriages are ones that weathered the biggest storms. Marriage takes a lot of faith and effort. Everyone's does.

Bottom Line

The marriage you are in right now is the marriage God calls you to preserve and protect. If you're struggling in your marriage right now, don't give up!

Go Team

Barnabas, however, took him and brought him to the apostles and explained to them how Saul had seen the Lord on the road and that He had talked to him, and how in Damascus he had spoken boldly in the name of Jesus. (Acts 9:27)

Risky Affirmation

An interesting dynamic arises in Acts 9. Barnabas, now a respected elder in the early church, takes a bold risk. While many doubted the validity of Saul's conversion from chief persecutor to believer, Barnabas puts his credibility on the line to affirm Saul's worth to the church. You could argue that without Barnabas' simple affirmation, the church might look a lot different today.

Barnabas displayed the qualities of a spiritual mentor. He stepped away from his own personal agenda and took up the job of guiding this young believer into maturity and leadership. You'll notice that Luke, the author of Acts, describes the duo as Barnabas and Saul until the end of Acts 13, when suddenly they are described as Paul and Barnabas. It would appear that this elder statesman in the church, who captained their missionary team, had coached Saul into Paul, who became history's greatest evangelist and church planter.

From Saul to Paul

Every Christian leader has Sauls in their midst—newly converted Christians long on zeal and short on wisdom. The easy thing is to view them as a nuisance, a sort of stumbling block to greater ministry. But God may be calling us to coach them, to ensure that when they leave our presence, they are more Paul than Saul, ready to lead for God.

Bottom Line

Leading like Barnabas means we help guide our team members toward spiritual maturity.

Wanted: Teachers

Although by this time you ought to be teachers, you need someone to teach you the basic principles of God's revelation again. You need milk, not solid food. (Heb. 5:12)

Prime Rib or Skim Milk?

It's no secret that in many churches men struggle with spiritual maturity. Perhaps it's because of two widely held myths.

The first is that discipleship and growth are somehow an option, like pursuing a hobby. This nonchalance keeps a lot of guys on the sidelines of their faith. The other myth is just as destructive: the myth of inability. If you could get the honest truth from most Christian guys, you'd find they really don't feel they possess the gifts to move forward in their faith. They see the pastor, the missionary, the church leader and believe these "professional Christians" are more spiritually blessed than they are.

Growth Is Possible

While personality and gifts vary widely from man to man, Jesus' radical call to fruit-bearing discipleship is neither optional nor impossible. In fact, it's the normal Christian life. That's why in today's verse the author of the book of Hebrews conveys a sense of disappointment over his readers' lack of growth.

The encouraging truth is that every Christian man has been empowered and equipped by the Holy Spirit to move toward greater Christlikeness. All God needs is our surrendered heart and our intentional desire to know Christ. The Spirit does the rest—convicting, teaching, transforming, and motivating the heart.

Bottom Line

God's will is for every man to move from milk to meat.

You're Not Alone

You are my rock and my fortress;
You lead and guide me because of Your name. (Ps. 31:3)

Beaten Down and Betrayed

An amazing sense of peace and comfort resides in the words of Psalm 31 because all of us can identify with David's sense of utter despair. At one time or another, we've all felt beaten down and betrayed. For any of a million different reasons, each of our lives has been rocked by difficulty and despair.

No matter how hard we try to control things, our circumstances are often beyond our control. Maybe the worst feeling of all occurs when debilitating doubt creeps in, causing us to feel completely and utterly alone. The situation can seem so desperate, like no one out there could possibly help or even understand our situation.

God Shows Up

And that's when God shows up. Whether things seem completely out of control in your day-to-day walk or in society in general, God is there. Our lives may change constantly for better or worse, but our Creator was, is, and always will be steadfast and in control. When we cry out to Him, He listens and helps us every time.

Psalm 31 seems to have been written specifically for those of us in crisis. Within its twenty-four verses, David pours out his heart and soul to God. When he refers to God as a rock of refuge and an impenetrable fortress, the implication is clear: no matter how uncertain our lives may be, God is our immovable, unshakable protector. We can count on Him.

Bottom Line

In your times of doubt and struggle, God is always with you, always in control.

Wonderful Creation

*I will praise You because I have been
remarkably and wonderfully made. Your works are wonderful,
and I know this very well. (Ps. 139:14)*

iPad

The iPad is an incredibly cool gadget. It can browse the Internet and send and receive e-mails. It's a portable music/video player, photo album, e-book reader, and video game player. The device is ultra-thin and weighs next to nothing, making it easy for you to check out this week's issue of *Sports Illustrated* or get in a round or two of your addictive game of choice.

Yet the iPad does have its limitations. Even with growing gigabytes of memory in each new release, only so much can be downloaded. Keeping smudges off the touch-sensitive screen is nearly impossible. Sometimes the apps don't work, and it crashes. And don't even think about dropping an iPad, because it probably won't survive the fall.

No Limits

The God we serve has no such limitations. His love, grace, and mercy know no bounds. His maximum battery life is not measured in hours but in eternity. And as amazing as an iPad can be, it simply cannot compare to God's most wonderful creation—us!

As humans, we can walk, run, jump, sit, talk, and think. We can reason. We can drive cars and fly airplanes. We can be happy or sad, rejoice or grieve. The most important purpose behind our creation, however, is to worship and serve our Creator. God knew what He was doing when He formed us—so thank Him today!

Bottom Line

God is far more interesting than any technological advancement ever made, and so are you— a person made in His image! Be amazed and give thanks!

Playing Offense

He gave Himself for us to redeem us from all lawlessness and to cleanse for Himself a people for His own possession, eager to do good works. (Titus 2:14)

Do the Right Thing

Steve was a new Christian. When he heard about the church basketball league, he thought it would be the perfect way to meet like-minded guys. Just one problem: Steve's competitive juices often took over on the court, and he ended up cursing and getting into fights. Every game he determined not to swear. Every game he failed. Finally, a friend told him to change his motivation. Instead of trying not to sin, he encouraged Steve to focus on doing something positive on the court.

Before the next game Steve decided to try and say three nice things to his opponents after they made good plays. Guess what? It helped! Not only did Steve's language improve, but he didn't get into any fights. That's progress!

Don't Be Passive

God doesn't want us to live passively, trying not to break one of His laws. He wants us to live powerful lives that not only change us but also change the people around us. His grace should not only make us glad to be forgiven but (as Titus 2:14 says) "eager to do good works."

Many men put all their efforts into avoiding sin yet end up either failing or living joyless lives. By actively looking to do good works and following God, we can live energized lives and avoid sin's trappings. Doesn't that sound more appealing than playing defense your whole life?

Bottom Line

Instead of trying to avoid doing the bad stuff, make an effort to do some good in the world. You were made for that.

When Happiness Hurts

See how happy the man is God corrects; so do not reject the discipline of the Almighty. (Job 5:17)

Honor the Bond

Happy is such a happy word. Just saying it can make you feel warm and fuzzy. It's natural for parents to want their children to be happy and be blessed with high self-esteem. But happiness also has a dark side. Studies show that gang leaders, violent criminals, and bullies often have high self-esteem. Self-esteem can also come from feeling powerful, so men who abuse women or executives who cheat their company can often feel happy about themselves.

Pain Equals Gain

When it comes to raising good kids, the goal shouldn't be happiness. Richard Weissbourd, a faculty member at the Harvard School of Education, says character comes from making sacrifices, facing challenges, and dealing with adversity—ideas rooted in the Bible. Serving others can give our kids a sense of happiness that doesn't fade. Even a little pain or discipline can ultimately lead to happiness, as the "happy" man in Job 5:17 attests.

Just as we shouldn't reject God's discipline, we shouldn't hold back in disciplining our children or allowing them to feel a little pain. Momentary sadness caused by correction or hardship can help our kids live more God-honoring lives. We should teach our kids to do the right thing, not because it makes them happy but because it's right. That may be countercultural, but it's God's way.

Bottom Line

God calls us to focus on our kids' character so they'll experience the right kind of happiness.

Pernicious Pride

Come now, you who say, "Today or tomorrow we will travel
to such and such a city and spend a year there and
do business and make a profit." You don't even know what
tomorrow will bring—what your life will be! (James 4:13–14)

Presumed Innocent

We humans are a planning species, endlessly making goals (for the day, the weekends, our vacations, and careers), always devising schemes to make us happy. This isn't surprising, really. God certainly makes plans, and we are made in His image. Our ability to plan is something He gave us. In our Scripture today James isn't speaking against us making plans but against the presumption that so often accompanies our plan making.

Many of us are probably surprised at the charge of presumption. After all, making plans is just a part of going about our business. But because of sin's influence, "business as usual" tends to be self-referential where we leave God out of the process if not by deliberation, then by default.

Reality Check

Surely this is crazy. As James says, "You don't even know what tomorrow will bring—what your life will be!" We need to recognize this subtle form of pride and take steps to resist the natural, godless way we go about much of our lives. Living out the details of life without reference to God is nothing short of arrogance and presumption. Let's put God back into the center of our daily planning and problem solving. In so doing, we'll have a much surer footing and the peace of knowing we aren't running the race in vain.

Bottom Line

Start by asking God to birth His plans in you, and then remember to submit all your thoughts, hopes, cares, and dreams to Him.

Measure of a Man

Patience is better than power, and controlling one's temper, than capturing a city. (Prov. 16:32)

A Lost Virtue

This sin-afflicted world of ours can offer us countless opportunities for conflict and disappointment. Even worse, the relationships that are most important to us often seem to end up being the most difficult.

Patience in the face of provocation can be challenging. After all, we pride ourselves on not taking any flak. When we've been hurt, our natural desire is to go on the attack immediately and with full force. We treat conflict like a pretext for full-scale war, be it psychological or physical. In addition to this instinctive response, a "real man" in our culture is measured by his physical strength, toughness, and ability to intimidate others.

What Is True Strength?

Interestingly, however, the Scriptures offer a wholly different measure of strength and maturity. According to today's verse, patience and self-control are the true measures of a man, at least of a man renewed in Christ. Of course, we know that there is "a time for war" (Eccles. 3:8), but this is reserved for danger to life and limb. When we treat all situations as if they're the basis for war, we invariably destroy those we were meant to build up.

Indeed, patience goes against the grain of our old nature and the prevailing culture, but it is surely the mark of spiritual maturity. We will not become what God wants us to be without it.

Bottom Line

Identify one area of your life in which self-control and patience don't come easy for you, and then pray for God's help.

The Blame Game

What is the source of wars and fights among you? Don't they come from the cravings that are at war within you? (James 4:1)

A Marriage Mystery

In marriage two people who thrill to one another's presence make public promises of love and devotion all their days. Yet many couples eventually find themselves enmeshed in chronic conflict and seeking to break their holy vows. How does such a thing happen? Where does such rancor come from?

Few of us would admit that we are disagreeable people. And if we concede to occasionally being so, we are quick to attribute the matter to outside influence. We point out how hungry we were, or how tired, or how sorely provoked we were by our spouse.

Mystery Solved

In contrast to our finger pointing, Scripture lays the matter squarely at our own feet, indicating the cause to be our own fleshly desires run amok. This is not to say that some desires are not legitimate. But if their thwarting leads us to wrath and anger, then these "legitimate" desires have gone beyond the bounds of legitimacy and transformed themselves into idols.

In short, the amount of conflict in our lives is a barometer of spiritual health. The only thing that will quench fleshly desire is a greater desire for God. If we recognize this fact, we have a chance of praying rightly, doing rightly, and turning our homes into a haven of peace rather than a swirl of stormy conflict.

Bottom Line

Instead of blaming everyone else, let's demonstrate true leadership by acknowledging our shortcomings and repenting when necessary.

Big Faith, Big God

Plane Truth

George wanted to fly his mother out for a summer visit. With a little research online, he found her a ticket on a fifty-seat commuter plane leaving from a nearby airport that connected to a larger plane in a major city. But when George called his mom, she hesitated.

"Do I have to fly in a commuter plane?" she asked. When he told her that those were the only planes that flew out of the airport closest to her, she said, "I don't think this is a good time to come."

"Well, if you drive an extra couple of hours to a bigger airport," George said, "you can take a 777 wide body." That's all she needed to hear to change her mind.

Faith Factor

When George's mom thought about the commuter plane, she didn't have much faith in its safety. But she did trust the bigger plane. We often act the same way when it comes to God. Our faith in Him is related to how we see Him. In Mark 11:22, Jesus tells His disciples to "have faith in God." A verse later Jesus says if you have the faith to move a mountain, it will move.

God deserves that much faith. His size is unfathomable. He is limitless. By having an accurate view of God, we'll naturally have the faith we need to serve and trust Him wholly.

Bottom Line

We can have big faith because we serve a big God. And that faith can help us act boldly.

Reject Passivity

Then the woman . . . took some of its fruit and ate it; she also gave some to her husband, who was with her, and he ate it. (Gen. 3:6)

Sinful Onlooker

If you grew up in the church, you've probably seen the flannel-graph scene of Eve being tempted by the serpent. As the snake slithers down the beautifully fruited tree, Eve looks mesmerized by Satan's temptations. We all know what happens next: Eve eats the fruit. But that picture of Eve standing alone with the serpent might not be accurate—Adam was right there with her. He wasn't out naming animals or hunting down dinner. According to Genesis 3:6, "[Eve] took some of its fruit and ate it; she also gave some to her husband, who was with her, and he ate it." When Eve was being tempted, Adam didn't step up and stop her.

Get in the Action

Adam could've knocked away the forbidden fruit before it ever touched her lips. Even better, he could've grabbed a stick and stabbed the serpent until his forked tongue lay limp. Instead Adam, "who was with her," stood back and did nothing as sin entered the world.

As men, we can't follow Adam's example. We need to set standards and protect our families from harmful influences. Experts say it's natural for men to shirk responsibilities. But God doesn't want us to live according to "natural" inclinations; He wants us to live supernaturally—motivated to protect and be involved with our families.

Bottom Line

God wants you to be active in protecting your family. Embrace that responsibility.

Whose Purposes?

David, after serving his own generation in God's plan, fell asleep, was buried with his fathers, and decayed. (Acts 13:36)

Your Times

It's morbid but true. Every one of us has an appointment with the worm, a time when our earthly body will decay in the grave. And no amount of Botox, liposuction, or medicinal herbs will delay that appointment.

The apostle Paul, in this sermon preached in Acts, says that before David died, he served God's purposes in his own generation. The Greek word behind the phrase "in his own" is *idios*, which is where we get our word *idiosyncrasies*. In other words, David served the purposes of God according to the uniquenesses of his own generation.

Their Times

Your generation is different from the generations that have come after you. Chances are, the way you would do things doesn't always square with the methods and opinions of those who are younger. But their differences aren't always wrong. Must your children have the same camp experiences, sing the same songs, and express themselves in worship the same way you did for their faith to be valid? Or is serving the purposes of God according to their own generation enough?

It's the arrogance of every generation to believe theirs is the best ever. The "how" of kingdom building is never as important as the "Who." Make sure you are serving *God's* purposes in your life, not your own.

Bottom Line

Learn the uniquenesses of your kids, and ask God to fulfill His purposes in their lives, not your purposes for them.

Two Great Gifts

*Grace to you and peace from God our Father
and the Lord Jesus Christ. (Phil. 1:2)*

The Gift of Grace

When was the last time you experienced grace? When was the last time you got something totally for free, no strings attached, that you didn't deserve or earn in any way whatsoever? It doesn't happen often. We're used to operating under the system of "you get what you pay for" and "no free lunch." That's just how things work in this world. Yet nothing is better than grace. We long for it.

The Gift of Peace

Peace is just about as rare as grace. We struggle to maintain a sense of personal peace, not to mention interpersonal peace. There are so many things in life that can rob us of peace, so peace is a gift we need and long for too.

Thankfully Paul delivers on both counts when he passes on the blessing of grace and peace from "God our Father and the Lord Jesus Christ." He's not just giving us a theological treatise on grace; he's actually offering it to us on behalf of God our Father and the Lord Jesus Christ. It's a personal blessing. Imagine what it would be like to live under that blessing all day, every day. Imagine God speaking grace and peace to you and over you personally. These are biblical realities. These are gifts just waiting to be received.

Bottom Line

Grace and peace are ours in abundance. But we need to receive them by faith.

Praying with Joy

I give thanks to my God for every remembrance of you, always praying with joy for all of you in my every prayer, because of your partnership in the gospel from the first day until now. (Phil. 1:3–5)

No Passing Thought

How many times has someone expressed a need to you and you've replied with, "I'll pray for you," only to realize a few days later that you forgot all about it? For many of us, our good intentions about praying for others are just that—good intentions. But rather than feeling guilty about coming up short in this area, maybe we ought to ask ourselves why we don't prioritize prayer for others more. Maybe the problem goes deeper than laziness or forgetfulness. Maybe it's really a problem of belief. Maybe we don't think it matters much whether we pray or don't pray.

Reading today's verse, you don't get the sense that the apostle Paul struggled to remember to pray for the Philippians. You also don't get the sense that he thought prayer was unimportant. Quite the opposite. He said he thanked God "for every remembrance of you, always praying with joy for all of you in my every prayer."

A Beautiful Partnership

Notice how Paul says that he prays for them because of their "partnership in the gospel." As Christians, we're all in this together. We desperately need the prayers of others, and others desperately need our prayers. Praying for others is a great joy and privilege. Don't neglect it.

Bottom Line

Praying for others is one of the best ways you can love them. Let your prayers be filled with thanksgiving and joy and faith.

Good Work

I am sure of this, that He who started a good work in you will carry it on to completion until the day of Christ Jesus. (Phil. 1:6)

Complete Confidence

Much in life is uncertain, but some things are for sure. Your salvation is definitely one of those things. Yet countless Christians go through life without complete assurance that they are forgiven, that God accepts them, that the good work He began in them will never end.

We need to know this assurance beyond a doubt because we are weak apart from God's persevering grace. The road of discipleship can seem long and difficult at times, and if we don't know that God is absolutely committed to strengthening us and being with us all the way to the end, we're not going to make it or at least we're not going to make it with the amount of joy and comfort we could and should have.

Who Is Your God?

Like a lot of spiritual issues, assurance really comes down to what we believe about God. Is He faithful? Is He good? Does He really love us? Can we trust His Word? How we answer those questions in our heart will determine whether we enjoy the freedom and joy He desires for us or whether we go through life doubting, fearful, and striving to somehow do enough to assure ourselves we won't lose His favor and protection. We will not risk much for God if we aren't sure whether He'll come through for us. Assurance is a big deal. Ask God to bolster yours.

Bottom Line

Assurance is a matter of faith. It's a matter of taking God at His Word and acting as if what He says is true—because it is.

A Fruitful Life

. . . filled with the fruit of righteousness that comes through Jesus Christ to the glory and praise of God. (Phil. 1:11)

A Life That Counts

Every man wants his life to count, to be successful, to make a difference in our short time on this planet. The problem is, our desire for success is often mixed with selfish ambition and pride. If we're honest, sometimes we want others to think well of us more than we want to put forth the effort to actually *be* people worthy of respect and admiration.

This desire for success, impact, and respect is as true for Christians as for anyone else. The difference is, we know that our definition of success needs to be redefined as faithfulness to Christ. We know we must live righteous lives characterized by much fruit-bearing, giving glory to God. But how do we do that?

A Better Way

The way to bear fruit for God is actually *not* to set out to bear fruit for God. Sure, we need to have a desire to bear fruit, but it's not something we can just go out and do in our own strength. Instead, we bear fruit by staying closely connected to God in our daily living and by being willing to do whatever He wants us to do. Of course, we probably won't have all the specifics we'd like—God doesn't give us a blueprint for our entire life—but we can always be praying and seeking and doing the next right thing. Our fruit comes only through our relationship with Jesus.

Bottom Line

Ministry is always done in the name of Jesus and in His power. He produces fruit through us. Make sure you stay close to Him.

A Strong Stance

Always be ready to give a defense to anyone who asks you for a reason for the hope that is in you. (1 Pet. 3:15)

Here I Stand

Martin Luther, known today as the Father of the Reformation, began teaching during the sixteenth century that forgiveness of sins was available through faith in Christ alone, not by the more customary practice of the day—buying a pardon from the religious authorities. His disgust over the issue came to a head in 1517 when John Tetzel, a representative of Pope Leo X, traveled throughout Germany raising money for a church building project by selling certificates of pardon signed by the pope. On October 31 of that year, the fiery Luther wrote up his angry challenge—known as the "95 Theses"—allegedly nailing them to the front door of the Castle Church in Wittenberg.

He was later accused of heresy and ordered to recant. But he took the position that he could not recant, based on both the Scriptures and common reason, believing he was speaking the truth. He famously said, "Here I stand, I cannot do otherwise. God help me. Amen."

What I Believe

As men, we need to know what we believe and be willing to take hard stands in defense of our faith, our families, and our biblical convictions. Too often we reserve our strongest opinions for things that don't really matter—"Who was the better running back? Barry Sanders or Walter Payton?"—but when God's Word is being twisted around to justify sin or promote untruths, we give it an anything-goes shrug and ignore the warning bells. Strive to know the truth and to champion it courageously.

Bottom Line

Do you know what you stand for and why?

Fire Warning

Look, all you who kindle a fire, who encircle yourselves with firebrands; walk in the light of your fire and in the firebrands you have lit! This is what you'll get from My hand: you will lie down in a place of torment. (Isa. 50:11)

Got a Match?

Sometimes we grow weary of waiting on God, confusing activity with accomplishment. The old adage, "Don't just sit there, do something," is inbred in every male. We tend to be "fix-it" kind of guys. And in darkness, it seems like things aren't being fixed very quickly. We are in a hurry, and God seemingly isn't.

Some of the fires a man lights during these dark times include the fire of direction (leaning on our own intelligence), security (trusting in our riches and wealth), or relationships (believing others can fill a void only God can fill). But if we live by the light of our own fire, we are sure to flame out.

Real Light

"Firebrands" are simply sparks. A spark is very small compared to the true Light of the World. All the different methods by which we would save ourselves are only small, shooting sparks compared to Jesus.

The contrast is simple to understand. The righteous can walk in darkness yet patiently wait for the light that God will kindle for them. Instead of growing impatient, taking things into our own hands, we can wait on the Lord, knowing that His fire is burning even when we can't see it.

Bottom Line

Give up your fear of the dark (your control issues) by learning that God can be trusted.

Picture His Name

God replied to Moses, "I AM WHO I AM." (Exod. 3:14)

Say the Name

When God revealed Himself at the burning bush, He said Moses was to call Him *YHVH*, which our English translates as "I AM." These four Hebrew letters sound like "Yode-Hey-Vav-Hey." Today, it is rarely pronounced by Orthodox Jews for fear they might use it casually. But Christians aren't afraid to call on the name of "Yahweh" or "Lord."

Ancient letters such as Egyptian hieroglyphics, the Chinese alphabet, and Hebrew letters were little pictures or symbols that represented an idea. They were "ideograms"—like the symbols for male, female, or disabled that you might see in various public places. When you look at the "picture meanings" for the Hebrew letters YHVH, God's plan for the world comes into sharp focus.

See the Name

Yode is a small letter that is also the symbol for "hand." *Hey* looks like an open window and represents the idea of "look" or "behold." *Vav* looks like and refers to a hook, nail, or peg. Ancient Hebrews might not have understood the significance of these symbols, but Christians are brought to yet another point of devotion as we consider the name of God.

Symbolically speaking, the holy name of God, YHVH, can be translated as "Behold, the hand. Behold, the nail." Behold, the Savior of the world who died for you. God's name spells love.

Bottom Line

When we take God's name in vain, we mock His work to redeem us through the cross.

Touch the Future

Children were brought to Him so He might put His hands on them and pray. But the disciples rebuked them. (Matt. 19:13)

Praying and More

Years ago a father brought his young son to a hotel where the famed Babe Ruth was staying. They knocked on Babe's door, and the ballplayer himself came out and said, "Hello, kid, want an autograph?" To which the father responded, "No, I just want my son to shake the hand of the greatest baseball player that ever lived."

Something special is conveyed through the gift of touch. The parents of those children in Jesus' day could have simply asked the Messiah to pray for their children. He could have easily done that and affected them even if they weren't present. But they brought their children to Jesus so He might also touch them.

The Ministry of Touch

Men are sometimes a little leery of touching a child for fear the touch might be misunderstood. Perhaps their own fathers were men of few words and fewer touches. No matter—by our touch we can encourage a child. We convey worth and warmth with that hug. We build up confidence with that pat on the back. We teach boys how to become men by looking them in the eye and shaking their hand.

How poor is the child whose father never touches him! In a world where children often lack for male Christian role models, may we never be guilty of the sin of the disciples—may we always make time to touch *and* to pray.

Bottom Line

Let Jesus touch a child through you today!

Walking in the Dark

Who among you fears the LORD, listening to the voice of His Servant? Who among you walks in darkness, and has no light? Let him trust in the name of Yahweh; let him lean on his God.
(Isa. 50:10)

A Light Has Come

Children typically fear the dark, and many of us never get over it. But consider darkness—it is nothing more than the absence of light. Before Jesus came, the world was walking in spiritual darkness. People didn't have a clear understanding of who God really is. It took the Light of the world to reveal the Father to us, to show us His heart and His redemptive plan. No wonder we worship Jesus as the "light of the world" (John 8:12).

Trusting When We Can't See

God ordained the Hebrew Sabbath to begin at sunset, when darkness swallows the daylight, when senses are heightened and the need for God is the greatest. He guided the children of Israel with a pillar of fire by night. In the darkness of the wilderness temptation, He sent angels to minister to His only Son. And darkness came over the land as that Son was crucified—yet God was still present.

The verse above instructs us to trust God as we walk in darkness. To be people of "the light" is also to be people of "the night" who lean on the Lord even when we can't see Him. There will be times when we don't understand what God is doing or saying, when He is cloaked in mystery. During those times don't simply celebrate the bright, empty cross of resurrection: celebrate the dark, occupied cross of Good Friday! Keep trusting, even in the dark!

Bottom Line

God doesn't need light to do His greatest works.

Glad to Work

*We rebuilt the wall until the entire wall was joined
together up to half its height, for the people had
the will to keep working. (Neh. 4:6)*

Gripe or Gratitude

It's so easy to complain about our jobs. Our cubicle is too small. The people we deal with are rude. We don't like the office politics. Our superiors don't listen or don't care. Health insurance costs keep going up. Our raises are getting smaller or our pay is decreasing. Promotions always seem to go to the other guy. We don't travel enough or we travel too much. Before we know it, our sour attitude affects our performance. Sometimes we get so caught up in circumstances, we miss the big picture. We miss that our work is a contribution to God's kingdom.

Will to Work

Nehemiah was a big-picture guy. The Old Testament tells how this cupbearer to a king rebuilt Jerusalem's walls. Enemies taunted and attacked, but Nehemiah was singularly focused on the job God gave him. Despite setbacks, Nehemiah remained grateful to God for the work, and he spurred the people to complete the project in just fifty-two days.

How did Nehemiah do it? The Bible says, "The people had the will to keep working." Wall building can be monotonous, hard work—and dangerous, too, when you're being attacked. But God's people worked quickly and skillfully. When we have a grateful heart and a strong will to work, it's amazing what we can accomplish.

Bottom Line

Train yourself to see the good in your work. Then do your best in your job without complaining.

Near to Us

What great nation is there that has a god near to it as the L<small>ORD</small> our God is to us whenever we call to Him? (Deut. 4:7)

Friend of God

You are a friend of God. Let that sink in. God calls you His friend. Our relationship with Him is what makes Christianity different from other religions. From the beginning of recorded history, God has been close to His people. When Moses asked whether any other nation had a god who was near at hand, who listened and heard from them, the answer was *no* and *none!*

No other people can say they're as close to their god as we are to the One True God. God is near to us all the time. The Creator of the universe is only a prayer away. And just as God guided His people in Moses' time, He guides us today by His Spirit and through His written Word, the Bible.

His Story

God gives us His Word so we can know Him. Though we can never know God exhaustively—the Infinite can never be fully apprehended by the finite—we can learn a great deal about our all-powerful, never-changing, ever-present Lord through the pages of the Bible. Yet statistics show Christians are getting into God's Word less frequently.

But if we're friends with God, certainly we'd want to know Him. What is His character? What does He say? What has He done? How does He want us to act? It's all there in the Bible.

Bottom Line

Are you giving your relationship with God the time it deserves? Try to learn something new about your Savior-Friend this week.

Down the Middle

Two are better than one because they have a good reward for their efforts. For if either falls, his companion can lift him up; but pity the one who falls without another to lift him up. (Eccles. 4:9–10)

The Right Aim

Imagine a bowling lane where each pin at the far end represents one of your responsibilities. Provide income, love your wife, spend quality time with your kids, please your boss, coach a soccer team—you get the picture. Rolling a strike and meeting all of those obligations is hard enough. Now throw in an illness, job loss, depression, family struggle, or something else, and it can feel like trying to bowl left-handed while being poked, pulled, and prodded.

Avoiding the Gutters

As followers of Christ, we have bumpers available to keep the ball from going in the gutter. These bumpers come in the form of God's Word, prayer, wise counsel, and our own spiritual discipline. We need to be diligent to make sure our bumpers are in place, that they stay in place, and that any flimsy areas are reinforced.

One of the best ways to ensure your protection against gutter balls is through seeking the help of other men who can assist in keeping your life rolling straight down the middle. Ask God to direct you to one or two other men you can start meeting with each week. Be honest with one another, share your weaknesses, and enlist their help in living right before God. It could keep you from going in the gutter.

Bottom Line

Meeting regularly with other guys who can hold us accountable can keep us from being bowled over by life's challenges.

Questions for Parents

"Why do you call Me good?" Jesus asked him.
"No one is good but One—God." (Luke 18:19)

What Would Jesus Ask?

Jesus knew how to ask the perfect question. The Gospels record more than a hundred questions He asked. Some were rhetorical, like when He said in Matthew 6:27, "Can any of you add a single cubit to his height by worrying?" Other times His questions made a person think, such as when the young ruler called Him "Good Teacher," and Jesus responded, "Why do you call Me good? . . . No one is good but One—God." Questions are a great, nonthreatening way to engage someone in conversation.

Ask and You Will Receive

As parents we can learn a lot from Jesus when it comes to the power of questions. Instead of talking at our children to teach a lesson or pass down our beliefs, we may be more effective by asking questions. Make sure your questions can't be answered in a simple yes or no. Try to ask your kids open-ended questions that get them talking so you can hear what they really believe.

As our children get into their teen years, it's especially important to ask questions to keep communication flowing. By encouraging your kids to think and formulate their own opinions, you'll help them build a stronger foundation. When we're forced to articulate what we believe, it fortifies our beliefs. Following Jesus' example in asking questions is one small way we can be like our Savior.

Bottom Line

Questions can be key in communicating with our children. Just make sure to have a conversation, not an interrogation.

Healthy Sex

Heat It Up

"Women are like Crock-Pots; men are like microwaves." We've all probably heard that adage when it comes to how husbands and wives view sex. While it may not be true for everybody, women tend to need more time to get in the mood. Instead of being frustrated by that fact, we may want to look at why God created our wives that way.

As men, we're visual and physical. It doesn't take much to get our motor running. Women, on the other hand, need to feel an emotional connection to enjoy sex. That connection takes time. And time is key to a healthy marriage.

Undercover Truth

Sex is important in a marriage. But as husbands, we must respect our marriages enough to put forth the effort to keep our life in the bedroom pure. Pornography paints a cheap, easy picture of sex. Real love takes hard work and patience. Be willing to wait for the right time to make love to your wife. Let the mood simmer as you enjoy talking and being with her.

By slowly building the heat in your love life, you'll honor your wife and the God who gave her to you. And you will enjoy a God-blessed sex life that will help your marriage stay strong—something every guy needs and wants.

Bottom Line

A good sex life brings many benefits. What are some ways you can make your love life more satisfying to you and your wife?

Trial and Error

*Remember that the LORD your God led you on the
entire journey these 40 years in the wilderness, so that
He might humble you and test you to know what was in your
heart, whether or not you would keep His commands. (Deut. 8:2)*

Observe Where We Failed

Today's verse comes from Moses' address to the Israelites as
they're camped across the Jordan River from the promised land.
They are just days away from doing what their people could have
done forty years earlier had they been obedient and not doubted
God.

Over and over again in Exodus and Numbers, we see Israel
described as rebellious, stiff-necked, and forgetful. And today
we often still struggle with the same, wrong heart attitudes that
the Israelites did. In this piece of Moses' address, we see God's
purpose for their trial and perhaps for ours.

Regain Our Focus

This text is both comforting and convicting. It's comforting
in the sense that God is always with us and has a purpose for
allowing us to go through trials. It's convicting, however, in that
He exposes our pride, impatience, doubt, prejudice, and ingratitude along the way. Simply put, we have two options in how
we respond to hardship: turn to God or grumble. Rather than
working harder to find our own solutions, we must spend time in
prayer and in the Word. Allow God to reveal Himself, His love,
and His purpose in whatever trials you face.

Bottom Line

God often uses our struggles to test our heart and teach us
more about Him. Use this time to adjust your expectations and
put your focus back on Him.

Listening to God

*All Scripture is inspired by God and is profitable
for teaching, for rebuking, for correcting,
for training in righteousness, so that the man of God may be
complete, equipped for every good work. (2 Tim. 3:16–17)*

God Is Not Silent

Part of the reason we don't always hear from God is that we don't always put enough stock in the primary way He communicates with us—through His written Word, the Bible. Many times we're looking for something more, some "personal word" that circumvents the hard work of actually listening to what God says in the Bible and wrestling with the implications of it.

That's not to say that God doesn't speak in other ways—through circumstances, through the counsel of others, even through a strong inner sense or prompting, directing us to say or do something. It's just that listening to what God says in the Bible should be first and foremost in our lives. In fact, when we're steeped in the Bible, when we're listening to God *that* way, we're much more able to hear Him speak in other ways.

The Spirit and the Word

The Holy Spirit and the Word always go together. When we have God's Word in us, the Holy Spirit has something to work with. He can bring to remembrance just the right Scripture at just the right time. This is how God speaks. This is how He guides us. This is how our relationship with Him grows.

Bottom Line

God speaks to us through His Word. Are you taking time to listen? Do you read the Word with a sense of anticipation? Ask the Holy Spirit to help you listen.

Whose Approval Matters?

This is the LORD's declaration. I will look favorably on this kind of person: one who is humble, submissive in spirit, and trembles at My word. (Isa. 66:2)

Compared to Others

Scripture doesn't promise an easy life for everyone who follows Christ. What it does promise, though, is God's approval when we reflect Him in our actions, attitudes, and motivations.

Stop and think about that for a second. *God's approval.* You may be thinking, *I'm a pretty nice guy. I treat people well. I work hard. I do good things. I'm even reading a devotional book right now!* But are you just approving yourself based on a comparison with the people around you?

Compared to Scripture

Look at a few examples of who Jesus says is blessed (see Matt. 5:3–5):

- *The poor in spirit.* Are you self-sufficient, or do you go to (and rely on) God for everything? Do you go directly to Him when you need help?
- *Those who mourn.* Have you developed a tolerance for small sins like white lies, or do you really grieve when you see yourself acting outside of God's will?
- *The gentle.* Do you have a right view of yourself in relation to God? Are you more self-confident than God-confident?

Bottom Line

Whose approval matters most to you? Reread the first eleven verses of Matthew 5, and let them challenge you.

Pollution Problem

The pure in heart are blessed, for they will see God. (Matt. 5:8)

The Problem

In Romans 7:24, Paul exclaims, "What a wretched man I am! Who will rescue me from this dying body?" Can you relate to this? Our sin nature is ever present, constantly tempting us to do what we know we shouldn't. If we are honest with ourselves—like Paul was in Romans 7—then we've got a real pollution problem. Instead of a pure heart, we have a tainted one.

Scripture shows us that sin hinders our ability to see God—to see where He's leading us, what His plan is for us, what He wants to teach us, and how He's answering our prayers (or why He's not).

The Cleanup

If we want to see clearly how to live for God, we have to deal with our pollution problem. Here's how:

Step 1. *Stop polluting the heart with sin.* Ask yourself, What kind of company do I keep? What kind of jokes do I laugh at? What kind of movies and entertainment do I watch? What websites do I visit?

Step 2. *Ask for God's help in dealing with the remnants of pollution already in your heart.* Is there any resentment or unforgiveness you need to deal with? Is there something you need to confess or apologize for?

Step 3. *Take a daily dose of grime prevention*—spend time in God's Word.

Bottom Line

Having a pure heart requires commitment and discipline that won't always come easy. The good news is that God offers His help.

And the Winner Is . . .

*"Be careful not to practice your righteousness
in front of people, to be seen by them. Otherwise,
you will have no reward from your Father in heaven." (Matt. 6:1)*

Pretending

Matthew 6 begins with Jesus teaching about the substance of our spirituality, specifically the reasons why we do what we do. His purpose is to show us what is pleasing to God versus what is empty and fake. To illustrate, He makes examples of certain "spiritual men" who did right things but with wrong motivations. He called them hypocrites, a word which means an actor under an assumed character. A stage player. A pretender—not the real thing.

These verses prompt us to stop and examine the authenticity of our spiritual lives. Ask yourself: Am I really seeking God or just going through the motions of church and a morning devotional? Am I really talking with God or just throwing words in His direction? Am I even listening? Am I trying to create or protect a reputation, or am I really working to develop godly character? Am I the real deal or a pretender?

For Real

We live in troubling and challenging times. Our media, our schools, even some of our churches are moving away from God's Word and His truth, relying on autonomous human thinking and an unbiblical notion of individual freedom. "Spirituality" as defined by our pluralistic, anything-goes culture isn't the solution. God's blessing is reserved for those who hunger and thirst for His righteousness, as defined by the Bible—the definer of what's real.

Bottom Line

It's time to get real about living for God. God isn't looking for actors; He wants the real thing.

All-powerful

God has not given us a spirit of fearfulness,
but one of power, love, and sound judgment. (2 Tim. 1:7)

Power

It's important to know what you've got, and God says that you have been given power—all the power (and love and sound judgment) you need to conquer fear. But if you don't think you've got what it takes, you won't rely on the resources God has given you to overcome the insidious enemy of fear.

Think of it this way: Can you imagine a race car driver who doesn't know what he has under the hood? Of course not! Those guys know exactly how much power they have, and they want as much as possible. As a Christian, you have all the power you'll ever need, but you've got to believe it and act accordingly. Otherwise your whole life will just putter along, bogged down by fear and unbelief.

Love

Love governs power and directs it. We're given grace not only for ourselves but also for the benefit of others. When our goal is to love and we feel empowered to do so, knowing that we are connected to the source of all love, the sky is the limit. Just imagine if your continual controlling thought was that you have been put on this earth to love, and you have the power of heaven at your disposal to fulfill this calling and mission. That kind of thinking leaves fear in the dust. And it produces the kind of "sound judgment" that doesn't waste time on lesser things.

Bottom Line

Today's verse is a great one to memorize, believe, and live out. Sadly, fear renders a lot of Christians ineffective and unhappy. Fight back with faith.

We Don't Always Know

*The L{ORD} answered Job: "Will the one who
contends with the Almighty correct Him?
Let him who argues with God give an answer." (Job 40:1–2)*

We Don't Understand

Job was a righteous man. We're told as much in the opening verse of the book of Job. And yet things didn't turn out so great for him. In fact, through no fault of his own, he basically lost everything—sons and daughters, houses and possessions, his health, the support of his wife and friends, everything. It's hard to imagine losing that much.

As he was going through these devastating losses, Job somehow managed to hold on to his integrity and faith for quite a while, as evidenced by his response to his wife's suggestion just to "curse God and die!" He tells her, "Should we accept only good from God and not adversity?" We're then told that "throughout all this Job did not sin in what he said" (see Job 2:9–10). That's remarkable.

The Breaking Point

Eventually, though, Job became angry at God. Not so much because of how things had turned out but because God was silent about the whole thing. Job wanted some answers! If he had done something wrong, he wanted to know about it. The silent treatment from God was killing him. Ever feel that way? The book of Job affirms that God is good but that we can't always understand what He's up to. We're called to trust and obey anyway.

Bottom Line

The book of Job is in the Bible for a reason—God deemed his story necessary for us to know. One takeaway is that God is far bigger than we can know.

Teaching Fathers

He established a testimony in Jacob and set up a law in Israel, which He commanded our fathers to teach to their children. (Ps. 78:5)

Church and Children

Father. A lot of responsibility comes with that title. The good news is you don't have to raise your children alone. Your wife, family members, and trusted friends can be a huge help. And you shouldn't overlook what an asset your church can be.

Research has found that kids who go to church with their parents behave better and have a more positive attitude than nonchurched kids. When our kids are around other like-minded families in a Christian environment, it builds their character and helps them be more self-sacrificing.

Train Up a Child

Well behaved. Selfless. Positive. Moral. Aren't those exactly the traits we want our children to exhibit? All of these qualities stem from spiritual training—which is one of a father's most important responsibilities. Today's verse says that God commands fathers "to teach to their children" the testimony of His Word and His mighty acts. God actually commands us to pass along His laws and His redemptive story to our kids.

When we follow this command, our children have a much better chance of beginning a personal relationship with Jesus. Then we not only receive the joy of knowing that our children will spend eternity with us in heaven but also the added blessing of having respectful, obedient kids on earth.

Bottom Line

Make sure you're teaching your kids about God and consistently attending church. It'll make a difference in your children's lives.

A New Body

*As for what you sow—you are not sowing the future body,
but only a seed, perhaps of wheat or another grain. (1 Cor. 15:37)*

The Seed

When you die, your earthly body is like a seed planted in the ground. The seed doesn't look like the fruit it will produce, but you can't get the fruit without the seed. If you want pumpkins, you don't plant watermelon seeds. If you want oak trees, you plant an acorn. An acorn doesn't look like an oak tree, yet it contains a forest of oak trees within its humble shell. It's the same with your physical body—what you plant is not what will emerge, and that's something to look forward to!

The Tree

As a believer, when you are resurrected from the dead, it will be you who comes up out of the grave, but you won't have the body you have today or the one that eventually dies with you in it. It will still be you, of course, but it will be a whole *new* you, vastly improved by God.

Think of it this way: you are to your resurrected body what an acorn is to an oak tree. Today you're just a tiny acorn, but when resurrected, you will be a mighty oak tree. It will be a radical change! The encouraging truth is that God is going to transform you in ways that are scarcely imaginable right now. And when it happens, you won't wish for your old body back with all its weaknesses and limitations. Not for one second. The new will be much better!

Bottom Line

Allow the promise of a new, resurrected body to give you hope today. What a great promise!

Departure or Arrival?

*As in Adam all die, so also in Christ
all will be made alive. (1 Cor. 15:22)*

The Journey

Imagine driving up to a five-star hotel where a valet parks your car and a doorman opens the door and escorts you inside. Your car is like your body that transports you through this world—a fallen world that's not your true, lasting home. Your soul needs a body so it can get around.

But at death your body is parked in a cemetery, the underground garage, put to rest, while your spirit is escorted to the gates of heaven. The gate is opened by the doorman, Jesus, the One who paved the way and paid the price for you to enter in. By the way, He doesn't just meet you on the other side. He also walks with you on this side and through the journey of death. He's there all the way through.

The Arrival

So while death at first seems to box you in, it actually frees you to go to God to experience the luxuries and amenities of an out-of-this-world resort (heaven). Death is often referred to as a departure when actually for believers in Jesus Christ it is an *arrival*. Death is the doorway through which you can leave the limitations and pains of this existence to enter into the heavenly realm, made completely and perpetually alive in the presence of God. So while the Bible describes death as an "enemy" (1 Cor. 15:26) it is also the doorway to much better things.

Bottom Line

The grave is not an entrance to death but to life. Have you made preparations for the journey?

An Unpopular Subject

He will also say to those on the left, "Depart from Me,
you who are cursed, into the eternal fire
prepared for the Devil and his angels!" (Matt. 25:41)

What's It Like?

It may surprise you, but Jesus said more about hell than all of the rest of the Bible put together. Jesus was serious about hell. It is not metaphorical but factual; not symbolic but logical. You can't have a heaven without a hell. You may try to deny its existence or rationalize it away, but Jesus said hell is real separation and eternal banishment from the most beautiful being (God) and the most wonderful place (heaven). It is a departure from everything that's right, true, wonderful, and good.

Who Will Be There?

According to Jesus, hell was made for those who deserve it—"the Devil and his angels" and the "cursed." Who are the "cursed"?—"Everyone who does not continue doing everything written in the book of the law is cursed" (Gal. 3:10). That means everybody.

But Jesus went to the cross for us. He was cursed so that we who deserved the curse could receive blessing instead. Jesus went through hell so we wouldn't have to go to hell.

Those who ignore the gift of eternal life He offered will be eternally separated from Him. Hell is the natural consequence of a life that has been lived in a certain direction—for self, rather than for God. But those who have run to the cross of Jesus for mercy and forgiveness no longer need to fear hell. They are heaven bound.

Bottom Line

Make sure you've received Jesus' gift of salvation. Make sure that you're heaven bound.

Final Exam

We must all appear before the tribunal of Christ,
so that each may be repaid for what he has done in the body,
whether good or worthless. (2 Cor. 5:10)

The Certainty

A day of judgment is coming upon all believers, when we will all appear before the judgment seat of Christ. In the ancient world the term *judgment seat* referred to a raised platform on which a judge rendered a verdict or a governor distributed awards to the victors at athletic contests. As a Christian—no less than for an unbeliever but in a different way—Christ is your Judge, and you will appear before Him to give an account of your life.

He doesn't want the efforts of your lifetime to go up in smoke. He wants to render His verdict, giving you eternal rewards. The judgment seat of Christ will be a time of commendation and celebration for believers, not condemnation. God will reward you for acts of love that perhaps no one else even noticed. Your rewards truly do go before you.

The Basis

The five-hundred-year-old play *Everyman* depicts all people. As Everyman faces Death, he looks among his friends for a companion. Only one friend would accompany him on the journey through death to final judgment. His name? Good Deeds. And so it is with us. Christ will judge us according to our deeds. The word *works* is not a dirty word. God condemns works done to earn salvation or to impress others, but He enthusiastically commends works done for the right reasons. After all, any good works we do are done through Him! (see John 15:5).

Bottom Line

If you understood that your works will have an irreversible effect on eternity, wouldn't you live differently in this world now?

Indescribable

*I also saw the Holy City, new Jerusalem,
coming down out of heaven from God,
prepared like a bride adorned for her husband.* (Rev. 21:2)

Can't Put It into Words

Elsie was blind from birth. She underwent delicate eye surgery and, upon seeing for the first time, rushed into her mother's arms and screamed with excitement, "Oh, Mama, why didn't you tell me it was so beautiful?" The mother, through tears of joy, answered, "My precious child, I tried to tell you, but I couldn't put it into words."

John the apostle, who caught a glimpse of heaven, couldn't adequately put it into words either. He used images. Heaven is "the Holy City"—a place of provision and plenty; "new Jerusalem"—something altogether different in kind; "a bride adorned for her husband"—a place of beauty and purity.

You Just Have to See It

The great pastor R. G. Lee said, "Heaven is the most beautiful place the mind of God could conceive and the hand of God could create." Heaven is so indescribable that the only way to fully understand it is to see it for yourself. It's like trying to describe the Grand Canyon or Yellowstone to someone who has never been there. Words fail you; pictures don't do it justice. Eventually you have to say: "Well, you've just got to go there." Once in heaven the thought will hit you: Why did I spend so much time trying to make my stay on earth more comfortable when I had the eternal joy and indescribable delight of heaven awaiting me?

Bottom Line

Heaven, the most beautiful place imaginable, is the one place you don't want to miss.

Forgiving Your Spouse

[Love] does not keep a record of wrongs. (1 Cor. 13:5)

The Importance of Letting Go

To be human is to blow it. We all sin, and we all need forgiveness from God and from one another. If you are married, you are going to have many occasions to seek forgiveness from your wife and to grant it as well. She might say some sharp words just based on exhaustion or hormones. You might do something inconsiderate or stupid, and it is critical to say those vital words, "I am sorry. Will you please forgive me?" You can't hold on to the hurt. Let things go. Even on those occasions when you feel you are completely in the right and she is 100 percent wrong, let it go. Don't compile a list of all the times she hurt you.

The Example of God

God forgave you, and He wants you to learn to do likewise. Having been forgiven everything, we are in no position to withhold forgiveness from our mate (or from anyone else).

One caveat here: this discussion of forgiveness presumes a certain degree of normalcy in your marriage. If there are grievous and ongoing sins, such as infidelity, substance abuse, or anything dangerous, you need professional help. Forgiveness does not mean ignoring patterns of out-of-bounds behavior. Forgiveness will still be needed in those situations, but reach out for intervention. And pray hard. You can't love and forgive in your own strength.

Bottom Line

Jesus has already forgiven you of far more than He will ever call upon you to forgive in your spouse. Choose to forgive and ask for His help.

Gifts and Talents

The man who had received five talents went,
put them to work, and earned five more. (Matt. 25:16)

Treasure Bestowed

God has given each of us spiritual gifts, and He wants us to put them to work for the progress of His kingdom. (See 1 Corinthians 12 for a list of spiritual gifts and the call to employ them.)

An unused gift is a buried talent, and a buried talent earns no profit for the Master. If you know what your gifts are, it is time to take an honest inventory. Are you using your gifts in a tangible, consistent way? How? Where? When? Who is benefiting from the gifts God has given you? You are a steward of them.

Unbury the Gold

It pleases God enormously when we use our gifts, talents, and time in the work of the kingdom. The ways we serve can differ radically, but each act of service delights God. Some guys love to mentor young believers. Some are gifted in acts of practical service for those in need. Some are teachers. Some are encouragers. Some share the gospel with ease. Some are outstanding administrators. Some excel at acts of mercy.

There is a ministry with your name on it. So if you have buried your talent, dig it up! You have a unique role to fulfill. Put your gifts to use for the benefit of the body of Christ. When you do, you'll discover that your relationship with God grows too.

Bottom Line

God has entrusted you with at least one powerful spiritual gift, and the more you use it the more He will accomplish through you.

Learning to Trust

"Why are you troubled?" He asked them. *"And why do doubts arise in your hearts?"* (Luke 24:38)

The Strange Ways of God

"Why are you troubled?" What a strange question from Jesus, considering that His followers were still reeling from His brutal murder, and He had now surprised them with His resurrection. For three years they had followed Him, invested their greatest dreams in Him, and hoped to see Him usher in the kingdom of God. Then for three days they had been trying to come to grips with losing Him to the most cruel kind of death dreamed up by Rome. Heaven had been silent. All seemed lost. They groped to understand. And suddenly He was standing before them! While they attempted to process the mind-boggling reality, He asked them why they ever doubted Him. Perhaps we would have doubted too.

Take the Leap

We learn a couple of big lessons from this exchange. First, God is willing to plunge us into confusing, scary, gut-wrenching situations. Second, He wants us to keep trusting Him no matter how bleak it looks, no matter how bewildering it seems. He is working out His plan, even if you can't make sense out of it. He is asking you the same question He asked Peter, James, and John—"Why do doubts arise in your hearts?"

Did He not create the universe? Did He not part the Red Sea? Has He not always kept His promises? Why would we think He would fail now? Why are we troubled?

Bottom Line

Like a muscle, faith must be stretched and exercised in order to grow. God often allows trials and confusion to give us the chance to trust Him.

Dual Identity

To the temporary residents dispersed . . . chosen according to the foreknowledge of God the Father and set apart by the Spirit for obedience and for sprinkling with the blood of Jesus Christ. (1 Pet. 1:1–2)

Loved and Accepted

Our governing officials attain their position when a majority votes for them. But as Christians we don't "attain" our salvation; it is given to us. God's vote is the only one that counts. And because the work of Christ has been imputed to us, our approval rating in God's sight is and will always be 100 percent. We can rest in that knowledge. Our responsibility and privilege is simply to keep believing the gospel, which He enables us to do.

Hated and Rejected

But at the same time that we are loved and accepted by God, we are also hated and rejected by the world. This is to be expected because Jesus said if the world hated Him, it will hate us also, because we are His followers (see John 15:18).

This dual identity—loved by God and hated by the world—guides our lives. We have security, joy, and purpose as God's children, but our trust and enjoyment of these things will be challenged by a world that largely rejects us and our message. It is up to us to decide which aspect of our identity will carry the greatest weight in our daily lives. When we allow God's love and acceptance to rule our hearts, the rest doesn't matter.

Bottom Line

Our identity as children of God is what enables us to bear up under the rejection of the world without losing our confidence and hope.

Responsibilities

Dear friends, I urge you as strangers and temporary residents to abstain from fleshly desires that war against you. Conduct yourselves honorably among the Gentiles. (1 Pet. 2:11–12)

Holy Lives

As God's children we bear some specific responsibilities in a world that often rejects us. One of those responsibilities is to live a holy life. This is what Peter is talking about when he tells us to "abstain from fleshly desires" and to "conduct [ourselves] honorably." To be holy is to be set apart. As Christians we are set apart; we are not like the world. Our lives must be distinct, reflecting the character of God to a watching world.

Witnesses

Along with a call to holiness is a call to be a witness. Really, the two cannot be completely separated. Our holy and distinct lives are meant to call attention to God, particularly in the eyes of those who are hostile to us. This passage teaches that it is possible for us to live in such a way that the enemies of God will turn to Him as they observe God's work in our lives. We are, as 1 Peter 2:9 puts it, "a chosen race, a royal priesthood, a holy nation, a people for His possession."

Of course, we're also responsible for graciously witnessing with our mouths (see 1 Pet. 3:15–16). Our verbal witness is meant to work in tandem with the witness of our lives. A holy, generous, and joyful life is attractive to others. It glorifies God and opens the door for sharing our faith.

Bottom Line

While we enjoy great privileges as believers, we must never forget our responsibility to live for Him and to make Him known to others.

What's the Problem?

The righteous cry out, and the LORD hears,
and delivers them from all their troubles. (Ps. 34:17)

The Blessing of Problems

An old African proverb says instead of asking God to take away your problems, you should pray for a stronger back. But a lot of men would rather take the first option. We don't like problems so we try to avoid them. Many of us ask God to clear out the traffic in our lives instead of relying on Him to help us through the roadblocks. After all, life feels good when you're cruising in the fast lane. But maybe we should change our view on problems. Instead of seeing them as a hindrance, we need to look at them as an opportunity to see God work.

No Problem

Jesus certainly didn't have any problem with problems. Every one of His miracles began with a problem. Sick, blind, lame—no problem. Out of wine? Not anymore. Dead? Seems like a big problem but not to Jesus. Just ask Lazarus (John 11) or Jairus' daughter (see Luke 8:40–56). Jesus took problems and turned them into opportunities to display God's power.

Running from problems or trying to avoid them doesn't help you grow as a person or become stronger with God. But embracing a problem and conquering it with God's help brings glory to your heavenly Father.

Bottom Line

Next time you find yourself stuck in a problem, pray that God would deliver you in a way that honors and glorifies Him or would help you persevere in a way that keeps the focus on Him.

Faith of a Father

*Abraham answered, "God Himself will provide
the lamb for the burnt offering, my son." (Gen. 22:8)*

Father of Faith

Abraham's faith is credited with leading him through God's test in Genesis 22. When God told Abraham to sacrifice the son he loved, the centenarian packed up his donkey, grabbed Isaac, and headed to the mountains. Abraham trusted God even when God asked him to give up what he loved most.

But what about Isaac's role in the story? Surely the strapping young man could've overpowered his hundred-year-old father or run away. Yet Isaac helped Abraham carry the wood and believed his dad when he said, "God Himself will provide the lamb for the burnt offering" (Gen. 22:8). Isaac even allowed Abraham to bind him, lay him on the altar, and raise a knife to slay him.

Faith Foundation

Have you wondered what gave Isaac the faith to follow God's plan? One word: Abraham. Isaac had seen God active and powerful in Abraham's life. He had seen his father's trust in the one true God. He had heard the stories of God's provision. He had seen Abraham walk consistently with God. He had heard Abraham talk to God, and he had witnessed God's answers to prayer. Isaac's foundation of faith was solid because of Abraham.

Just as Isaac watched Abraham, our children are watching us. Would they be willing to put their lives on the line for the Lord because they've seen great faith in us?

Bottom Line

Do you talk about what God is doing in your life and share His goodness with your children? Set aside some time to do just that.

Road Rage

A fool's displeasure is known at once,
but whoever ignores an insult is sensible. (Prov. 12:16)

Mad Driver

Maybe it's a Jekyll and Hyde thing. But it's not unusual for a seemingly mild-mannered man to get behind the wheel of a car and suddenly turn into a NASCAR driver. There's something about horsepower and metal that makes men want to trade paint at 175 mph . . . or at least causes them to lose their cool when somebody cuts them off.

Road rage is a huge issue for both followers of Jesus and for guys who would never set foot in church. But sometimes it's hard to tell the difference between the two groups when they're driving.

Swerve Away from Anger

As a wise king once wrote in the verse above, "A fool's displeasure is known at once, but whoever ignores an insult is sensible." That's good advice to follow at work, at home, at the grocery store, and behind the wheel. While it may seem natural to doubt someone's intelligence who comes to a complete stop in the merge lane, we need to temper our emotions and act sensibly. By overlooking other drivers' offenses, we'll be less likely to cuss at them or display frustrated gestures and more likely to make it to our destination safely.

We need to let the peace of Christ rule in our hearts all the time—even in the car when some idio-. . . er, person made in the image of God cuts us off or fails to use his turn signal. Our driving is part of our walk with Christ.

Bottom Line

Take the high road when you drive. Steer clear of anger.

Deflated Ego

Everyone who exalts himself will be humbled, and the one who humbles himself will be exalted. (Luke 14:11)

A Thousand Miles

A signing had been scheduled for Rick's first book, and there was no way the fledgling author was going to miss it. Rick hates to fly, so he drove nearly a thousand miles from his house to the bookstore. Along the way he had visions of fans lined up around the block clamoring for his signature on their newly purchased book.

If only it worked out that way. After that long drive, one book was sold and signed. One. Make no mistake about it. A disappointed writer drove away from the bookstore that night and then the thousand miles back home. Other book signings went reasonably well, but Rick would never forget that first one.

No Better Lesson

Rick had never had a better lesson in humility. His book had been published, yes, but somebody else's project was going to make the best-seller lists. In the end he decided that a book on his shelf with his name on the spine was good enough for him.

It's easy to get caught up in the pursuit of personal and professional accomplishments. But that's not what it's all about. Christ set a far different example, and He isn't impressed by much of what the world considers important. What He's after is for us to humble ourselves, serve other people, and seek approval from Him only.

Bottom Line

If you're seeking to impress others with your accomplishments, you're barking up the wrong tree. Seek Christ's approval.

Righteous Protest

"Is it not written, My house will be called a house of prayer for all nations? But you have made it a den of thieves!" (Mark 11:17)

No Trivial Matter

For many weeks now Art had noticed an issue cropping up at church that greatly concerned him. This went far beyond the color of the hymnals or the size of the pages in the church directory. It was a matter he felt would eventually hamper the work of the church if something wasn't done about it.

Thing is, Art had never said much about such things. During business meetings, he usually kept quiet and let others do the talking. This issue, however, was far too important for him to sit back and say nothing. When it came time for new business to be discussed, Art raised his hand, cleared his throat, and stood up to speak.

Pick and Choose

Nowhere in the Bible does it say that Christians should stand idly by and accept things with which they truly disagree. On many occasions Jesus Himself spoke out against those He saw as hampering the work of His Father's kingdom. He didn't just sit back and take it, afraid of what others might think of Him.

It's important for Christians to pick and choose their battles. Is the issue really that important? Or does it have more to do with the individual's own stubborn pride? If biblical fidelity is at stake and it's not a case of bickering about inconsequential details, a Christian's responsibility is to stand up and be counted.

Bottom Line

Standing up for what's right is the right thing to do. Just be sure that you're doing it in a godly, honorable way.

Sports Dads

Fathers, don't stir up anger in your children, but bring them up in the training and instruction of the Lord. (Eph. 6:4)

A Desperate Attempt

As soon as the ball trickled through the poor kid's legs, his dad was screaming at him from the stands. "You'd better get down on that ball! What have I told you?!?" When he next came up to bat, he struck out, bringing more harsh, loud criticism. Another error in the field, another strike out, and the father was all but apoplectic.

The scene repeated itself every single game of the season and even carried over into other sports. Instead of listening to his coaches on the field, the youngster looked to his father in a desperate attempt to please him. Yet every time he missed a basket or failed to get a hit, his father's disapproval rang out.

Raving Lunatic

Some of the nicest men in the world turn into raving lunatics at their kids' ball games. Does your child get most, if not all, of his or her validation from you through sports? If so, there's something wrong with that picture. There's a huge difference between pulling for your child to do well in sports and pushing them to be perfect.

Sports are supposed to be . . . what's the word for it? Fun. Yeah, that's it. There's another major problem with "acting out" at your child's game. What kind of example does it set for spectators and participants? You have only one chance to make a first impression, and you're going to spend it yelling at a youth-league umpire?

Bottom Line

Unless you're a pro baseball or football hall of famer, keep your athletic tips in perspective. It's only a game.

In Everything

*Give thanks in everything, for this is God's will
for you in Christ Jesus. (1 Thess. 5:18)*

Feel Thankful?

It's such a simple verse, but it's like a powerful vitamin pill. We know it will benefit us, but it's hard to swallow at times. Give thanks in everything? What about when the car breaks down and your child leaves for college and the promotion goes to someone else?

First of all, thanks is something we *give*. We don't just *feel* thankful—we express it to someone else. A mature Christian mixes all his thoughts with thanks, and all our worldly possessions look better when we realize they are gifts. A sense of entitlement never takes us far down the road of gratitude.

Give Thanks Away

"In everything" doesn't mean everything that happens to us is good or that we should be thankful for everything that comes along in life. (We can't be thankful for our sin, for instance.) But we can be thankful that God is good, in all things, in all ways, at all times. In this way thankfulness and faith go hand in hand.

And this is a part of God's will for our lives. If we're not obeying this simple instruction, giving thanks to God in all things, why would we think God would show us deeper aspects of His will? The phrase "in Christ" is the foundation for our thanksgiving, not our circumstances. Every other gift comes and goes. But Jesus stays. Now *that's* something to be thankful for!

Bottom Line

Take your vitamin daily. Tell God what you're thankful for.

How to Fire a Pastor

If I say, "I won't mention Him or speak any longer in His name," His message becomes a fire burning in my heart, shut up in my bones. I become tired of holding it in, and I cannot prevail. (Jer. 20:9)

Pastors Want the Fire

The prophet Jeremiah was not unlike any other pastor. He had his ups and downs. But he was reminded that God had a calling on his life, and he described God's calling to preach the Word like a "fire" within his inmost being. All pastors want to feel that fire as they preach and minister.

But our overfed generation can breakfast with Lucado in the morning, feast on Swindoll in the afternoon, and have MacArthur for dinner. And then we wonder why our local pastor doesn't measure up! His illustrations aren't as sharp, his jokes not as funny, and his points not as lucid. So we go home and have roasted preacher for lunch.

Be the Spark

Do you want to fire your pastor or "fire up" your pastor? He needs faithful men standing in the gap for him. Here are some ways you can help:

Pray for him and then tell him you did. Take him out for a meal and just listen. Go to his office and compliment instead of complain. Take him to a ball game or play golf with him. Buy him a book. Better yet, buy him a techie gadget that you know he can't afford. Make your pastor glad to see you coming. You'll be surprised how it will affect your ears as you hear his next sermon.

Bottom Line

Your pastor needs you more than you can imagine.

Know What You Know

*The one who has accepted His testimony
has affirmed that God is true. (John 3:33)*

A Gray World

Is there absolute truth in the world? Or is every idea equally valid? While people may say, "Don't impose your beliefs on me," you never hear them say, "Don't impose your mathematics on me." Why don't we say that? Because we assume math is connected to reality. In math, answers are either right or wrong, and it's the same with moral and spiritual beliefs.

A lot of people think they can create their own morality. But just try to explain that to the IRS at tax time! Relativism is unlivable. You don't want your spouse to be "relatively" faithful, do you? You don't want a brain surgeon who simply has an opinion about what's in your head; you want one who knows what he's talking about! Morality is no different. Truth exists.

Truth Is a Person

Nobody wants to live in a world where Nazism or hedonism or materialism is granted equal moral status with the Golden Rule. We know better. At the heart of reality is a Person who is truth, and this Person is someone you can know. He is God, the One of unimaginable love and goodness who has communicated to us what He is like.

Ultimately God doesn't just call us to believe Him. He calls us to know Him. The apostle Paul said, "I know the One I have believed in" (2 Tim. 1:12). Don't just believe the truth; know its Author.

Bottom Line

If you know the words of Jesus, you know God is true, and you know that all truth comes from Him.

Filtered

*We demolish arguments and every high-minded thing
that is raised up against the knowledge of God,
taking every thought captive to obey Christ. (2 Cor. 10:4–5)*

How Do You Decide?

Whether you like it black and thick as mud, or semiclear with a shot of cream and sugar, nobody likes grounds in their coffee. The quality of good coffee depends on the quality of the filter to strain out that which isn't good. Likewise, the quality of a good Christian life depends on having a biblical filter by which we strain out all information that doesn't line up with God's Word.

Everyone has a worldview, a systematic way of looking at the world. Everything we hear, see, and think passes through a filter as it goes into our minds and hearts. Questions for the Christ follower are: Do you have a biblical worldview? Do you see the world and people the way God sees them? Or does something else determine how you go about choosing what information is true and what is not?

Every Thought Captive

How do you develop a worldview? By taking every thought captive to obey Christ. Every image you see, ask yourself the question, "Does dwelling on this honor Christ?" Every word you are tempted to say, ask yourself, "Does this further the kingdom of God?" Every news report you hear, ask yourself, "Does what they are saying line up with what the Bible says is true?" Before long you will develop a strong biblical filter that will develop wisdom and discernment inside of you. And you will find this wisdom and discernment sweet to your soul.

Bottom Line

Ask God to develop a strong biblical filter inside your heart and mind.

Bird's-eye View

Ask the animals, and they will instruct you; ask the birds of the sky, and they will tell you. . . . Which of all these does not know that the hand of the LORD has done this? (Job 12:7, 9)

By Accident?

The agnostic astronomer Sir Fred Hoyle argued that life is so complex, the chance that it originated by accident can be completely ruled out. "Divine design" is all around us.

Consider the woodpecker. This living jackhammer hits its head against a tree hundreds of times a minute with a force of deceleration up to a thousand times the force of gravity. He survives this because woodpeckers have extra strong neck muscles and a special layer of cartilage in the skull that acts like a shock absorber. They also have extremely tough beaks and a special film that closes over the eye, keeping the eyeballs in and the wood chips out.

Or by Design?

A woodpecker feeds on insects it reaches with its sticky tongue, which is 4.5 times longer than its skull! But this poses another problem—what to do with the tongue when it's not in use? Fortunately, woodpeckers have another special feature—a tongue storage compartment, which wraps around the skull and attaches in the beak region. It's like a tape measure that winds up. In evolutionary thinking, which came first: the storage compartment or the long tongue? Without the tongue the birds would starve; without the storage compartment they would choke on their long tongues. Do woodpeckers look like the product of chance and accident? No way! They are the product of Divine design.

Bottom Line

How much more fearfully and wonderfully has God made you than the woodpecker!

Turn Around

Repent and turn back, so that your sins may be wiped out, that seasons of refreshing may come from the presence of the Lord.
(Acts 3:19)

What It Does

How often have you stopped at a gas station to ask for directions only to have the attendant say, "You're going in the wrong direction; you need to turn around." To repent means to turn around.

Repentance finds its origin not in religion but from a culture where people were essentially nomadic and lived in a world with no maps or street signs. It's easy to get lost walking through the desert where everything basically looks the same. One could walk and walk and eventually come to the realization he was going in the wrong direction. Turning around, he would head in the opposite direction. That's repentance.

What It Is

Repentance does not mean to feel sorry or cry over a mistake or blame someone else for the wrongs in one's life. Repentance is the act of changing the direction in which the heart is inclined. It is a spiritual about-face. It is a change of mind that calls for a change of way.

Repentance is the decision to turn from selfish desires and seek God. It is a genuine, sincere regret that creates sorrow and moves us to admit wrong and desire to do better. It is becoming aware of the awesome love of God that motivates you to change. No one is happier than the one who has sincerely repented of wrong. Far from being drudgery, it is a doorway to life, joy, and peace.

Bottom Line

The sooner you get started back, the sooner you'll feel at home again.

The Key to Patience

Love is patient, love is kind. (1 Cor. 13:4)

God Made Us Different

There are subtle but significant differences in the emotional makeup of women and men, just as there are subtle but significant differences between a daisy and a bazooka. Men and women are wired so very differently. Any guy who wants to be happily married should expend some effort in studying the emotional and biological differences between men and women.

Things that bother women don't bother us. Little distractions and annoyances can really impact a woman's willingness or even ability to enjoy sex, while men would not be distracted even if mortars were falling. And while small gifts and flowers may do zero for you, it is amazing how important these tokens of affection can be to your wife.

Take Time to Understand

Understanding these male-female differences will go a long way in helping a guy learn to be patient with his wife. For a woman everything is connected to everything else. In many cases fixing the faucet or the noise in the dryer or some other little household thing for your wife can make a huge difference in how she feels. On some days it may be that the most romantic thing you can do is the dishes, or to take the kids to the park so your wife can curl up with a book.

Accommodate your differences rather than let them frustrate you. Take the time to understand how God made your wife. You'll both be much happier.

Bottom Line

The more you understand and celebrate the way God made men and women different, the more patient and happy you will be with your wife—and vice versa.

Side by Side

One of His disciples, the one Jesus loved,
was reclining close beside Jesus. (John 13:23)

Everyday Family

Nobody has more influence over your children than you do. As your kids grow, they watch you to develop their beliefs and value system. This means that being a good father doesn't demand a ton of biblical wisdom and excellent speech-making skills (although both of those may help). Being a good father does mean taking an active role in your child's life. Coaching a sports team, going fishing, teaching a hobby, or working on household chores together can go a long way to encourage emotional connectedness.

Being There

When John records the events of the Last Supper, he writes, "One of His disciples, the one Jesus loved, was reclining close beside Jesus." This disciple was close enough to whisper into the Lord's ear. The physical proximity of Jesus and John demonstrated the love they shared for each other.

In the same way, we show our kids love by being close to them. Kids desire to hang out with their fathers. They want to "recline close beside" you when you're watching a movie. Often the little things make the biggest difference in parenting. Don't hesitate to hug or wrestle playfully with your children. When you stay close to your kids, they'll stay close to you. And if your teenage children try to push you away, hold them close anyway. They still need you even if they don't always act like it.

Bottom Line

Stay close to your kids and they're much more likely to stay close to you.

Good Directions

Plans fail when there is no counsel,
but with many advisers they succeed. (Prov. 15:22)

Behind the Wheel

What do Christopher Columbus, Amerigo Vespucci, Meriwether Lewis, and Ferdinand Magellan have in common? They're explorers, but more important, they're men. The itch to explore runs in a man's blood. Maybe that's why when we get behind the wheel of a car, we feel the burning desire to just go. Forget directions. Unplug the GPS. We'll get to our destination by using our internal compass and sheer force of will. That doesn't always work so well, though, does it?

Not surprisingly, many men view their marriage a lot like their driving. We have some idea of where we want to go, and even if it means getting lost a couple of times, we're confident we'll get there in the end. But this attitude can sometimes ruin the journey for our passenger.

On the Right Road

Asking for directions is good advice while driving and in a marriage. Like the proverb says, look for "counsel" from other "advisers." Check with people who are familiar with the territory to make sure you're heading in the right direction. Seek marital advice from godly friends, your pastor, Christian resources, a church small group, and even your wife. By getting some good counsel, you'll get where you want to go on time and intact.

Bottom Line

To have a safe and fun journey in your marriage, ask for advice. With a little direction your relationship with your wife can thrive.

Homesick

We do not have an enduring city here; instead,
we seek the one to come. (Heb. 13:14)

Pain Is Inevitable

We are fallen people living in a fallen world, and we bear the emotional and physical scars to prove it. Just look around. Damaged relationships. Cancer diagnoses. Neglected children. Lost jobs. Foreclosed homes. The strong are preyed upon by the weak, and too often justice is not served. If you are not suffering now, it is just a matter of time before something hits. That's simply the nature of a world caught in the ravages of sin. But God tells us that His redeemed people have been given a new citizenship in heaven. This sin-torn world is not our home anymore. We are visitors. Sojourners. We are passing through this life, making our way to our Father's house.

The Relief of Heaven

When life hurts, take your eyes off your current problems and look ahead to a glorious, pain-free future in heaven. Whether you have a broken heart, a wounded body, a financial problem, a deep struggle in your faith—this is not the end of your story. There is great hope for you. And this hope grows as you look to your real home, the place Jesus has prepared for you, where God makes His presence especially known. In that place paralyzed limbs will move again, and the blind will see colors never before imagined. Loved ones lost to death will greet you with joy. Just think, you are closer today than you were yesterday.

Bottom Line

No matter how things are going for you now, remember that heaven is your final destination and that you will soon be there.

Rich Rewards

God is not unjust; He will not forget your work and the love you showed for His name when you served the saints. (Heb. 6:10)

The Least Little Act

Evangelical Christians rightly proclaim that our good works do not save us, but let's not forget that God carefully records and rewards the service we render to Him. He will "not forget your work" when you serve Him by serving the family of God. What kind of reward-worthy deeds is He talking about? Jesus set the bar pretty low when He said, "Whoever gives just a cup of cold water to one of these little ones because he is a disciple—I assure you: He will never lose his reward!" (Matt. 10:42). The smallest, simplest, easiest task done for Jesus' sake will be rewarded in eternity.

Storing Up Treasure

Some Christians get a bit uncomfortable with the idea of being rewarded by God. Sounds too mercenary, too self-centered, too much about us. We need to get over that feeling. God repeatedly says that He plans to reward our service. He wants to motivate us by the promise of a reward for a job well done. It is part of His nature to want to bless us in return for what we do for Him.

Take advantage of the opportunity to perform the good works for which God created you, and your reward will be multiplied in heaven. Remember, that's a good, healthy, biblical motivation for doing good. There's no need to try to be more spiritual than God!

Bottom Line

Find meaningful, enjoyable ways to serve God, and throw yourself into them. God wants to richly reward your service to Him.

Second Chances

The word of the LORD came to Jonah a second time. (Jon. 3:1)

The First Mistake

We don't always get second chances in life. Ask the kid who didn't make the Little League team or the divorced person who got dumped or the employee who embezzled company funds or the golfer who left his putt short on the eighteenth hole. But Jonah got a second chance.

God had directed Jonah to travel east over land to Nineveh. But Jonah booked passage on a ship headed west toward Spain. During that journey a tremendous storm arose, and Jonah ended up in the Mediterranean Sea. That's when the fish swallowed him. Within a short time of gulping down the prophet, the fish suffered an attack of indigestion. Jonah was vomited onto shore. Why?

The Second Chance

In the middle of the book of Jonah a most interesting phrase appears—"a second time." Deliberately, consciously, stubbornly, Jonah had run away from God. Yet God came to the prophet a second time and allowed him to carry on his ministry. Jonah's story is more about God than a man and a fish.

God is the God of the second chance, the fresh start, the new beginning, and the rebirth. If you miss this discovery, you miss the message of the book of Jonah, not to mention the entire Bible. God doesn't turn a deaf ear or a cold shoulder to the repentant, no matter how blatant the rebellion or which border the runaway crosses. God gives second chances. Sometimes even in the exact place where we failed!

Bottom Line

If you are running from God, turn to Him. He will grant you a second chance.

Reclamation Business

Jonah got up and went to Nineveh according to the LORD's command. Now Nineveh was an extremely large city, a three-day walk. (Jon. 3:3)

Wrong Thinking

Disobedience to God doesn't automatically disbar us from later usefulness. David committed adultery and murder, but God renewed him to teach transgressors His ways through beautiful psalms and hymns and to rule over the nation of Israel. Peter denied Jesus not once but three times, but God reinstated him for service to His people as a great leader of the early church. John Mark, helper to Paul and Barnabas on the first missionary journey, defected along the way, but God reshaped his life, and he later wrote the second book of the New Testament. Jonah also rebelled, but God restored him for service. This is the heart of God for His children.

Right Action

We should reject the notion that if we turn away from God's will, we are forever disqualified. Satan likes to muddle us into thinking we are beyond salvage, doomed to God's second best. Don't believe it. God is in the salvage reclamation business. He delights in taking mistake-prone people like you and me and transforming us into something beautiful and useful. God never discards a repentant life. No matter what the disobedience, God wants to renew, reinstate, and reshape the life.

Perhaps you feel like you are beyond help. But He's not through with you yet. Your life is not over. You are useful to Him.

Bottom Line

No matter how defeated you feel, God cherishes taking broken people and making something beautiful out of us.

Finding a Better Dad

*The LORD will not forsake His people
or abandon His heritage. (Ps. 94:14)*

AWOL Fathers

A lot of guys have a deep wound caused by their dads bailing out on them. The father was either not there at all, was in and out, was emotionally distant, or was abusive. In many cases, no matter how much the wounded son longs for the restoration of the relationship, it is never going to happen. Guys can waste a lot of emotional energy hoping things will change, waiting for the affirmation that never comes. As hard as this sounds, sometimes we just need to let go of the bad dad and get a new one.

New Day, New Dad

God offers to be a "father of the fatherless" (Ps. 68:5)—the Dad who never lets you go, never lets you down, never rips you off, and never breaks your heart. He loves you beyond what you can imagine, His commitment to you is rock solid, and He will bring ultimate justice to the unrepentant people who have hurt you. No words can capture what you mean to Him.

Ask God to open your eyes to the Father love He has for you. And almost as important, let God love you through other men who walk with the Lord. None of us is strong enough to go through life without the help and encouragement of our brothers. We need the love of our heavenly Father, but we also need a band of brothers to make it real.

Bottom Line

If your dad is out of your life, your Father in heaven wants to fill the aching void. Invite Him to do that, and get the help of other men too.

Foolish Things

*God has chosen what is foolish in the world
to shame the wise, and God has chosen what is weak
in the world to shame the strong. (1 Cor. 1:27)*

Fool for Christ

When most people think of the late Manute Bol, they think of a man with pencil-thin arms and tree saplings for legs, a basketball player who was ridiculed for being a physical anomaly rather than a star athlete. And when his career was over, he appeared to be just another one of those "hungry for the spotlight" athletes as he dabbled in other sports.

But a closer look at this athlete from Sudan reveals a heart of courage and compassion. As a young man growing up in Africa, he once killed a lion with a spear while protecting the cattle he was herding. Upon his arrival in the NBA, many believed the gangly center was just a circus act to sell tickets for his team. But Bol knew God had a plan for his life.

Whose Fool Are You?

At a time when many athletes go broke on cars, houses, jewelry, and groupies, Bol spent his salary building hospitals and schools in his war-torn Sudan. And when he retired from basketball, he continued to raise money, strapping on boxing gloves, skating on a minor-league hockey team, even racing horses as a jockey. He looked foolish in such efforts, but he wasn't afraid to humble himself for the sake of others. How about you? Looking like a fool for Christ for the right reasons is anything but foolish.

Bottom Line

Want to be really free? Give yourself to Christ today, with no thought of your reputation.

Eye Exam

*They have eyes full of adultery and are always
looking for sin. They seduce unstable people and have hearts
trained in greed. Children under a curse! (2 Pet. 2:14)*

Spiritual Myopia

What do others see when they look into your eyes? Bold commitment? Or pride and arrogance? Our eyes really can be a window to our soul.

From the beginning, man was seduced by Satan with the thought that he could have eyes that would be opened so he could "be like God" (Gen. 3:5). Later in Proverbs 6:17, "arrogant eyes" are listed first among seven things God hates. We're also told that "a fool's way is right in his own eyes" (Prov. 12:15) and not to set anything worthless before our eyes (see Ps. 101:3). Our eyes are important.

Looking into the Light

Jesus declared that our eyes are either good or bad, depending on what we fix them on (see Matt. 6:22–23). If we see Jesus as truly worth following, our bodies will be filled with the light of Christ. If we don't, our bodies will be full of darkness. We see a picture of this darkness in today's verse where Peter warns against false Christians with corrupt, fleshly eyes that lead both them and others into sin.

It's only by "keeping our eyes on Jesus" (Heb. 12:2) that we're able to follow Him in obedience. It's a matter of focus, and it's not impossible. Thankfully, we have been given the Holy Spirit and the Word of God to help us see.

Bottom Line

Your spiritual eyes reflect what is already in your heart, but they can also change your heart. Keep your eyes on Jesus, and you'll have a good heart.

Finish Well

The end of a matter is better than its beginning;
a patient spirit is better than a proud spirit. (Eccles. 7:8)

The Starting Blocks

King Solomon had one of the greatest starts in life any human has ever had. He grew up in the palace of his father, King David. At the start of his reign, Solomon chose to ask God for wisdom rather than riches or honor—and God gave him all three! The Bible declares that no one was equal with Solomon in terms of the splendor of his riches and excellent wisdom. Rulers traveled from distant lands to marvel at this king.

The Finish Line

But as Ecclesiastes 7:8 reminds us, "The end of a matter is better than its beginning." Despite his excellent jump out of the starting gate, Solomon didn't finish his race well. Most men are challenged to keep their marriage to just one woman healthy and whole. Over the course of his reign, Solomon married seven hundred wives and had three hundred concubines. He allowed his fleshly appetites to flourish and rule and began to lean on his own wisdom to guide him.

Even the wisest man today can become the greatest fool tomorrow if he stops listening to the voice of truth and instruction. It doesn't take long for a runner to stray from his lane. And many men have grown cold toward God in their later years despite being hot-hearted for Him in their youth. A man never outgrows his need for grace. A humble, patient spirit is rewarded in the end.

Bottom Line

Purpose to keep your eyes on the prize and to end your race of faith well.

Don't Get Burned

Can a man embrace fire and
his clothes not be burned? (Prov. 6:27)

Sin by Any Other Name . . .

OK, so it's not hard-core porn. Does that make it any less sinful? Be honest—when you see an old girlfriend on Facebook, does your mind wander off into fantasy land? Is her marital status one of the first things you check? Do you start wondering what life would have been like if you had married her instead of your current wife? If so, let's hope you're wearing asbestos pants because you're scooping fire into your lap.

An affair doesn't have to be physical in order to defraud your wife and dishonor God. An emotional affair can hurt just as deeply. It's a slippery slope, a slow burn, moving from an innocent "Hey, how are you?" to sharing more intimate details about your life. Have you shared any inappropriate information about your marriage with another woman on Facebook?

. . . Smells Just as Fishy

"People loved darkness rather than the light because their deeds were evil," says John 3:19. Do you quickly delete anything on your computer or text messages on your phone? Are you currently having a conversation with another woman that you would not want your wife or pastor to know about? If so, you're walking in darkness. Make no mistake—your deeds will be brought to light. You're playing with fire, and even asbestos pants won't save you. It's not a question of *if*, but *when*, you will get burned.

Bottom Line

Your heart is capable of great deception—don't fall for its lies!

The Line of Faith

A Sure Promise

Parenthood is full of unpredictable twists and turns. But God's Word provides us with steady, unchanging truth about family relationships. This psalm is a promise to all parents. As a dad fears the Lord, God directs His love toward that man's children and His righteousness toward the grandchildren.

What does it mean to fear the Lord? It's not a destructive fear that God will act unlovingly toward us. Yet it is much more than simple respect. To fear God is to revere Him and His Word, to know that this Sovereign Being could snuff out our lives with one breath but chooses not to because of His great love for us. To fear the Lord is to value His ways and His Word above all others. It is a complete trust in Him that He is with us and will also be with our children and our children's children.

A Spiritual Legacy

How can you impact the lives of those you haven't seen and may never see? Highlight your Bible with verses special to you. Keep a prayer journal. Write a note to your unborn children and grandchildren. Above all, live a life worthy of the Lord. Imagine if you had such a note or Bible from your ancestors—would it go a long way toward convincing you that God has His hand on your life? Your faithfulness will impact generations.

Bottom Line

Live for Jesus now to impact the lives of your descendants later.

Zip the Lip

A shrewd person conceals knowledge, but a foolish heart publicizes stupidity. (Prov. 12:23)

Prayer Request or Gossip?

Do women gossip more than men? Or can men be just as guilty of sharing someone else's personal information? Get a bunch of guys around a pool table, at a hunting lodge, or even on social networking sites, and you'll quickly see that there's a lot of 411 being shared—and some of it can sink somebody's ship.

Often gossip is shared in pseudospiritual forms like a prayer request. "Pray for Bob as he tries to get back on the wagon again." "What? We didn't know he fell off!" And the conversation quickly deteriorates. Whether in a Sunday school room or Starbucks, word spreads quickly.

Building Bridges?

Just because you know something to be true doesn't mean it needs to be shared. That's true even about your own life. Sometimes we think we need to confess all our sin publicly in order to get right with God and others. Actually, it's best to confess sin only as publicly as you commit it. If you only sinned against one, you don't need to share that with an entire group.

Sharing the struggles of others without their permission makes it very hard for them to return to the group. More than one guy has changed churches after seeing information he shared in confidence spread all over the Internet—or the church. Information shared inappropriately doesn't build bridges; it burns them.

Bottom Line

Gossip in any form hurts others and dishonors God.

Bitterness

Good, Bad, and Ugly

God gave you anger as an early warning system against evil, danger, or abuse. When an enemy violates boundaries—whether against you, your family, your nation, or the vulnerable—your anger kicks in. It motivates you to take righteous steps to protect yourself and those who need it. Jesus got angry when He protected His spiritual sheep from wolves in sheep's clothing (see John 2:15). When anger motivates righteous action, it has served its God-given purpose.

But when anger is left simmering, it turns toxic. Bitterness, resentment, and an unforgiving spirit are symptoms of simmering anger. God did not design you to store up anger. He graciously commands, "Don't let the sun go down on your anger" (Eph. 4:26).

Bitter Fruit

Bitterness poisons relationships—and not just the relationship with the person you're mad at. Bitterness toward one person harms all your relationships, including your marriage, family, and work relationships. Bitter people make for lousy friends, and Scripture warns against partnering with a chronically angry man (see Prov. 22:24). You need to release the pressure from your simmering cauldron of anger. Decide if the relationship is worth salvaging—sometimes it isn't. If it is, talk through your conflict, enforce appropriate boundaries, forgive, forbear, and move on.

Bottom Line

Unresolved anger puts a bitter taste in your mouth and spoils your relationships. Grow in Christ and develop a forgiving spirit.

Depression

He heals the brokenhearted
and binds up their wounds. (Ps. 147:3)

Deep and Dark

Most every man, even the most faithful Christ follower, will face depression. Sometimes depression has a physiological basis, and it is wise to use God's gift of doctors and medicine. Other times depression has an emotional or spiritual basis; it is your soul's response to heartbreak, trauma, or loss.

God promises to heal the brokenhearted. He promises to bind up your soul's wound. He may use friends, family, therapists, or counselors. He may bring healing directly in answer to prayer. But God does not leave you alone. He comes alongside you to comfort and restore. In fact, one of His most healing remedies may be the painful "gift" of depression.

God's Gift?

It may surprise you to read that some Christian psychologists view depression as a gift from God. When you are depressed, your range of emotions shrinks. Your highs aren't as high, and your lows aren't as low. You become numb toward life. Disinterested. You pull back from activities. You hunker down and lick your wounds.

Almost like the soul's equivalent of going into shock, depression conserves energy and life. It is a God-given mechanism to buy time for healing. It creates a quiet space in which you can receive grace from God and others. Don't fight your depression. Don't deny it when it comes. Quiet your life, and move toward God and a life-giving community.

Bottom Line

Depression hurts, but God deepens us and heals us through it. When you're low, don't give up. Turn to God and others for help.

Envy

What Is Envy?

Envy is the feeling you get when somebody else has what you want, and you resent them for having it, even if you don't really need it. Envy persuades you that you'll never have enough money or stuff to be happy. It turns you against others for simply enjoying their blessings from God. It rots you from the inside out (see Prov. 14:30).

Once you succumb to envy, you can never be satisfied. Even if you receive today what you so desperately longed for yesterday, tomorrow you will envy something flashier and better. Envy detonates a chain reaction: envy, scarcity, self-pity, and hatred. Today's verse calls it "demonic." Dark forces nurture envy to such a degree that Jesus died because of it (see Mark 15:10).

Releasing Envy

Two secrets can move you toward contentment:

1. *Operate in the opposite spirit.* When envy tempts you to criticize, offer praise instead. When envy tempts you to acquire and hold, choose open-handed generosity. Instead of wishing a person ill, pray for God's increased blessing on them.

2. *Operate in the Holy Spirit.* There's nothing wrong with desire. Our problem is that we sometimes desire stuff more than God. We need a stronger bond with God so He can trust us with the other desires of our hearts.

Bottom Line

The biggest problem with envy isn't that you want other people's stuff—it's that you don't want God enough.

Safe Landing

Trust in the LORD with all your heart, and do not rely on your own understanding; think about Him in all your ways, and He will guide you on the right paths. (Prov. 3:5–6)

Spiritual Vertigo

A pilot who has vertigo may lose his sense of balance and try to fly his plane by "feeling." When he's in a storm or dense clouds, he may begin to think up is down, north is south. If he doesn't trust his instrument panel, he'll soon be flying by the seat of his pants. Any aviator should know the warning signs of vertigo and how to reduce the danger: avoid flight conditions that may cause vertigo, never take it lightly, be familiar and proficient with the plane's instruments, and most important, trust the instrument panel.

If we're not careful in our walk with the Lord, we can be vulnerable to spiritual vertigo. Sometimes we're surrounded by problems—an account lost at work, a troubled marriage, a rebellious teenager. We don't know which way is up. We feel like we're not standing on solid ground, we begin making all kinds of poor decisions, and our life spins out of control.

Spiritual Victory

We need to be like the seasoned pilot who doesn't give in to the confusion of vertigo. This means we need to avoid situations where we could lose our spiritual focus, never take lightly the continual temptation to ignore spiritual truth, be familiar with biblical principles, and always—above everything else—trust the Bible, the spiritual instrument panel that will guide us to a safe landing. Flying according to God's flight plan is always best.

Bottom Line

Avoid spiritual vertigo by staying grounded in the Word of God on a daily basis.

Weakness and Strength

He gives strength to the weary
and strengthens the powerless. (Isa. 40:29)

Who, Me?

It isn't in the DNA of most men to admit their specific weaknesses or their overall weakness in general. Many of us have spent a large part of our lives trying to convince ourselves that despite our frequent feelings to the contrary, we're actually pretty OK . . . well, at least better than average. It's human nature to avoid feeling shame. But the problem with being OK is that Jesus didn't come to change people who are OK; He came for those who are weak and helpless.

Isaiah shares a powerful truth. He says that God gives strength to the weary and strengthens the powerless. But in order to receive strength, we actually need to acknowledge our weakness and powerlessness. Until our souls are so completely broken, until we realize that we honestly have no goodness in us, God cannot work to conform us to the image of Christ.

I'm OK, You're OK

What often keeps us from admitting our frailties is the nagging suspicion that God cannot be trusted with our most intimate details. We think that He, like the guys at work or at church, might use the embarrassing revelations of our lives against us. But what we don't understand is that God delights in our weakness. And when we depend upon Him completely, He raises us up and gives us supernatural strength. In the upside-down kingdom of God, weakness attracts strength.

Bottom Line

Admitting weakness is the first step toward discovering God's power.

The Great I Am

Jesus said to them, "I assure you:
Before Abraham was, I am." (John 8:58)

Mind-Boggling

The person and work of Jesus has been and always will be the greatest theological issue confronting the church. Our entire faith is built upon Jesus—who He is and what He did. We're called to teach about Him, preach about Him, witness about Him, and defend His claims. In light of this, we ought to know what He said about Himself. The better we know Him, the more our lives will be caught up with His in worship and witness.

In the Gospel of John, Jesus makes several "I am" statements about Himself—between seven and ten (or so) depending on how you add things up. We'll take a look at several of these, starting today with perhaps the most mind-boggling of them all—His claim that He simply is the "I am."

God Up Close

In describing Himself this way, Jesus evokes the same language of God's self-disclosure in Exodus 3:14: "God replied to Moses, 'I AM WHO I AM.'" When Jesus says that He was "before Abraham," He is saying that He has *always* existed. This is a claim to divinity. The Jews certainly understood that. That's why they wanted to stone Him (see John 8:59).

Jesus said in John 14:7, "If you know Me, you will also know My Father." Jesus is God and reveals God. He wasn't just a good teacher. He is the eternal God come to earth in human flesh. He's the divine Savior that we need.

Bottom Line

Remember, when you see Jesus, you're seeing God in human form.

The Bread of Life

"I am the bread of life," Jesus told them.
*"No one who comes to Me will ever be hungry, and no one who
believes in Me will ever be thirsty again."* (John 6:35)

Hungry Souls

We get hungry. Often. It's not uncommon to hear ourselves
or others say things like, "I'm starving! I haven't had anything to
eat all day." When we can hear our stomach growling and we're
beginning to feel a little weak, it's hard to think about anything
other than getting some food. Satisfying our hunger becomes
our number-one priority at that point.

The truth is, we need food. We can't live without it for too
long. Asking for our daily bread just makes sense because we
need it (see Matt. 6:11). But as much as we need our daily bread
to sustain us, we also need the spiritual sustenance that only
Jesus can provide. Only He can feed our starving souls.

A Satisfying Savior

In John 6:35, Jesus says, "I am the bread of life." His listeners were asking for a sign like the manna God provided the
Israelites as they were traveling through the wilderness (see
Exod. 16:4). To this request Jesus replied: "I assure you: Moses
didn't give you the bread from heaven, but My Father gives you
the real bread from heaven. For the bread of God is the One
who comes down from heaven and gives life to the world" (John
6:32–33). Jesus is the real bread from heaven. Spiritual hunger is
satisfied only by Him. Don't go hungry!

Bottom Line

The world offers a lot of substitutes, but our spiritual hunger can be satisfied only by Jesus. Ask Him to fill you up with
His love for you.

Light of the World

Jesus spoke to them again: "I am the light of the world. Anyone who follows Me will never walk in the darkness but will have the light of life." (John 8:12)

In the Dark

Ever get lost in the woods at night without a flashlight? Not a good feeling. Or maybe you can recall a time when the power went out at your house and you were stumbling around in the dark trying to find a flashlight without running into something. It's always a relief when the lights come back on and we can see what we're doing.

Light is important. We need to be able to see where we're going in this life, and only God can illumine our path. In the Bible, light and truth are closely related. To walk in the light is to walk in the truth. Alternatively, when the Bible talks about walking in darkness, it is talking about being disconnected from God—the source of all spiritual light and truth. People living in this condition experience confusion, chaos, and pain. How could it be otherwise? They are separated from the Creator of everything, including meaning and purpose.

Into the Light

One of the great joys of being a Christian is knowing the truth. Knowing that salvation is found only in Jesus. Knowing that He is our Savior. Knowing that He is the source of all life. As John 1:4 puts it: "Life was in Him, and that life was the light of men." So let your life shine brightly with the glorious light of Jesus.

Bottom Line

Let Jesus shine the light of His truth into your heart so that you can shine brightly for Him in a dark world.

The Door

"I am the door. If anyone enters by Me, he will be saved and will come in and go out and find pasture." (John 10:9)

Place of Decision

Doors are transition points, places of decision and future change—whether big or small. When you enter through a door, you enter into someplace new. At the same time you leave the place you've been.

Perhaps the best kind of doors are doors of opportunity. The apostle Paul prayed for such a door in Colossians 4:3: "Pray also for us that God may open a door to us for the message, to speak the mystery of the Messiah." He knew that God is the great door opener. We can plan and hope and dream, but ultimately God is the One who opens doors of opportunity for us.

The Ultimate Door

Jesus offers the ultimate opportunity: "I am the door. If anyone enters by Me, he will be saved and will come in and go out and find pasture." Notice that Jesus says that He is *the* door to salvation, not one door among many. To give you some context: a shepherd in biblical times actually slept in the one doorway to the sheep pen. In that sense he literally *was* the door. In using this metaphor, Jesus is once again making a claim to deity and teaching that salvation is found only through Him. Of course, this kind of exclusivity isn't popular today. It's one of the most common objections people have to Christianity. And yet it's the truth. Jesus is *the* door.

Bottom Line

When you walked through the door of salvation, you entered into eternal life—the greatest opportunity any of us could ever have.

The Good Shepherd

"I am the good shepherd. The good shepherd lays down his life for the sheep." (John 10:11)

Personal Concern

God has many titles for Himself in the Bible, but few, if any, are as warmly personal as "shepherd." Psalm 23, "The LORD is my shepherd . . ." is one of the most beloved passages in the Bible for good reason—its simple beauty and comfort are perfectly designed to meet the many needs of the human heart. The truth is, we *are* like sheep in many ways—often confused, helpless, needy, dependent. We need a good shepherd to guide us, protect us, provide for us, and sacrifice for us. And that's exactly the picture the Bible paints of God the Father in Psalm 23 and other passages like Isaiah 40:11: "He protects His flock like a shepherd; He gathers the lambs in His arms and carries them in the fold of His garment. He gently leads those that are nursing." What a gracious heavenly Father we have!

Man on a Mission

Jesus calls Himself "the good shepherd." This designation is in stark contrast to the religious leaders whom He refers to as the "hired man" (John 10:12). The hired man, having no real interest in the sheep, runs at the first sign of trouble. Jesus, on the other hand, "lays down his life for the sheep" (John 10:11). Jesus knew His mission. He knew the cost He would have to pay to secure the lives of His sheep. And He was willing to pay it for us. He is the Good Shepherd.

Bottom Line

Let the knowledge of God's personal care for you give you both comfort and great hope.

Key to Success

He stores up success for the upright; He is a shield for those who live with integrity. (Prov. 2:7)

The Owner of Success

Despite the American Dream, a man's talent, experience, and work ethic are not enough to bring success. You can possess uncanny gifts, a broad and rich background, and the ability to burn much midnight and weekend oil, but you do not have the ability to make something succeed. No one does. A biologist can have "the building blocks of life," but she cannot make life. A farmer can have soil, seed, manure, and rain, but he cannot make the corn grow. We can't just make things happen on our own.

But there is One who can. There is One alone who makes life. There is One alone who makes crops grow. And there is One alone who brings success. He is Creator, Sustainer, Provider. "I am Yahweh, and there is no other. I form light and create darkness, I make success and create disaster; I, Yahweh, do all these things" (Isa. 45:6–7).

Redefining Your Goal

The Lord alone decides whether you succeed, and if so, how much. As with your talent, experience, and work ethic, He will dole out success and failure however He chooses. It is all from the Lord—everything you have and are—and to Him it will all return.

So what must you do to earn His blessing of success? Don't spin your wheels on this one, brother. It's the wrong question. Ask rather, "How can I please You in both drought and deluge, mountain and valley, in every time and in every way?"

Bottom Line

Seek to please the King; therein lies your true success.

Get Out of There

"Look, I'm sending you out like sheep among wolves. Therefore be as shrewd as serpents and as harmless as doves." (Matt. 10:16)

Know Your Weaknesses

Gentlemen, let's face the facts: sexual temptation is rampant in our society. From the titan of Internet pornography to the hoards of suggestive shows, from the covers of supermarket magazines to the prevalence of adulterous affairs, the slippery slope of sexual immorality lies all around us.

And many of us, at one time or another, sink neck deep in the filth. Regarding sexual purity, we can be nothing more than whitewashed tombs—clean by appearance, vile within. How are we to live "as shrewd as serpents and as harmless as doves"? How can world-savvy men live with innocence? Three words . . .

Cut and Run

In specific reference to adultery and lust, Christ said to cut off the cause (see Matt. 5:27–30). While your eye or hand is not the cause or source of sexual temptation, Christ taught that nothing is to come between us and purity. So cut off the flirtatious relationship with the woman at work. Move your computer to the living room, ask your wife to manage "parental controls," or cut off the Internet. "For it is better that you lose one of the parts of your body than for your whole body to go into hell" (v. 30). As Joseph fled from Potiphar's wife, we too are to "run from sexual immorality!" (1 Cor. 6:18). Against some evils you stand and fight; not so with lust. Run from it!

Bottom Line

Sexual temptation is a stumbling block for most men. We must acknowledge our weakness and follow His guidance: cut and run.

Belt of Truth

Stand, therefore, with truth like a belt around your waist. (Eph. 6:14)

Ready for Battle

We're in a war, a spiritual war, and the stakes are as high as they can be. Our enemy, the devil, throws everything he can at us to render us ineffective for God. More than that, he's out to make us miserable—the worst kind of witness to a watching world. If we don't recognize the battle, or if we just wish it away, we'll get clobbered.

The warfare language in Ephesians 6 and throughout the Bible is there for a reason—a cosmic clash is going on all around us, pitting God and His people against Satan and the forces of evil. We can't escape it; we have to fight. And to fight well we need to be dressed for battle in the armor that God provides.

Starting with Truth

Using the imagery of a Roman soldier's armor, Paul lists the Christian soldier's spiritual armor, piece by piece, in Ephesians 6:10–17. The first five articles of clothing are defensive in nature—they help us stand firm against the enemy. Over the next few days, we're going to take a look at each one, starting with the "belt of truth."

Without the truth we're simply defenseless. Jesus said that the truth sets us free (see John 8:32). Confidence in God's Word is a must. That's where the battle starts. The enemy is constantly feeding us lies, so we must fight back with truth.

Bottom Line

Mentally putting on our spiritual armor each day is a great practice. It reminds us we're in a war and that God has provided protective armor for us.

Breastplate of Righteousness

*Stand, therefore, with . . . righteousness
like armor on your chest. (Eph. 6:14)*

Pride and Unbelief

Even as Christians we can sometimes fall into the trap of trying to justify ourselves through our own righteous behavior. That's impossible, of course, considering that the standard we'd need to live up to is absolute perfection. And yet, there is something in us—the Bible calls it *pride*—that has a hard time admitting sin and receiving grace. A Christian is, by definition, someone who has given up all hope of self-righteousness and has embraced Christ's righteousness instead. This great exchange is the heart of the gospel and the spring of all joy in the Christian life.

Heart of the Gospel

It's not surprising, then, that Satan would attack Christians in this area. He is called "the accuser of our brothers" in Revelation 12:10, and that's exactly what he does. His strategy is two pronged and subtle. If he can't get us to try to justify ourselves through our own moral performance (which actually results in living in denial with unconfessed sin), he will constantly attempt to cast doubt in our minds about the sufficiency and reality of our justification in Christ. It's all-out warfare for us to rest in Christ.

The breastplate of righteousness—the firm and secure knowledge that we are righteous in Christ apart from works—is absolutely critical to protect our hearts from self-righteous pride or crippling despair. Without it, we're vulnerable to attack.

Bottom Line

Our righteousness in Christ—our justification before God on account of Christ—is crucial to our standing firm.

Shoes of Peace

*Stand, therefore, with . . . your feet sandaled
with readiness for the gospel of peace. (Eph. 6:14–15)*

Dig In!

We've been talking about putting on the full armor of God in order to protect ourselves from the attacks of the enemy. Continuing to get dressed for battle, the next essential piece of armor we need is a good pair of shoes—"gospel of peace" footwear, as Paul puts it. Even though shoes are made for walking, they are also helpful for digging in deep and defending your turf.

In spiritual terms we need God's peace if we hope to stand firm against Satan's attacks. A troubled heart simply doesn't defend itself well. By contrast the peace of God that comes from the gospel helps keep us balanced and clearheaded. It's a peace that "surpasses every thought" (Phil. 4:7). So while chaos and trouble prevail on the outside, peace reigns on the inside.

Advance!

While our armor is mainly defensive in nature, our gospel shoes enable us to take peace wherever we go, impacting all of our relationships. We are called to be peacemakers. This certainly includes working for peace among believers, but it also includes sharing the good news with unbelievers who are not yet at peace with God. In seeing ourselves as ambassadors for Christ in this way, we experience more of God's peace ourselves. Christianity was never meant to be a private affair. He wants His peace to extend to others, and He wants to use us as instruments of His peace.

Bottom Line

Satan hates peace. God loves it. The gospel of peace gives us peace within and peace without.

Shield of Faith

In every situation take the shield of faith, and with it you will be able to extinguish all the flaming arrows of the evil one. (Eph. 6:16)

The Battle

Imagine if you went through your day with a continual awareness that the devil is constantly firing flaming arrows at you in the form of lies, accusations, and temptations. Imagine, also, that you have been given a shield able to deflect these arrows harmlessly to the ground.

Well, both things are true. That is the reality you face every day. You are constantly being fed lies and deceptions from the enemy. That's all he traffics in. Too often, though, we don't recognize what he's up to. (He is deceptive, after all.) We wrongly assume that every thought that enters our minds originates with us. Not so. We have an enemy, and he is out "to steal and to kill and to destroy" (John 10:10). We need the shield of faith!

The Strategy

In 2 Corinthians 10:3–5, Paul outlines what taking up the shield of faith looks like: "For though we live in the body, we do not wage war in an unspiritual way, since the weapons of our warfare are not worldly, but are powerful through God for the demolition of strongholds. We demolish arguments and every high-minded thing that is raised up against the knowledge of God, taking every thought captive to obey Christ." Taking up the shield of faith means subjecting all of our thoughts to the Word of God, and if something doesn't line up, we reject it.

Bottom Line

Faith is a gift that grows by exposure to the Word. The stronger our faith, the more we can recognize and dismiss the enemy's lies and deceptions.

Helmet of Salvation

Take the helmet of salvation. (Eph. 6:17)

Fighting from Victory

One of the devil's most effective strategies is to try making us question our salvation. Satan constantly whispers condemning lies, conveying the message that we must not really be Christians given how we still struggle with sin. It can be effective, too, because we *do* still struggle with sin. We know our failures and duplicity all too well. He takes advantage of that and tempts us to doubt our salvation based on our performance.

When we doubt our salvation, all kinds of things go wrong in our Christian life. We lose our joy. We lose our courage. We lose our love for God. It's pretty hard to love someone who you feel doesn't love you or only loves you conditionally. It's especially hard to love a perfect God who we can (wrongly) believe requires perfection out of us before He will love us. Jesus, however, has secured our salvation once and for all. His performance was perfect, and so is ours in Him.

Free to Fight Back

The gospel is so free, we have a hard time believing it. It's really hard to accept salvation as a free gift, no strings attached. We revert back to performance mode so easily. But when we do, the devil wins because trying to earn God's approval is both unnecessary and impossible. More than that, it has the exact opposite effect of what God desires for us—holier lives and security in Him.

Bottom Line

Your eternal security is the result of Christ's saving work. Wear that knowledge like a helmet protecting your mind from doubt.

The Restored Life

"Go up into the hills, bring down lumber, and build the house. Then I will be pleased with it and be glorified," says the LORD. (Hag. 1:8)

Pressure from Below

The book of Ezra tells the story of the return of the Jews to Jerusalem to rebuild the temple. Though they knew better and had been warned over and over, they disobeyed God's law, slid further and further into sin, and were eventually taken captive by a conquering nation. When they finally turned back to God (see Ezra 1:5), the process of spiritual restoration began.

But it wasn't long before they faced opposition from those in the land. Some of that opposition came in the form of an insincere offer to help, which sounded well intentioned. Other opposition was a more direct, in-your-face kind of legal and physical pressure. Before long it became too much, and Israel's journey toward restoration came to a halt.

Help from Above

It was at this point that the prophets Haggai and Zechariah arrived on the scene. They encouraged the Jews to renew their commitment and continue their work. Today's verse is part of that rally cry. Yes, it's an uphill journey. Yes, it's hard work, but don't give up! Stay the course. Your restored life will bring glory to God and He will bless you! Living the restored life is not without opposition and discouragement, but it is not without help either. Beware of the habits, friends, or activities that oppose your walk with God. Stand firm in your commitment to Him and receive His help. He will help you rebuild!

Bottom Line

You will face opposition in returning to God or attempting to draw closer. Stay the course!

Returning to God

They set up the altar on its foundation and offered burnt offerings for the morning and evening on it to the Lord even though they feared the surrounding peoples. (Ezra 3:3)

The Trip Down

Most of us could point to periods in our lives when we weren't walking closely with God or seeking His will. Perhaps you or someone you care about is there right now. Well, thankfully, in the book of Ezra, God gives us an open invitation to return to Him and a neat biblical model for spiritual restoration. Ezra tells the story of the Jews who returned to Jerusalem after being exiled to Babylon a generation or two earlier. They had been taken captive because they had perpetually disobeyed God's commands, living life to please themselves rather than walking closely with God.

The First Step Up

Most certainly there was much work for the Jews to do when they arrived. We might imagine the excitement and eagerness they felt to rebuild their homes, their businesses, and their city. But instead, what we see them do first is rebuild the altar. The altar was where the Jews confessed their sins, offered thanks, and prayed. In other words, it was their central point of communication with God.

Likewise for us, restoring our communication with God must be our highest priority. Before serving in the church, signing up for a men's group, or doing some other activity, we must restore our direct, personal, ongoing communication with God. Our spiritual vitality depends on it. Real prayer, real relationship with God, must be our primary objective. The rest is secondary.

Bottom Line

Returning to God starts with restoring our prayer life.

Christic, Our Substitute

He made the One who did not know sin to be sin for us, so that we might become the righteousness of God in Him. (2 Cor. 5:21)

He Took Our Sin

The cross of Christ was the scene of the greatest exchange in history. Jesus did not die merely as a moral example or a martyr. He died as our substitute. God made Him "to be sin for us." That means He carried every moral failure you have ever committed. Every hatred, every deception, every evil lust, every act of selfishness, and every immorality—past, present, and future. You cannot invent a sin that has not already been placed on the shoulders of Jesus Christ. God gathered up as a singular sum the sin of the world and laid it all on Jesus. Then God punished Christ for our sins instead of punishing us. Christ was our great substitute in death. He died so we wouldn't have to.

We Take His Righteousness

We gave Him our sins; He gives us His righteousness. Righteousness is simply the quality of being good enough for God. Instead of measuring us by our own merits and goodness, God now measures us by the righteousness of Christ. He sees us covered over and filled with the righteousness of Christ. In Christ alone you are good enough for God forever. That's the great exchange that takes place, and it's something we can experience moment by moment in our walk with the Lord. The more we understand and believe it, the more thankful we'll be.

Bottom Line

The gospel of grace offers the good news that a Substitute died in our place for our sins and exchanged His own righteousness for our filthy rags.

Christer, Our Champion

He disarmed the rulers and authorities and disgraced them publicly; He triumphed over them by Him. (Col. 2:15)

The Great Battle

The cross of Christ was the climactic battle of an ages-old cosmic war. At the cross Jesus battled against every evil force that had attacked humanity. Sin was there in all its ugliness, demanding condemnation and wrath. When sin galloped in, death came riding on its back. Hell clamored to devour the Savior. Satan and his hosts swooped in to destroy Him. The concentrated powers of darkness did battle against one Man, all alone: the God-Man versus the powers of evil that would destroy our lives and bring darkness over the universe.

The Triumphal Procession

When the battle seemed fiercest, Jesus cried out the words humanity had longed to hear since the fall. He announced to angels, demons, humans, heaven, hell, and the devil: IT IS FINISHED! Sin was paid in full. The death of Christ meant the death of death. Hell lost its claim on humankind. And Satan and his hosts were disarmed and put to public disgrace.

One day we will join Him in a triumphant procession, celebrating our Champion and casting our crowns at His feet. Death, hell, and Satan will have received their just punishments. And God's people will step into their full victory in Christ. Until then we live by faith in the One who gives us the victory—the Lord Jesus Christ, our Savior and Victorious King! Thanks be to God! Victory is assured!

Bottom Line

The cross was a battlefield, and Jesus Christ emerged the all-time, undisputed, undefeated Champion over sin, death, and the enemies of God.

Leadership in Marriage

He said to them, "The kings of the Gentiles dominate them, and those who have authority over them are called 'Benefactors.' But it must not be like that among you." (Luke 22:25–26)

Tearing Down

In our verse for today, Jesus referenced the Gentile kings who were known for their ruthless domination, and He used them as an example of how not to lead others. Dictionary.com defines *dominate* as "ruling, controlling, and towering above." Consider this: One of the ways husbands "tower above" their wives is by displaying a critical nature and pointing out deficiencies and failures. Sometimes the criticism is disguised in the form of a joke or a teasing tone, yet it's more harmful than funny. In fact, it has the effect of tearing down, leaving the wife's need for her husband's love and affirmation unmet.

Building Up

It is not to be like that among us, Jesus says. The godly husband doesn't consider himself the "benefactor" as if he were solely responsible for everything good that happens (see John 3:27). Instead, he sees his wife as a unique and beloved creation of God. His focus is on what is good and right about her rather than what's not so good or could use improvement. This doesn't mean he puts her on a pedestal or is blind to her weaknesses, but his focus is on her strengths. His only need for understanding her weaknesses is to keep from causing injury with a careless word or deed. He uses them to add layers of protection, to help build her up. He affirms her significance as his coheir.

Bottom Line

Notice how often you offer criticism or "suggestions" instead of praise and affirmation.

More Marriage Lessons

"It must not be like that among you. On the contrary, whoever is greatest among you must become like the youngest, and whoever leads, like the one serving." (Luke 22:26)

On Defense

The context of our verse today is a dispute that arose among the disciples over who would be the greatest. The prior verse reveals that this silly exercise stemmed from a comment Jesus made that one from their ranks would betray Him. The disciples defended themselves to each other, leading to an argument driven by pride. In this setting Jesus shows the contrast between servant leadership and domination.

On Offense

Isn't that sometimes true of us? When our marriage reveals a character flaw, we try to reestablish ourselves as head of the house (as if someone had taken that away), making decisions and exercising authority without also showing humility and servitude. When this happens, our wives are left without a voice and the consideration they deserve and need.

Servant leadership, on the other hand, calls for humility and a commitment to meet the spiritual, emotional, and physical needs of our spouse. One of the most important ways we can do that is by listening. This doesn't mean we subjugate our opinions or defer every decision. Rather, we stop to consider her needs and concerns, seeing how our decisions will affect her and the rest of the family. Instead of arguing until we win or insisting on having the final word, we promote and nurture our wife and the perspective she brings.

Bottom Line

Being the "dominant male" is best left to apes and lions. Jesus taught us to lead with humility, service, and a listening ear.

Judgment Day

When they persisted in questioning Him,
He stood up and said to them, "The one without sin among
you should be the first to throw a stone at her." (John 8:7)

The Bigger They Are . . .

It happens far too often these days. A sports star, politician, actor, or some other rank-and-file celebrity messes up, and the public pounces. Fueled by an insatiable 24-7 news cycle, we can examine the fallout from every conceivable angle—and then some. Consumers say they're tired of scandals, yet ratings skyrocket nonetheless.

Some people seem to take an almost perverse pleasure in seeing the mighty tumble. Stars who were once heroes cheered by millions are now drowning in a sea of accusation with virtually no hope of being rescued. They've gone from hero to zero in no time flat, and no one really seems to care.

Throwing Stones

To figure out how Jesus feels about this, a Christian needs to go no further than John 8:1–11. In the well-known story of the woman caught in adultery, the scribes and Pharisees are sure they've painted Jesus into a corner. They feel morally superior to this woman. There is no love or compassion in their accusations.

Yet Jesus' answer is perfect in its simplicity. Go ahead and kill her, He seems to be saying, but only if you are without fault. Remember His counsel the next time a famous person, or even someone you know, is disgraced. Rather than pile on, offer grace and mercy.

Bottom Line

Celebrity scandals show all too clearly that famous people aren't perfect. But then again, neither are you. No one is. Judgmentalism is prideful.

Preaching to the Preacher

Should I not care about the great city of Nineveh, which has more than 120,000 people who cannot distinguish between their right and their left, as well as many animals? (Jon. 4:11)

The Out-There People

Christians with Jonah's attitude sometimes suffer from the "out there" syndrome. We think all of the sin, wickedness, and injustice are with *that* particular group of people we despise. For Jonah it was Nineveh. They were among the most feared, hated enemies of the Jewish people. So when Jonah's reluctant mission produced revival in Nineveh, Jonah's heart burned with rage.

The story of Jonah reminds us that while God is at work among the wicked, He sometimes saves His greatest revival for the heart of the preacher. Jonah was a patriotic Jew, whose imbalanced devotion to Israel led first to pride, then prejudice. So God sent Jonah to Nineveh. Not just because Nineveh needed Jonah but because Jonah needed Nineveh.

Skipping Chapter Four

What we learn from God's final words in the book of Jonah may be the most important lesson in the book. God cares about all people! Like Jonah we can allow ourselves to form prejudices that keep us from extending God's grace to the "Ninevehs" of our world. We forget that we, too, arrive at the cross with our own Nineveh-sized baggage, atrocities that seem genteel in a permissive culture but violate God's standard of perfect righteousness. So God consistently allows circumstances in our lives that will challenge our natural self-righteousness. The more we appreciate the grace we've received, the more we will offer it to others.

Bottom Line

Sometimes the faithful servant of God needs the most revival.

What Kind of Tree?

He is like a tree planted beside streams of water that bears its fruit in season and whose leaf does not wither. Whatever he does prospers. (Ps. 1:3)

Are You an Oak?

It's easy to take trees for granted until you live in the desert where trees do not flourish because the climate is so dry. They need lots of water to develop a strong root system in order to be healthy and fruitful.

Think of majestic maples framing a riverbed, oaks fed by an underground spring, or cypress trees reaching for the sky out of a swamp. The tallest sequoias grow in valleys where year-round streams flow. But you won't find these beautiful trees in the Mojave Desert.

Where have you chosen to plant your heart? In a parched desert? Or in a verdant rainforest, getting spiritual nourishment every day? It's a choice every man must make.

Or a Tumbleweed?

In a unique twist Psalm 1 foreshadows John 14:6, where Jesus says to His disciples, "I am the way, the truth, and the life. No one comes to the Father except through Me." Psalm 1:1 says, "How happy is the man who does not follow the advice of the wicked," for Jesus is "the way." Verse 2 says, "His delight is in the LORD's instruction," for Jesus is "the truth." And verse 3 says that you are like "a tree planted beside streams of water," for Jesus is "the life." The man who lives in this way lives a prosperous life indeed! Are you following the way, the truth, and the life?

Bottom Line

Take a look at a strong, healthy tree outside, and ask God to show you how your life can be like that.

Packing for Vacation

Let us be concerned about one another in order to promote love and good works, not staying away from our worship meetings, as some habitually do, but encouraging each other, and all the more as you see the day drawing near. (Heb. 10:24–25)

What'd You Forget?

Maybe you're the "travel agent" of your family, the one with all the travel brochures, with your tickets booked months ahead, the one who knows the fastest lines at Adventureland. Or maybe you're headed to a secluded cabin in the woods, ready to enjoy simple time away from the cell phone and the TV.

But of all the things you could forget to pack for your vacation, make sure you don't forget God. Not trying to be legalistic here; just trying to encourage you to teach your children by example that gathering together regularly to worship God wherever you are is important.

Is God Coming with You?

Sure, that visit to grandma's country church may seem boring to the kids. But show them how lifelong faith has sustained people from older generations, even without the latest music and lighting systems. Or find a church of a different stripe or background and worship there. It will promote lots of discussion among your family.

If you're a long way from civilization, lead a family worship service yourself. Sing along with a CD. Share a favorite Scripture verse, or tell what God is currently teaching you. A family time of worship will be a great memory for your kids, and it will honor God as well.

Bottom Line

Take the Lord on vacation—you may have one of the best worship services of all time!

Worship Wars

*While they were in the field, Cain attacked
his brother Abel and killed him. (Gen. 4:8)*

The Heart of Worship

How ironic that worship, the gift God has given us to love
Him and declare His worth, was also an impetus for the first
murder. Who would've thought that someone could get so upset
during a worship service? But just as in the days of Genesis, "sin
is crouching at the door" when we worship (Gen. 4:7), and we
must master it.

The issue in Genesis 4 was not over the mode of worship, whether God preferred livestock or produce as an offering. Instead, the acceptability of their worship had everything
to do with the motive of their hearts. Cain presented "some" of
the land's produce as an offering, but Abel offered some of the
firstborn of his flock and their fat portions. Cain merely "tipped"
God while Abel gave from his very best.

One Pure Motive

How quickly we judge others in their worship, deeming
theirs to be less than our own. Whether it's the style of their
music, the formality of their dress, or the outward expression
of their praise, both young and old have been guilty of assum-
ing their own worship of God is the acceptable version. We've
assumed "our way" and "God's way" are the same. Don't let the
way others worship become a heart hang-up for you. Instead,
keep your eyes on Jesus, and focus on how your worship offering
might please Him. If you do that, you will be blessed and God
will be honored.

Bottom Line

Purpose to give God your best in worship this coming
Sunday.

Self-sacrifice

Self-Giving or Self-Preserving?

Any good father knows that love sacrifices its own pleasure, agenda, time, comfort, and life for the sake of another. Jesus loved you to the maximum. He laid down His life "that He might bring you to God" (1 Pet. 3:18). He could have demanded His rights and clung to His comforts, but He let them go. Instead, He emptied himself (see Phil. 2:5–8). He rescued you "from the domain of darkness" and died in the process (Col. 1:13). For Jesus, self-preservation was not the ultimate priority; *love was!*—love for His Father, for you, for the world.

Big Ways, Small Ways

True love gives. When you love as Jesus loved, you will sacrifice yourself for others. It may mean offering up some kind words, a helping hand, a gentle touch, or a cup of cold water. Or it may even mean offering up your life in the service of the gospel. Sacrifices like these prove that "God's love has been poured out in our hearts" (Rom. 5:5).

There's a great paradox in Jesus' kind of love: you give your life away to gain it (see Mark 8:35). You don't count your life dear to yourself if it prevents you from loving others (see Acts 20:24). Like David Livingstone, the great explorer and missionary to Africa, you come to feel that you really never made a sacrifice. This is only possible when you are so satisfied in Christ and awed by His sacrifice, anything you give up feels like nothing in comparison.

Bottom Line

Love is a joyful and willing self-sacrifice to meet another's needs.

Love and Power

Love one another earnestly from a pure heart, since you have been born again—not of perishable seed but of imperishable—through the living and enduring word of God. (1 Pet. 1:22–23)

God's Life in You

Jesus didn't die on the cross and rise again just to call you to an improved version of your presaved life. He calls you to a whole new life, a "born again" one. God planted His life in your soul like a seed into soil. That life brings with it all the qualities of God's heart: His kindness, compassion, gentleness, honesty, integrity, courage, and love. For the follower of Jesus, love is not simply an action to choose but a divine power to unleash. It is the fruit of the Spirit, not of self-effort. You can't love others the way God wants them to be loved by your own power. You need the power of God.

God's Love through You

Fortunately, you can have the power of God working in your life. Today's Scripture identifies three sources of His power: (1) *God's Word*. When you learn and obey Scripture, you don't just gather information; you access divine power to love others. (2) *God's Spirit*. The Holy Spirit indwells you starting at conversion, and He continues to work in you, conforming you to the image of Christ, producing the fruit of the Spirit in you. (3) *God's life*. The "imperishable seed" is Christ in you. He enables you to love people you would otherwise find impossible to love. You can let His love shine through you as you abide in Him.

Bottom Line

You are meant to be a conduit of God's love to your family, friends, coworkers, and the world.

Spiritual Maturity

*Leaving the elementary message about the Messiah,
let us go on to maturity, not laying again the foundation. (Heb. 6:1)*

Love Is a Choice

You can decide to run a marathon in a moment of inspiration, but your ability to complete one comes only after much preparation and hard work. Depending on the kind of shape you're in, it can take six months or more to create an adequate base of fitness that enables you to traverse the 26.2 miles without a high probability of injury and a certainty of great pain. So while running a marathon is a choice, it's the kind of choice that requires you to keep on deciding you really want to run a marathon after all. A lot of things in life are like that. There's the initial decision and then a lot of confirming decisions along the way.

Can You Choose It?

Jesus invites you to a manly, mature, self-giving life of love that grows as you mature in Him. Really, your ability to love is the best measure of your spiritual maturity. As you learn to continually walk in the Spirit, Christ's love will flow through you to others.

It's a supernatural thing. It requires active abiding in the vine. Christ enables you to love the people in your life, even when they're at their most unlovable, but you have to let Him—and keep on letting Him—consistently walking in the Spirit.

Bottom Line

Love is a choice, but the supernatural love of Christ grows stronger in you as you grow deeper in Him.

Avoid the Noise

*He said to them, "Come away by yourselves
to a remote place and rest for a while." (Mark 6:31)*

Caught in the Chaos

Many men have their on/off switch stuck in the up position. We're so busy doing, achieving, succeeding, and conquering things, the concept of rest is almost foreign to us. *Isn't resting what the people in Fiji do?* Yet rest is important—even biblical. In Mark 6:31 Jesus says, "Come away by yourselves to a remote place and rest a while."

But how do we rest in a society that bombards us with information and entertainment? From the Internet to exciting hobbies to movies on demand, not to mention full-bore, full-time work that leaks over into the evenings and weekends, we can easily fill our minds (and days) with seemingly beneficial things. If we live with a nonstop mentality too long, however, we don't end up feeling successful. Instead we just feel tired and burned out.

Grounded in Silence

Studies show God created our minds to work best in silence. In the quiet we can more effectively think, sort our thoughts, and feel God's presence.

To grow closer to God, we need to rest. Filling our minds with new information or working hard to accomplish a goal isn't bad, except when it distracts us from God. The world is filled with so many distractions, it's important to plan quiet time in a solitary place. Whatever happened to sitting down with a good book—or the Good Book? Try it, and watch your relationship with God grow.

Bottom Line

Seek silence. That's where the Lord can be heard the loudest.

What's Next?

Everything that was a gain to me, I have considered
to be a loss because of Christ. More than that,
I also consider everything to be a loss in view of the surpassing
value of knowing Christ Jesus my Lord. (Phil. 3:7–8)

The Eagle Has Landed

Hundreds of millions watched on TV as Neil Armstrong and Buzz Aldrin became the first men to walk on the moon. Twelve men eventually stepped out onto the lunar surface in subsequent Apollo missions, and several later struggled with what to do next in their lives. After all, how do you possibly top something like that? At an average age of early to mid-forties, the most impressive accomplishment of their lives was over and done with, never to be repeated.

Addicted to Adrenaline

Of course, millions of men tend to get caught up in that next big thing. They didn't walk on the moon, but they might have written a book or brokered a huge deal at the office. Later the emptiness is hard to shake. It's almost as if they're addicted to the adrenaline rush that comes with accomplishment.

God understands (and created) our need for adventure and achievement, but we must also understand that our enemy, the devil, will trick us into thinking we can only scratch our itch for excitement in a small handful of arenas. Ask God to widen your scope, discovering His full joy and enthusiasm wherever you are—at home, with your family, in serving Him, in worshipping Him.

Bottom Line

No matter how impressive your accomplishments might be, a right relationship with Christ matters most in life.

Out of the Darkness

My heart is glad and my spirit rejoices;
my body also rests securely. (Ps. 16:9)

The Lightning Bolt

The words of the e-mail shot off the computer screen like a lightning bolt. "I will be calling you to offer a full-time j-o-b," the note began. Little else needed to be said. After picking up short-term deals here and there for so long, the promise of a "full-time j-o-b" was absolutely stunning.

He had had a great many disappointments along the way. At times it seemed that the prayers he prayed simply seemed to bounce off the ceiling. Although it had often taken every ounce of optimism he could muster to maintain a positive attitude, here was the confirmation he'd waited so long to receive. Amen, amen, and amen.

Weight of the World

As hard as the darkness can be to deal with, it makes coming out on the other side all the more special. When you feel like you've had the weight of the world on your shoulders, how great it is for you to appreciate the feeling of not carrying that burden anymore. Honestly, you feel you could take on the whole world.

But you won't do it single-handedly. Remember all those times you didn't seem to get an answer to your prayers? The Lord took into account every single word, whether you realized it or not. He had a good plan for your life all along! So when the next big trial comes along, be sure to remember the Lord's faithfulness, "the One who lifts up my head" (Ps. 3:3).

Bottom Line

Don't give up hope when it feels like you're in the pit. Wait for the joy of stepping back into the light.

Down, Down

I am bent over and brought low;
all day long I go around in mourning. (Ps. 38:6)

The Darkest Hours

Nighttime is the worst. In the quiet darkness, there's nothing to distract you from the weight of the world that's crashing down around you. You try to go back to sleep, and when you don't, it leaves you that much more frustrated. You turn on the television, and there's nothing on but infomercials and reruns of SportsCenter.

Doubt and fear take over. Sometimes, in the worst times, you can't even put a finger on exactly what's wrong. The only thing you know for sure is that there's no way you're going to be able to pull yourself out of this one. You feel like a failure, plain and simple. Depression has taken over your life.

Light at the End?

Many of us are all too familiar with depression. We recognize the signs in our own lives and in the lives of people we know. Despondency, hopelessness, and despair seem to take over. The world seems permanently gray with no chance of the sun ever coming out again. It's far more than just having a case of "the blues." Depression is an insidious enemy that can sap every ounce of joy from your life. Know this, however. You are not alone! Help can be had in the form of trusted friends and professional counselors. And help can be found in our good God who "is near the brokenhearted" and who "saves those crushed in spirit" (Ps. 34:18).

Bottom Line

If you're struggling with depression, fight it with every ounce of your strength! And get all the help you can—from others and from God. There is hope.

Put God First

"Do not have other gods besides Me." (Exod. 20:3)

The Thrust

In her book *My Memories of Ike*, Mamie Eisenhower tells that after she had been married only a month, Ike was given a new assignment and announced to Mamie that he must leave. She said to him, "Ike, you are not going to leave me this soon after our wedding day, are you?" He put his arms around her and said gently, "Mamie, there is one thing you must understand. My country comes first and always will; you come second."

Likewise, God always comes first too. He will not share His place with anyone or anything. The words "besides Me" mean "in preference to Me." The central thrust of this commandment can be summed up in one word—*priority*. God wants to be our number-one priority, not just one among many. He wants to be first, not a close second.

The Tests

Does God really have first place in your life? There are two simple tests to determine if He has first place. The first one is the love test. You are called to love God "with all your heart, with all your soul, with all your mind, and with all your strength" (Mark 12:30), but if you give your first love to someone or something else instead, then you are serving some other god. The second test is the trust test. What do you trust or cling to? "To trust anything more than God is to make it a god," Puritan divine Thomas Watson wisely stated. Is God first in your life?

Bottom Line

Continually examine your life to make sure God is first. When He is in His proper place, life gets a whole lot simpler.

Accept No Substitutes

"Do not make an idol for yourself, whether in the shape of anything in the heavens above or on the earth below or in the waters under the earth." (Exod. 20:4)

The Competition

What do you have that commands your attention and your affection? A '56 Chevy? An original piece of art? Financial portfolio? Children? Football team? The cottage at the beach or in the mountains? Anything that competes with God for your first affection and attention is an idol. When you allow anything apart from God to rule you, compel you, or control you, you have created an idol.

The Detection

God wants to set you free from enslavement to idols, so detecting and exposing the idols in your life is essential. Prayerfully consider the following list of questions, which are designed to unmask any idols in your heart: What preoccupies or rules your heart, your thoughts, and your time? What compels you, controls you, drives you, motivates you? What gives you a sense of worth? What defines your identity before others? If everything else were taken away, what is the one thing you could not bear to live without? Are you looking to something or someone to provide what only God can?

Always be on guard against anything that pulls you away from God. Tear away the idols from your heart, and devote yourself to God.

Bottom Line

You can make idols out of a lot of good and worthwhile things, even within the church, if they become more important than God. Guard your heart.

Take God Seriously

Be Serious

You can hardly watch a movie, read a book, or engage in a conversation that does not use profanity or cursing. It has become commonplace and acceptable. At first sight this commandment seems to be banning such talk, but after careful study this directive is not just about swearing or using four-letter words. The issue is whether or not you take God's name *seriously* both in language and in lifestyle.

The idea of *name* transmits much more weight in the Bible than in our culture. God's name represents His reputation, His character, and His authority. The word *misuse* means ineffectual, useless, or empty. To "misuse the name of the LORD," therefore, means to let God's name and all that it implies be ineffectual and meaningless in your life.

Be Selective

How do you prevent misusing the Lord's name? Be selective with your words, especially those you use about God. Watch what you say, guard your mouth, control your tongue. In other words, think before you speak!

Do you realize that as a believer in Christ, you bear His name? Paul writes in 2 Corinthians 6:3–4: "We give no opportunity for stumbling to anyone, so that the ministry will not be blamed. But as God's ministers, we commend ourselves in everything." *Everything!* Your behavior and your speech reflect on Jesus. Make sure you are representing His name well.

Bottom Line

Be mindful and careful of the words you use about God.

Take a Day

*"Remember the Sabbath day, to keep it holy:
You are to labor six days and do all your work,
but the seventh day is a Sabbath
to the LORD your God." (Exod. 20:8–10)*

Day of Rest

Our great-grandparents called it the Holy Sabbath; our grandparents called it the Sabbath; our parents called it Sunday; we call it the weekend. We have forgotten to observe the Sabbath, and we are paying the price.

The word *Sabbath* means a day of rest to desist from labor. God tells us to "remember the Sabbath" and "to keep it holy." *Holy* means set apart or different. You are to set apart one day a week to do something different from what you do the other six days a week.

Reason to Rest

Rest and relaxation are not optional to healthy living. Rest was never meant to be a luxury but a necessity for growth, maturity, and health. You do not rest because your work is done; you rest because God commanded it and created you to have a need for it. The Sabbath was made for you because God knows that your physical, emotional, and spiritual well-being demands periodic breaks.

The Sabbath is not just a psychological convenience; it is a spiritual and biological necessity. "Remember the Sabbath" is more than just a lifestyle suggestion; it is a commandment. To forget it is dangerous—personally, morally, and spiritually. Your body will last longer and function better if you take time to rest. And in the long run you'll accomplish far more by resting.

Bottom Line

The old adage is true: If you don't "come apart," you will come apart.

Outsourced Parenting

*A rod of correction imparts wisdom, but a youth
left to himself is a disgrace to his mother. (Prov. 29:15)*

Are You There?

My father was forty-five when I was born. And to top it
off, I came as a set—I was a twin. As a parent myself now, I'm
exhausted some days and don't feel like playing with my daughter. I can only imagine how my daddy must have felt when my
twin brother and I reached early adolescence. But he was available, always involved in our lives.

Passive parenting is like passive farming. Without involvement one can expect little more than a harvest of weeds. You
cannot outsource parenting. You can't bully or buy your way to
successful kids. They are not raised on "quality time" but on real
time—your time and lots of it.

Will You Be Present?

In the business world a lot of tasks and projects are out-
sourced to other companies to save money and time. But parents
cannot outsource their presence with their children to teachers, coaches, babysitters, or the church. You can't give your kids
money and send them on their way and think you have fulfilled
your role. Children need parents to be involved and connected
with their lives. Parents are not required to be perfect, but they
are required to be present.

Look for ways you can spend time with your children.
Develop a hobby together. Go shopping together. Play a sport
together. Schedule regular nights to go out and have fun. The
possibilities are endless. Just remember: there is no substitute for
time spent with them.

Bottom Line

Nothing can ever replace the times and the memories
shared with a child. Make a memory today.

It's Not Yours

Yours, LORD, is the greatness and the power and the glory and the splendor and the majesty, for everything in the heavens and on earth belongs to You. Yours, LORD, is the kingdom, and You are exalted as head over all. (1 Chron. 29:11)

The Reality

"I see that the new owners made some changes to your old house," a man said to his former neighbor. "Yes," he replied, "I can't believe they cut down my trees." *My* is one of the most misused, if not dangerous, words in our vocabulary: my job, my money, my talents, my wealth, my belongings, my family, and even, my life.

King David reminds us that God owns all, and we are only managers of what He has entrusted to us. David knew the kingdom was not his—it was God's; the soon-built temple was not his—it was God's; his wealth was not his—it was God's. This outlook made it easy for David to give of the vastness of his wealth to the temple's construction.

The Response

The first law of biblical stewardship is this: God owns it all. Because God is the rightful owner of everything we have, we have a responsibility to manage well all He has entrusted to us. Here we discover the essence of stewardship or management. God has furnished us resources that we are to use for His purposes. Those resources encompass our time, talents, and material possessions. Pledge to use your God-given and God-owned resources to accomplish God-ordained purposes. You won't be sorry.

Bottom Line

How will you demonstrate God's ownership today?

Go!

Go to the great city of Nineveh. (Jon. 3:2)

Don't Stop

Many Christ followers think God's basic call on their life is to stop doing this or stop doing that. People often tell their faith stories by saying something like, "I gave my life to Jesus, and then I stopped doing this, and that, and . . ." listing the sins they've tried to put off. Isn't there more to Christianity than trying to stop doing things?

Yes, it's good to set aside habits and behaviors that are sinful or harmful or not of God. But the heart of Christian discipleship is not the word *stop*. If it were, we'd all be better off just staying home, hiding behind the shutters.

Just Go

At the heart of Christianity is movement, an outward focus, a *going* that we can easily forget as we face the demands of our lives. But God didn't forget why He had called Jonah. He was called to go to Nineveh. It was his mission whether he liked it or not.

Nineveh is not just the place you don't want to go. It's the place that is seemingly out of God's reach. It's the friend or family member you've prayed for but who never seems to change. It's the peer or colleague who laughs at your faith or how you live. It's the person you try to love, but he just responds like a jerk no matter how gracious you are. It's the situation that never seems to get any better, which never inspires hope. It's the place God has called you to go, and it's the place where you must rely on God to survive.

Bottom Line

The gospel begins with *go*. So what are you waiting for?

God Can Reach Anyone

The men of Nineveh believed in God. (Jon. 3:5)

The Impossible

The man's father was a highly functional alcoholic—bright, energetic, and engaging. The son prayed for his father for more than thirty years, but nothing changed. No breakthroughs, no conversion, no surprise outcomes. He started to think, "I've had it. Prayer is no use. My father won't change."

Maybe you have a story or know someone like that, something that makes you stop expecting, believing, hoping, praying.

The Possible

But whenever we think things are heading down, God is always up to something great. After Jonah delivered his seven-word sermon, the Bible says, "the men of Nineveh believed in God." The people farthest away from God came to God. God didn't look at Nineveh and say, "No way, not possible." He said, "I am the Lord, the One who rescues people from their sins, and I'm going to do something in your days that you would not believe even if you were told." He makes the impossible possible.

The man who had been praying for his father said that a few months before his dad passed away, he heard him tell his family he had finally turned his life over to God. The son said, "I still think of it and laugh." Isn't that so true? Because the joke is on those of us who stop believing that all things are possible with God. The book of Jonah reminds us that God can reach the unreachable.

Bottom Line

Don't stop believing. God can reach those you may be tempted to think are unreachable.

Turning It Around

Though we are slaves, our God has not abandoned us in our slavery. He has extended grace to us in the presence of the Persian kings, giving us new life, so that we can rebuild the house of our God and repair its ruins, to give us a wall in Judah and Jerusalem. (Ezra 9:9)

History of Mistakes

From Genesis through 2 Chronicles we read the history of the Jewish people—delivery from slavery, the inheritance of a land rich with God's blessings, the rise and fall of government, and then the results of their disobedience to God. Sadly we find characteristics in their history we can relate to: the tendency to substitute our goals and methods for God's, compromising what we know He wants from us. Disobedience to God had a high cost not only for the ancient Israelites but also for us and for those around us.

Future of Hope

Ezra 9:9 reveals an awesome truth for those still carrying the consequences of poor choices. Though we're still dealing with the effect of our sins, God is still with us and is still working in our situation. He has not abandoned us in our slavery. He provides a way for us to be freed from our bad habits and sinful tendencies, to be restored to a right relationship with Him, and to be useful to Him despite our pasts.

Don't listen to the voice that says you've messed up too badly or are disqualified from service. That's the enemy's tactic to keep you from accepting God's gift of redemption.

Bottom Line

If you or someone you know is burdened by regret, take heart. You're not alone—God is right there with you, ready to give you new life!

Be Prepared

Precious treasure and oil are in the dwelling of a wise person,
but a foolish man consumes them. (Prov. 21:20)

Living It Up

Many Christians today struggle to find balance in their financial lives. Some are overextended, having lots of stuff but little savings, while others are at the other extreme, living below their means to the point they'd be embarrassed to have coworkers over for dinner. We know Proverbs is full of warnings against accumulation of "things" and getting into debt, but then we have Scriptures like Ecclesiastes 5:19 that encourage us to enjoy our wealth and possessions. So where's the middle ground? How should we think about the money God has given us to steward well?

Laying It Down

Perhaps the questions start with: "Does having this _____ make me a slave to my job, salary level, time away from home? If God were to take this away for a time, would my reserves be sufficient?"

Today's verse reminds us to expect hardships and be prepared for tough times. So rather than spending every penny as soon as we have it, we must discipline ourselves to be prepared for adversity, whether our own or that of others around us. Being spiritually and physically prepared for God to use you for His work is a mark of a mature believer.

Bottom Line

In Matthew 25, Jesus reminds us of the importance of helping others in need—something we can't easily do if we're barely treading water ourselves.

Putting Passion to Work

It was You who created my inward parts;
You knit me together in my mother's womb. (Ps. 139:13)

Trudging Along

Is what you do for a living the same as what you do for an income? Pause for a moment to think about this question. How closely aligned are your interests and talents with where you spend your time? Does your income-providing job make you feel alive? Does it use the strengths and talents God purposely gave you when He designed you?

If the answer to any of the above is "no," it doesn't mean you should rush out and quit your job! That's not likely the wise path. Many of us have jobs that don't use all of our strengths. But Scripture teaches us that God was purposeful and deliberate when He made us. He knows us better than we know ourselves, and He has a plan for using each one of us "to build up the body of Christ" (Eph. 4:12).

Running with Purpose

Take some time this week to evaluate where your interests and particular skills are. Make a list of your interests on a piece of paper, then spend time in prayer asking God to show you how He wants you to use those interests to serve Him. You might even talk with someone on your church's staff, since many churches have tools to help men discover their place of service within the body of Christ and their communities.

Bottom Line

God created you to be a useful, necessary part of His body. Serve Him with your strengths.

The Soldier's Life

Share in suffering as a good soldier of Christ Jesus. (2 Tim. 2:3)

The Call to Hardship

Fortunately, conditions for soldiers have improved greatly since the time of the Civil War. Still it is no easy life. Today thousands of young men and women are putting themselves at risk on behalf of the country they love.

People aren't drafted or conscripted to serve in the United States armed services anymore, but every Christian man is called by God to live the soldier's life. He may never don an army or navy uniform, but he must accept the commission to give his life sacrificially for those he is called to love and serve.

A Countercultural Message

Paul reminded the young preacher Timothy that he was in a battle. Living out the faith in a hostile culture is a war against the flesh, war against the world system, war against an unseen but fierce enemy, Satan. So Timothy shouldn't have seen difficulty as something unexpected. It's what he signed up for as a follower of Christ. As a soldier he was always ready to engage in battle.

How do we apply this to the noise and confusion of daily life? By viewing each difficulty as one more skirmish in a long war. We need to keep in mind that we will take fire along the way, but we're fighting on the winning side and equipped for battle by the Holy Spirit. We can't avoid the war, but it's a fight worth fighting and one we're ultimately going to win.

Bottom Line

Christian men are called to the soldier's life of hardship, sacrifice, and honor.

Faith Factor

Teach a youth about the way he should go;
even when he is old he will not depart from it. (Prov. 22:6)

Floundering Faith

Shane and Nancy never thought they'd be having this conversation with their son. But after his first year of college, he returned home for summer break and said, "Mom and Dad, I don't believe in God anymore." Sadly many Christian parents deal with the heartbreak of children who walk away from their faith. The good news is that research shows a majority of those kids come back to the church once they marry and have kids of their own. But that doesn't help as you deal with the shock of a child who's turned his back on Jesus.

So what's a father to do? The Bible doesn't promise that if we teach our kids about God, everything will be rosy and they'll never doubt their faith. But it does say the truth of God's Word is hard to escape.

Faith Builder

If you have young kids in your home, model what it means to live a Christian life. Let them see you reading the Bible, praying, and having a vibrant relationship with God. Your example goes a long way in letting your kids know God is real. Then encourage your kids to get into God's Word on their own. While you may not be able to control the decisions your kids make in the future, you can certainly be faithful to what God has called you to do as a father.

Bottom Line

Your children's faith will be tested in college, so do all you can to help them build a firm foundation while they're at home.

Good Investment

"When you reap the harvest of your land, you are not to reap all the way to the edge of your field or gather the gleanings of your harvest. Leave them for the poor and the foreign resident; I am Yahweh your God." (Lev. 23:22)

Smart Money

Who can predict the stock market? Sure, Warren Buffett has done a nice job over the years. But the typical investor doesn't have the time, expertise, or energy to figure out where he should put his money. During certain downturns in the market, a lot of investors have decided to stuff their money under their mattresses (at least, figuratively), tired of Wall Street crashes and roller-coaster volatility.

But the Bible says there's one investment that can always be counted on to pay dividends: *giving to the poor.* Back in Leviticus, God commanded His people not to reap to the edge of their fields or gather the gleanings of their harvest. "Leave them for the poor and the foreign resident," He said. Instead of looking for every little profit or possible gain, God wanted His people to provide help for the less fortunate.

Give It Away

In tough economic times we all want to be wise with our money. Planning for the future and looking for ways to grow our wealth are good things. But God doesn't want us to lose focus on the bigger picture. He doesn't command us to be rich; He does command us to help the needy. Ultimately life is about giving away what you've received from God.

Bottom Line

Look for the needy in your area. What can you do to help? If you can't invest your money, invest your time.

Stay Engaged

*Absalom resided in Jerusalem two years
but never saw the king. (2 Sam. 14:28)*

Relational Breakdown

After David's sin with Bathsheba, he experienced family problems of all kinds. Especially heartbreaking was the situation with his son Absalom. After committing a serious crime, the young man fled the country for three years (see 2 Sam. 13:38). Eventually David granted mercy to Absalom and permitted his son to come home. However, David refused to see his son (14:24). They went five years with no face-to-face communication. No wonder Absalom would later commit the heinous sins of rebellion and adultery. When he needed love, companionship, and time with his father, he was met with only separation and silence.

Repeating Mistakes

In his day Charles Lindbergh, the great aviator, was one of the most admired men on earth. His travels took him around the world several times each year, but he seldom landed at home. His wife came to find his presence an intrusion and his absence an insult. Without a relationship with their father, Lindbergh's six children became dispirited and confused. One son remained alienated from his father right up to Lindbergh's death. Like all children, Lindbergh's kids definitely needed time with their father.

Men need to be constantly investing in their family relationships. This means devoting time and effort to maintaining good communication. As we've seen, the alternative can be disastrous.

Bottom Line

There is no substitute for an attentive and affectionate husband and father.

The Mercy of God

You, Lord, are kind and ready to forgive,
rich in faithful love to all who call on You. (Ps. 86:5)

Recognizing His Mercy

Psalm 86:5 assures us that God is "rich in faithful love." This faithful love is a *merciful* love—meaning we don't receive what we deserve (punishment) but rather the opposite (pardon and restoration). God in His great mercy has rescued us from our sinful, sorry, helpless condition and given us a whole new life in Christ.

Ephesians 2:4–5 puts it this way: "God, who is rich in mercy, because of His great love that He had for us, made us alive with the Messiah even though we were dead in trespasses. You are saved by grace!" Like the magnificent Niagara Falls, the mercy of God overflows freely and continually for us.

Demonstrating His Mercy

Did you know that in the natural world vicious wolves show mercy? When a wolf realizes he is losing a fight, he will expose his throat to the victor, who permits the weaker wolf to live. That's mercy, but it pales in comparison to God's mercy toward us. And because we have received such mercy, we should show mercy to others.

Does someone in your life right now need mercy? A suffering brother? A financially afflicted friend? Jesus said, "The merciful are blessed, for they will be shown mercy" (Matt. 5:7). And we all need mercy, don't we? God is pleased when we show mercy to others because He has shown such great mercy to us.

Bottom Line

The cross of Christ displays God's justice toward sin and His mercy toward the sinner.

Parting Ways

*There was such a sharp disagreement
that they parted company. (Acts 15:39)*

All Too Human

Paul and Barnabas—two New Testament leaders of enormous faith, character, and commitment to the kingdom of God—had such a sharp disagreement on ministry tactics that they parted company. Barnabas wanted a guy named John Mark to join their missions venture, but John Mark had bailed on an earlier missionary effort, and Paul lost confidence in him. Barnabas was willing to offer him a second chance. Paul wasn't. The rift was so deep that it blew up their fellowship and they parted company.

Make Peace a Priority

Apparently Paul and Barnabas were just as human as we are. Even the men of God we hold in highest esteem sometimes fail to iron out their differences. Maybe you've seen this played out in your own church or in your own life. Interestingly, God did not send an angel to clarify the issue for Paul and Barnabas, and He's not likely to do it for us. No revelation came as to the right course of action. Perhaps God sometimes leaves us in confusion and ambiguity so we can learn the art of disagreeing without being disagreeable. No matter who is "right" or "wrong" in a gray area, both parties are in the wrong if they do not handle their differences with graciousness. If you have a disagreement with a fellow believer, honor Christ in how you disagree. Basically, don't be a jerk! A little humility goes a long way.

Bottom Line

God wants us to conduct ourselves—even in our disagreements—with love, peace, and kindness, and all of the other fruit of the Spirit.

Choosing Peace

If possible, on your part, live at peace with everyone. (Rom. 12:18)

Walk the Path of Peace

Some people want to be cantankerous. They have a chip on their shoulder. They are looking for a fight. You find them in the workplace, at school, and even in the church. We can't keep them from being that way, but we can choose how to respond. In today's verse the apostle Paul says we should try to live at peace with everyone. That can mean giving up the right to get in an argument even when you know you are right—even when you can prove it! It takes wisdom to know when making your point is useful to the other person and when it just feeds more conflict.

Draw Healthy Boundaries

Just because someone is fishing for a fight doesn't mean you need to take the bait! Instead of reacting immediately, take a deep breath and pray for that person who is sadly trapped in a destructive habit of picking fights to feed some unsanctified inner compulsion for conflict. You can choose not to energize that person.

But note that Paul says to avoid unnecessary conflict "if possible." Sometimes it is not possible. The other person is simply out-of-bounds in word or action. In that case be assertive, be direct, and be tough. You do not have to let anyone violate personal boundaries. Indeed, letting someone walk all over you might only be feeding their sin habit. But generally speaking, as much as possible, strive to live in peace with all men.

Bottom Line

What if you were to consistently think of yourself as a peacemaker? It would change things, wouldn't it? Well, God says you are a peacemaker.

Music to God's Ears

May the God who gives endurance and encouragement allow you to live in harmony with one another. (Rom. 15:5)

A Sweet Sound

God loves harmony in interpersonal relationships. When Christians live in harmony, it is music to the ears of the Lord. When husbands and wives are loving each other, looking out for each other, and serving each other, it is like a symphony for the angels. If you are musically inclined, you know that harmony is not achieved without effort. You have to work at it and practice until you get it right. Interpersonal harmony is no different. In today's passage we are not simply commanded to live in harmony; we are encouraged by the fact that God "gives endurance and encouragement" to our efforts.

The Real Deal

Interpersonal harmony is not the fake patching over of disagreement. It is not living a shallow life to avoid conflict. It is not avoiding all discord. On the contrary it is doing the hard work required to live in peace and understanding. The honest, respectful working out of disagreements is akin to practicing music together until it starts to sound really good. And when it does sound really good, relationships are often strengthened. So don't avoid healthy conflict. Work out those interpersonal issues with grace and patience. The end result will be a beautiful song that delights you, your loved ones, and the God who is empowering you to make a beautiful sound.

Bottom Line

Working out interpersonal difficulties is like learning to sing harmony. The fact that it takes time and energy to get it right doesn't mean it isn't worth it.

Keep On Keeping On

*May the Lord direct your hearts
to God's love and Christ's endurance. (2 Thess. 3:5)*

Marathon Man

Think of endurance as a long, steady march in the right direction. Endurance is a mark of maturity in our faith. We need to cease the "on again, off again" life with God that characterizes the lives of so many believers. Too often we sprint when our emotions are high, then give up on God when life gets hard. Endurance is the ability to keep on keeping on when things are tough and you want to quit.

The Key to Endurance

But don't miss the secret of endurance, which is spelled out in today's verse. Surprisingly this Scripture doesn't speak of *our* endurance at all. It's actually a prayer that God will direct our hearts into "Christ's endurance." The Christian life is not about your capacity to whip up enough grit to cross the finish line. The Christian life is lived in the keen awareness that we do not have enough power within ourselves to endure. We might have enough internal willpower to slog through with something that looks like endurance, but it will not be accompanied by joy or peace or any of the hallmarks that make the journey the exhilarating adventure God intends.

If the kind of Christianity you are living is grinding you down, perhaps you have been relying on your own strength to endure. Keep returning prayerfully to God, and ask Him to give you the supernatural strength and endurance of Christ. That will make all the difference in the world.

Bottom Line

Christianity is a supernatural life, fueled by supernatural power. You need the endurance of Christ, not the endurance of you.

The One and Only

Turn to Me and be saved, all the ends of the earth.
For I am God, and there is no other. (Isa. 45:22)

What to Believe?

The world offers a smorgasbord of religions, with wildly different views of God. Some teach that there is but one supreme being (monotheism), while others are of "the more, the merrier" school of thought (polytheism). In contrast to the religious chaos that engulfs the globe, the true Supreme Being, revealed in the pages of the Bible, makes this declaration: "No god was formed before Me, and there will be none after Me" (Isa. 43:10). He is the one true and living God, above all other lesser gods.

No Ambiguity

In today's verse God invites "all the ends of the earth" to turn to Him alone to be saved. He understands that there is rampant religious confusion and a cacophony of truth claims. But into this confusion He speaks with perfect clarity: "There is no other God but Me, a righteous God and Savior; there is no one except Me" (Isa. 45:21). He has no competition. There is no one else in His league.

Furthermore, He is not hiding from us. He sent Jesus to be the "light of the world" (John 8:12) and beckons us to come to the One who died for us and rose again from the grave so that we could be rescued from our sin and misery. With the revelation of Jesus, all religious searching can come to an end. He calls everyone to turn to Him for salvation.

Bottom Line

Once we turn to the one true God as revealed in the Bible, our search for the source of truth, life, and meaning is over. It's all found in Him.

Oh, Brother!

Judah fathered Perez and Zerah by Tamar,
Perez fathered Hezron, Hezron fathered Aram. (Matt. 1:3)

One Messed-up Family

Most of us would be delighted to discover that we're related to nobility. But imagine if someone did a history of your life and included all the *infamous* people in your bloodline—the murderers, the prostitutes, the cheats.

Those are not the kind of people you'd want to be associated with. You may even try to hide them from your family's history. So it's a little surprising to open up to the early pages of the New Testament and discover that Jesus' family tree is far from perfect. In fact, you may realize that God not only chose some sordid characters to be in the line of the Messiah, He deliberately showcases them.

Enter Judah

One of these characters is a man named Judah. If you look at his story in the Old Testament, you'll quickly discover that his legacy is anything but stellar. He was a deceiver, a sellout, and an unfaithful husband and father. In fact, if you could choose anyone from the house of Jacob to bear the seed of the Messiah, it would be Judah's brother Joseph, whose life bore the marks of faithfulness to God.

Yet God didn't. He chose Judah. Why? Because Jesus didn't come for the righteous; He came for sinners. Working through unsavory characters like Judah highlights the fact of God's grace toward sinners—and that's a message we all need to hear.

Bottom Line

A scarlet thread of grace runs through the people in Jesus' family tree. That thread calls sinners into the loving embrace of His grace.

Even Her?

*Jesse fathered King David. Then David fathered
Solomon by Uriah's wife. (Matt. 1:6)*

An Unlikely Heroine

She had an affair while her husband was out on the battlefield defending the country. Then her lover plotted to have her husband killed, and together they covered up her pregnancy. Because of their sin, God caused their child to die. For the rest of her life her name was attached to one of the most disgraceful chapters in Israel's long history. Her name, of course, was Bathsheba, and for many people she represents illicit temptation, unfaithfulness, and sin. So imagine how surprised the early readers of Matthew's Gospel must have been when they saw Bathsheba's name appear prominently in the genealogy of Jesus.

Grace behind the Promise

God had promised that the Messiah would come from the family of David. This was an unconditional, unbreakable vow. But why choose a child from the unholy union of David and Bathsheba to be in the bloodline of the Savior? And why does Matthew highlight it in his history? Because—again—the sin is the story. The not-so-subtle message of Matthew is that Jesus didn't come for those who are self-righteous but for those whose lives are stained by sin.

Which is what makes the concept of grace so radical and surprising. The gospel doesn't invite good people to do better; it invites sinners to throw themselves at the mercy of Christ, the Messiah who came from a family with a checkered past. No matter what your past is like, God's grace is for repentant sinners.

Bottom Line

Grace means that Jesus came for immoral, unfaithful sinners like David and Bathsheba. We may have different sins, but we all need the same grace.

No Labels

Salmon fathered Boaz by Rahab, Boaz fathered Obed by Ruth, Obed fathered Jesse. (Matt. 1:5)

Losing the Label

When God empowered the Israelites to an improbable victory at Jericho, one lady and her family were saved. But it was a very unlikely lady—Rahab. You see, Rahab was known primarily for one thing—her harlotry. In fact, the Bible calls her "Rahab, the prostitute." Not a very flattering title. So Rahab was a prostitute, just the type of person you'd least expect to find celebrated by proud Jewish people. To top it off, she was a Gentile "sinner," an outsider, a woman of ill repute, a disgrace! Yet like the other misfits that comprise the opening genealogy in Matthew's Gospel, Rahab is mentioned as part of Jesus' lineage. What's more, when we visit Hebrews 11:31, her name is prominently displayed as a charter member of God's Hall of Faith.

Join the Family

Rahab represents those who find themselves outside of God's family, too sinful to be considered eligible for grace. "Rahabs" inhabit every community. They're the people who carry around damaging labels that aren't easily removed. Jesus offers these people the same radical grace Rahab received. Just as she was saved by the scarlet thread in her window, Jesus offers His blood as a pathway to a relationship with God. Outsiders are welcome. Everyone is welcome. No one is beyond the reach of God's grace. Be careful not to label people in a way that God doesn't. We're all saved by grace.

Bottom Line

God doesn't invite us into His family because of what we've done or not done but on the basis of His grace. Offer that kind of grace to others.

Cross Your Heart

*The heart is more deceitful than anything else,
and incurable—who can understand it? (Jer. 17:9)*

What Kind of Heart?

It is common in Christian circles to hear people speak about giving their hearts or their lives to Jesus. The intent behind such statements is good insofar as it reflects a total abandonment to God and His will for our lives. But language can sometimes shape our understanding of life as much as it reflects it, and for that reason it is vitally important that our language reflect biblical truth. The truth is that anyone who offers his heart to Jesus is offering Jesus something that is "more deceitful than anything else, and incurable." Seen in that light, maybe it's not such a great gift after all.

God's Gift to Us

The basis of our life with God is His gift to us, not ours to Him. God is always the Giver; we are always the receivers. We must not be confused about this. Keeping this reality straight gives us a constant source of encouragement and joy because we don't have to trust in the purity of our hearts as the basis of our acceptance by God. It reminds us that our trust is in the perfect goodness and righteousness of our great Redeemer.

Of course, this kind of thinking—biblical thinking—is counterintuitive. Natural thinking would never arrive at the conclusion that looking away from ourselves to Another would be the one thing that could set us free and make us righteous. But that's the cross-your-heart truth.

Bottom Line

When you focus on your righteousness in Christ, you will actually become more righteous. When you focus on your own heart, you will grow discouraged.

Why Can't I Get Better?

*I know that nothing good lives in me, that is,
in my flesh. For the desire to do what is good is with me,
but there is no ability to do it. (Rom. 7:18)*

Paul's Struggles

The apostle Paul may be the most well-known Christian in history. The Holy Spirit inspired him to author much of the New Testament, and the churches he planted became the seedbed of God's work in the early decades after Christ. So we often think of Paul as one of the holiest, best Christians who has ever lived. But Paul didn't think of himself that way, at least according to Romans 7.

God's Gift to Us

Paul had been a Christian for more than twenty years and had accomplished much for the kingdom of God. He was a paragon of Christian holiness and maturity. Yet here, as in 1 Timothy 1:15, he confesses himself to be riddled with sin. Because of this, some people suggest that Romans 7 speaks of Paul's preconversion days.

But his use of the present tense, among other things, leads most interpreters to believe he was speaking of his ongoing experience. So why, after all this time, could Paul not find within himself anything good? Romans 7:25–8:1 suggests a reason: that Christ might get all the glory, not Paul. Paul may not have sensed that he himself was getting better, but his sense of appreciation for Christ's work on his behalf continued to get better throughout his life. And there is little doubt that his looking away to Christ actually made Paul better.

Bottom Line

If you sense that you are not getting better, let this be what causes you to grow in your appreciation of Christ.

Action Prayers

Talk to God

Sometimes prayer merits our full attention. Sometimes we can pray while we're also working or doing some other kind of activity. But some tasks require such complete concentration, we need to break off our praying so we can give it our total energy and effort.

Soon after Moses led Israel out of bondage in Egypt, the people discovered that Pharaoh's army was hot on their trail. Terrified, the Israelites began to pray to the Lord for help. Of course, that was an appropriate response (except for their fear). God soon answered by telling Moses, in effect, "Men, it's time to quit praying and take action." God says the same thing to us more often than we typically recognize. There comes a time for getting out of the prayer closet and getting on with what you've been praying about.

Take the Next Step

It isn't always easy to know when to stop praying and charge ahead. How can we know when it's time to take action? His Spirit, His Word, and our own sanctified common sense can help guide us. But praying as we go, we can take the first step and believe that God is with us and will guide us, redirecting our course where necessary. God is honored by a faith that risks obedience without guarantees. So make sure you're not over-spiritualizing prayer as an excuse for a lack of action. At the same time recognize that prayer is the most important thing you can do.

Bottom Line

Learn to be sensitive to God's promptings, and then prayerfully round up the courage to take appropriate action.

Married for Good

The LORD God said, "It is not good for the man to be alone. I will make a helper as his complement." (Gen. 2:18)

Healthy Relationship

For decades scientists have studied the health effects of being married versus remaining single. While some recent studies have suggested the health advantages of marriage may be fading, experts still agree that people live longer, healthier, and more satisfying lives as couples rather than individuals.

Of course, researchers could've saved themselves a lot of time and money by reading the first few pages of the Bible because as the verse above explains, "God said, 'It is not good for the man to be alone.'" And as it always seems to happen, scientists have proven God right . . . again.

Marriage Checkup

Did you know that a divorced man is six times more likely to die of cirrhosis of the liver than a married man? Or that men who socialize with their wife and friends tend to live nine more years than socially disconnected people? Also, multiple studies have shown that on average, married people are happier than unmarried people of the same age.

So the next time your marriage goes through a bumpy stretch, take time to thank God for your wife and remember all the benefits of being married. Then lean over to your lifelong partner and give her a big kiss. For a 180-pound man, kissing burns about a hundred calories per hour—and that's good for you too.

Bottom Line

Work hard to have a good marriage. The health, spiritual, and relational benefits are worth it.

Holy Fire

The LORD your God is a consuming fire, a jealous God. (Deut. 4:24)

Camp Out

Summer is the perfect time to gather the family and go camping. According to the National Association of RV Parks and Campgrounds, thirty million Americans go camping every year. While getting away from it all and enjoying the beauty of God's creation is wonderful, many men (and especially boys) would argue the best part of camping is the campfire. The crackle of the logs. The smell of burning pine. The glow of the embers. The conversation and the stories. A campfire provides safety, warmth, and pleasure—all things that God gives to us.

Consuming Fire

In the Bible, God is compared to or appears as fire or light more than a hundred times. Who can forget God speaking to Moses through the burning bush or leading His people by a pillar of fire? The prophets Zechariah and Malachi said God will use fire to refine us to make us more like Him. And in Deuteronomy 4:24—as well as in a number of other places throughout the Bible—God is referred to as "a consuming fire."

The Lord wants to consume us. He desires total devotion in every area of our lives. His fire burns in us—purifying us and helping to strengthen us to stand strong for Him. But just as a campfire must be stoked, we must also fuel our flame for God through prayer, Bible reading, and Christian fellowship. Then we will glow brightly in His power.

Bottom Line

God demands every part of our being. Burn brightly for Him.

Keep Fighting

*I say then, walk by the Spirit and you will
not carry out the desire of the flesh. (Gal. 5:16)*

The War Within

Do you ever grow weary of yourself? Weary of struggling
with the same temptations? Weary of having good intentions
but lacking the seeming ability to follow through? If so, you're
not alone. Every Christian is engaged in a war against sin, and
the battleground for this war is located within his own heart.

No peace treaties are forthcoming. No possibility of surrender by our flesh—that stubborn, self-willed part of us that
opposes God and His rightful rule. No, we're locked in a fight
to the finish. So given our situation, what should we do? How
should we think about this war? Should we just throw in the
towel and give up since complete victory is unobtainable in this
life?

Growing the Right Desires

The first thing to be said is that this war must be necessary because God has allowed it and He tells us to fight it. The
second thing that should be said is that it's always better to face
reality than to flee from it. Therefore, we should embrace this
fight courageously rather than running from it or pretending it
doesn't exist.

The battle itself is won or lost at the level of our desires.
That's why it's so important to be constantly feeding our minds
with what the Spirit desires, not what the flesh desires. That
means being in God's Word and praying for His help.

Bottom Line

Never give up. You may lose some battles, but if you keep
fighting with God's strength, you'll win the war.

Plan B

I will repay you for the years that the swarming locust ate. . . . You will praise the name of Yahweh your God, who has dealt wondrously with you. My people will never again be put to shame. (Joel 2:25–26)

Not What You Imagined

Look around. Do you know anyone whose life has turned out exactly the way he scripted it? (Well, OK, there may be that one guy who just seems to get every break.) But seriously, most of us, at least some of the time, are tempted to think we must be on God's "Plan B" at this point, if not some other letter much farther down in the alphabet.

But whether we feel we're off-track because of our own unwise decisions or because of things life has thrown at us that seem completely out of our control, or some combination of the above, we are tempted to despair when our plans, hopes, and dreams come crashing down around us. We think God has abandoned us. And when that happens, we're in serious danger of making things worse by living faithlessly and compounding our situation with more bad decisions.

Faith and Hope

Consider this: your Plan B is not necessarily God's Plan B. Theologically, it can't be. Besides, He's the master of piecing together beautiful, redemptive stories out of lots of broken, disparate parts. So when you're confused and discouraged by life, choose to live by faith anyway. Choose to maintain your hope in God's faithfulness and His good plan.

Bottom Line

When life is confusing and discouraging, cling to God's promises. Choose to live with hope even when it's hard.

Forget about It

*One thing I do: forgetting what is behind
and reaching forward to what is ahead. (Phil. 3:13)*

Completely Pointless

Missed opportunities. Mistakes. Bad decisions. Ignorance. Willful disobedience. The unfairness of life. There are plenty of things that can cause us to live with regret. Almost everyone struggles with regret to some extent. We can easily think back on some wrong turns we've made and wonder how much better our life could be now had we only known better or chosen differently along the way.

So regret is understandable, but that doesn't mean it's helpful. Regret keeps us stuck in the past while God is calling us to go forward with Him into the future. Ultimately, regret does us no good since we can't change the past. Looking back is helpful only insofar as we're gleaning lessons from past mistakes and receiving healing and forgiveness from God. That's about it.

High Stakes

The truth is, regret is one of Satan's greatest tools in wreaking damage in the lives of believers. The devil is out to discourage us and defeat us any way he can. Keeping us stuck in the past, feeling guilty over past sins and mistakes, is one of his go-to strategies. He lies to us, telling us that God can't redeem our past. He chips away at our faith and destroys our hope. But we don't have to believe his lies. We can live in the hope of lessons learned and grace received.

Bottom Line

By God's grace, you don't have to stay stuck in the past, overwhelmed with regrets. He doesn't want you there, and you don't want to be there either.

Joy at Your Fingertips

The righteous are glad; they rejoice before
God and celebrate with joy. (Ps. 68:3)

As Much as You Want

Abraham Lincoln once said, "Most of us are just about as happy as we make up our minds to be." He had a point. Happiness is largely a choice. No, we can't control all of our circumstances, but we can certainly control our attitude about our circumstances. We can choose to look on the bright side in any situation. And we can adopt habits and practices that will likely increase our happiness too—things like counting our blessings, getting enough sleep, exercising, or serving others in some way. We simply have more control over our happiness than we're generally willing to admit.

Takes a Little Faith

But a Christian need not settle for a happiness based on circumstances or even obtained through wise, mature strategies (helpful as those may be). A Christian has direct access to the source of all happiness, the source of all joy—God Himself. So complete joy is possible for the Christian because God is an inexhaustible fountain of joy for those who believe. Today's verse matter-of-factly states that the righteous are "glad" and can "celebrate with joy." The life of joy that God promises us is truly possible. Joy is not some distant pipe dream; it is right at our fingertips.

Bottom Line

Expectations do impact experience. Recognize that God wants to fill you with joy, and then ask Him to do so. He promises that He will.

Loving God

*"Love the Lord your God with all your heart,
with all your soul, and with all your mind. This is the
greatest and most important command." (Matt. 22:37–38)*

In the Abstract

As Bible-believing Christians we understand and agree in principle that we are supposed to love the Lord with all our heart, and yet this command can remain somewhat of an abstract concept to us. When we're pressed to say exactly what it means, we can come up empty. So how does a man of God show his love for God? Well, the specifics will vary, but we can find a good example of the kind of heart God is looking for in a few scenes with Mary, the sister of Lazarus (see John 12:1–3).

In the Concrete

First, Mary spent her money—an amount probably worth a year's wages—on oil to anoint Jesus. She had to know that others would think her act of worship was wasteful, but she was willing to risk the ridicule of others, further demonstrating her love.

Mary served Jesus by washing His feet with her hair—an act of extreme humility since a woman's hair was often seen as her personal glory. She also anointed His feet, not His head, which was another demonstration of all-out worship. No doubt Mary had an extravagant, unashamed love for Jesus. And that's what God wants from us. It can take a million different forms, of course. The key is to be obedient to the clear instructions of His Word and sensitive to the leading of the Spirit on all occasions.

Bottom Line

Live in obedience to God's commandments, thus showing your extravagant love for Him.

Loving Others

"The second is like it: Love your neighbor as yourself." (Matt. 22:39)

Love Turned Inward

We've probably all heard preachers, teachers, or others say that before a man can love other people, he must first love himself. Countless scores of the famous and not-so-famous have echoed the thought. Lucille Ball, television and film star of yesteryear, once said: "Love yourself first and everything else falls into line. You really have to love yourself to get anything done in the world."

But Benjamin Franklin may have hit the nail on the head more accurately when he observed, "He that falls in love with himself will have no rivals." It's true—the man who is stuck on his own selfish goals won't have a lot of friends hanging around.

Love Turned Outward

Worldly wisdom appeals to our selfish nature. But Jesus assumes that self-love is our natural state. It doesn't really take a lot of work to love ourselves, not in a deep, realistic sense. What's hard is applying the second greatest commandment—to love *others* as we love ourselves.

It may be a challenge, but with God's empowering we can do it. We can see that the poor have a bed to sleep in, the cold have a coat to wear, and the hungry have food to eat. Jesus says in Matthew 25 that when we serve those in need, we actually serve Him. By loving them, we come full circle and demonstrate our love for Him. Remember that God Himself is a lover and a giver. He is our Source.

Bottom Line

List three ways you can demonstrate love for others, and then follow through on it.

Heart and Soul

His armor-bearer responded, "Do what is in your heart. You choose. I'm right here with you whatever you decide." (1 Sam. 14:7)

Shall We?

Let's face it. Just because a man is a pastor doesn't mean God has told him everything that's going to happen in the future. A pastor leads by faith. That new building may or may not get built. That new staff member may or may not be the right hire. That new church budget may or may not be fully supported. There are no certainties.

Young Jonathan led his armor bearer into battle one day with the less-than-inspiring, "Perhaps the LORD will help us" (1 Sam. 14:6). But the armor-bearer knew the heart of his leader, and he trusted him. His response filled Jonathan with courage. "I'm right here with you whatever you decide," he said. In other words, "I'm with you heart and soul."

Yes, We Shall

Your pastor doesn't know all the answers. He's like Moses leading the children of Israel through the wilderness, one Red Sea at a time. He's often up against circumstances he's never seen before. Seminary doesn't prepare a man for many of the situations he encounters in ministry.

So go to him sometime soon and echo the words of the armor-bearer. It will turn a "perhaps" into a "yes, God will." By the way, Jonathan and his armor-bearer were victorious against great odds, and their action sent the Philistines into confusion. On that day the Lord saved Israel (see 1 Sam. 14:23) because an assistant filled his leader with courage.

Bottom Line

Is your pastor facing a decision crisis? Be a part of the solution, not the problem.

Playing Hurt

*"If anyone is not offended because of Me,
he is blessed." (Matt. 11:6)*

First Half

It's probably not a question of if but when you get hurt in a church. Your leaders might make mistakes and offend you at times. But your job is to play through the pain. Jesus understood this when He challenged His followers not to fall away even if they were offended by Him (see Matt. 11:6).

Sometimes an athlete goes into the locker room at halftime, his team is losing, blood is coming out of the side of his nose, his ankle hurts, and his pinky is sticking out at an odd angle. But a strong team player says, "Wrap it, tape it, stitch it. My team needs me today."

Second Half

Yet often in the church when people get hurt or offended, they don't come back onto the field. They stay in the locker room and whine to themselves and anyone else who will listen. They leave and never come back. Satan has them just where he wants them—out of the game.

David was a servant to King Saul for a time. Later Saul grew jealous of David and tried to kill him. But David never struck back. Though greatly offended and hurt, David held no grudges. Instead, he faithfully and obediently withstood Saul's harsh treatment. The result was his own eventual promotion to a place of honor. How about you? Have you been treated unfairly and become bitter? If so, maybe it's time to let it go and get back in the game.

Bottom Line

Play hurt. Your team (your church) needs you. Victory awaits the one who plays hard to the end.

The Law of Inversion

"Your kingdom come. Your will be done on earth as it is in heaven." (Matt. 6:10)

Invasion

The Lord's Prayer is not a hopeful wish that someday we'll have a piece of the "sweet by and by" in heaven. When we pray "Your kingdom come," we're asking for a full-out invasion of even greater proportions than D-day in World War II. We're asking God to invade our world and bring about radical changes on earth.

When God's kingdom comes, all the price tags get switched. The world's way of thinking gets overturned. The rich share with the poor. The authorities in power sling a towel over their arms and serve the weak. Those at the head of the line are demoted, and those at the back of the line are promoted.

Be a Kingdom Bringer

If you decide to pray this prayer—I mean, really pray it— you should know that when God's kingdom storms the beachhead of this world, many little kingdoms will be threatened and start pushing back. The ultimate rule and reign of Jesus always faces opposition. His mission to bring the kingdom to this world puts Him on a collision course with some powerful forces. And a follower of Christ should expect no less.

How can you be a part of the invading force? Forgive someone you've been resenting. Confront someone you're afraid of. Demonstrate humility when everyone else is climbing the ladder. Because in the kingdom of God, the law of inversion is the law of the land. Giving becomes receiving.

Bottom Line

Be a kingdom bringer by being a constant kingdom receiver of the grace and power of God.

Extended Family

*Simon's mother-in-law was lying in bed with a fever,
and they told Him about her at once. So He went to her,
took her by the hand, and raised her up. (Mark 1:30–31)*

Meet the Parents

Marriage starts out so innocently, doesn't it? You have a wedding and then start living with the woman of your dreams. She's everything you've ever wanted in a wife. You can't imagine that the flame of this wedded bliss will ever die down. But hold your horses there. What's her family like?

You didn't just marry a woman. You married a product of two people, also known as "two sinners." She got some traits from her mother and some traits from her father. She's also got these other siblings and aunts and cousins, and how are you ever going to keep track of who's who when you see them?

They're Your Family Too

The apostle Peter's care for his mother-in-law suggests something other than the gruff fisherman we picture him to be. One of the best ways you can love your wife is to love her family—even with all its quirks and awkwardness at times. Hey, your own family is quirky too! So how do you love her family? The same way you love anyone else.

Be present and attentive in conversation. Participate in activities they like to do, not just the stuff you're into. Always speak the truth in love to them. Sometimes you may need to go the extra mile for them due to health or financial issues. It's all a part of being a Christ follower. It's also one of the best ways you can ever love your wife.

Bottom Line

Love your wife's family as your own.

Face in the Crowd

They devoted themselves to the apostles' teaching, to the fellowship, to the breaking of bread, and to the prayers. (Acts 2:42)

Life on the Sidelines

For many of us, attending a ball game is nothing short of an "event." We pack the kids into the car, cooler into the trunk, and we're off. We may even have a bumper sticker or flag flying from the window touting our favorite team. Then at the stadium, we sit and watch.

The outcome is completely out of our hands. We never actually make it onto the field of play ourselves; in fact, we're prevented by law from doing so. Stepping out of the grandstands to interrupt play is a bad idea. Those who do will probably be tackled, tasered, and arrested.

Get in the Game

When it comes to our experience in church, however, taking this same spectator approach couldn't be any further from what God desires for us and calls us to. So prayerfully ask yourself what you're good at and what seems to bless others. If you think you might be able to teach, give it a shot. If you can sing, sing in the choir. If you're outgoing, be an usher.

The church is the last place anybody should just watch from the sidelines. God gave you interests and abilities so you could actively use them for His glory. If you're not already doing so, it may take some time to find your niche. Whatever the case, don't settle for just being another face in the crowd. Ask God to show you an area of opportunity, and then go for it.

Bottom Line

Don't be content just to sit back and watch at church. Get in the game and help out!

Forgiven

Be kind and compassionate to one another, forgiving one another, just as God also forgave you in Christ. (Eph. 4:32)

Forgive and Forget

In theory, reconciliation seems to be a fairly simple concept. Someone hurts you and maybe you hurt them. But you get over it, forgive each other, and live happily ever after. No problem, right? No grudges are ever held, no hurt feelings ever nurtured. The world would be a far better place if it were really that easy.

Few things in this life, however, are harder than true forgiveness. You know the old saying about forgiving but not forgetting? Right there, that's the root of the problem. To resolve such deeply felt anger and resentment is to let loose forever the wrongs that were committed in the first place. It's far from easy. It requires a lot of perseverance and grace.

Break Down the Walls

But what if God judged us by the same standards we use for those who have hurt us? We all have family, friends, and coworkers who have let us down over the course of time. How many times, though, have we failed God? Does the same kind of wall go up?

Forgiveness through Christ's life, death, and resurrection is at the root of Christianity. By His example, it is possible to break down those mile-high, mile-wide walls that separate us from others. Pursuing reconciliation with others shows that we understand and appreciate the forgiveness and reconciliation we have received from God.

Bottom Line

Forgiveness and reconciliation with others is possible through Jesus Christ, who forgave and reconciled us to Himself.

Man among Men

The Word became flesh and took up residence among us.
We observed His glory, the glory as the One and Only Son from
the Father, full of grace and truth. (John 1:14)

The Incarnation

Jesus Christ—Lord of all. Sometimes in worship the emphasis falls more heavily on Jesus' divinity than on His humanity. He was, after all, the Son of God, and He wouldn't be worthy of our worship if that weren't the case. That being said, it's just as important to remember that Christ was also fully human. He walked, talked, ate, mourned, suffered, and died. In many ways He was a man just like us. Part of the miracle of the incarnation is that in entering our world as a man and eventually going to the cross for us, Jesus knew exactly what He was leaving behind. He gave up bliss for pain, power for weakness. Yet He did it anyway.

Third Day

Because Jesus was fully human, He can relate to the things we go through. He knows from firsthand experience what it feels like to be happy, sad, tempted, angry, frustrated, and so on. In that sense we approach Him on even ground, knowing He understands our struggles as finite human beings since He's been one Himself.

Of course, the story doesn't end with the crucifixion. On the third day after His death, Jesus was raised from the dead. And He wasn't just some ghost—far from it. He was very much alive, a fact to which several hundred people could testify. Today He lives to intercede for us from heaven as the eternal God-Man worthy of all our worship.

Bottom Line

Because Jesus became a man, He truly understands our human struggles. Because He is divine, He deserves our worship.

Staying on Track

A man's steps are determined by the LORD, so how can anyone understand his own way? (Prov. 20:24)

A Pinch of Perspective

At one time or another, many of us will wonder, *How'd I wind up doing this for a living?* or *How'd I end up working here?* Today we'll touch on two antidotes for work dissatisfaction: perspective and purpose. Both are absolutely critical.

Despite our culture's life-planning and self-fulfillment emphases, we're not the ones in charge. God is. When we became Christians, we forfeited our self-serving ways and became a part of the body of Christ, whose sole purpose is to glorify Him. It isn't about us anymore; it's about God. Yet we often don't fully understand the story God is writing for our lives. It can seem like a lot of unnecessary side stories and painful episodes are going on. Nevertheless, by faith we must choose to trust that God is working a masterpiece in our lives, so we've got to show up and play our part the best we can.

A Dash of Purpose

We can also become so entangled in deciphering our professional calling, we forget that the Christian life is less about what we do and more about how, why, and for whom we do it. A God-honoring janitor is vastly more useful than a self-serving executive; the first earns heavenly gold, while the second makes fuel for the fire. So while your life may feel confusing at times, it doesn't mean you're off-track.

Bottom Line

Whether digging ditches or negotiating mergers, earthly work always includes the potential for eternal impact. So do the best you can right where you are.

Ju$t Another Tool

Whoever is faithful in very little is also faithful in much, and whoever is unrighteous in very little is also unrighteous in much. So if you have not been faithful with the unrighteous money, who will trust you with what is genuine? (Luke 16:10–11)

The Nature of Money

Always remember that the world is on its ear. The practices and priorities of the world are backward, misguided, and hell bound. An important distinction, though, is that money is not necessarily bad in and of itself; the value judgment comes from what we do with it and why we do it. As the apostle Paul says, "We do not focus on what is seen, but on what is unseen. For what is seen is temporary, but what is unseen is eternal" (2 Cor. 4:18).

Only One Master

We must guard ourselves against the false promises of the financial slave master. Money seems to provide, but it is not the Provider; money seems to sustain, but it is not the Sustainer; money seems to protect, but it is not our Fortress and Rock. So let's loosen our grip. We serve a God who owns everything everywhere. Our security in Him is like an impenetrable mountain, while our finances and the economy are like the weather. It can snow, rain, hail, or shine, but the mountain is unmoved.

Money is nothing more than a tool. Whether you have little or much, acknowledge Christ's ownership of everything. Whether bankrupt or debt-free, live thankfully. No matter your financial situation, invest in His kingdom and refuse to let money be your master.

Bottom Line

Money isn't a bad thing, but too much focus on it can ruin us. Like everything else, if we worship God first, the rest falls into place.

The Listening Husband

The intelligent person restrains his words, and one who keeps a cool head is a man of understanding. (Prov. 17:27)

Multitasking Mania

The personal electronic device revolution has taken multitasking to a new low: we speak on the phone while checking e-mails; we attend meetings while typing on a BlackBerry; we chat with our coworkers while scanning scores on the Net. In so doing, we confuse busyness with productivity, juggling with accomplishment, and one-eighth of two as greater than one. Rarely are our minds fully focused.

Can the eyes focus on two things at once? Despite our high-distraction culture, that isn't how human vision works. We need both eyes focused on the same object in order to have depth perception. Can the *mind* focus well on two things at once? Consider drivers chatting on cell phones, conductors texting on trains, or pilots doing anything else while flying a plane. Foolish calamity and avoidable blunders occur when we divide our attention.

Bringing It Home

The folly of multitasking involves more than listening to our wives while looking at the computer or TV. It also applies to conflict resolution. While striving for peace, we tend to juggle our adamant desire to be heard with our responsibility to listen. But listening, which can be halfhearted at best, is often drowned out by our own words and anger. We interrupt to be heard, then plug our ears because we're mad. Not smart. Not godly. We need to just listen.

Bottom Line

Listening is critical to conflict resolution and requires our full attention. So let's single-task listen by restraining our words and keeping our cool.

Trying Our Patience

*A patient person shows great understanding,
but a quick-tempered one promotes foolishness. (Prov. 14:29)*

Wise Versus Foolish

Impatience is like opening doors with an explosive charge; damage always follows. The patient man knocks, turns the knob, or waits until he can find the key. Impatience always includes aftermath: a broken doorjamb, a loss of trust, the need for an apology, an added expense. Patience carries no such baggage. The patient man reaches his goal and pays no fines.

Impatience always causes excess: too much force, too much willfulness, too much haste. The patient man does only what is needed: the necessary effort and no more, the necessary assertiveness and no more, the necessary timing and not sooner. Patience is a way of the wise. Impatience is a path of fools.

Fathers and Patience

Which path do you tread? Sometimes one and sometimes the other? Do you act patiently at work, let your frustration build, and then unleash at home? Is that fair to your family? What fines of impatience do you pay? What's the cost to your wife and kids?

Among other things, good fathers are part teacher, part coach, part shepherd, part mentor, and part captain. Students need teaching; athletes coaching; sheep, shepherding; mentees guidance; and soldiers, direction. The givers give because the needy need. In your family you are a giver. If your children didn't need to learn and grow—and have the safety and license to make mistakes—then they wouldn't need a father. By God's grace, be patient.

Bottom Line

Good fathering requires patience. Ease into it.

God the Pursuer

The Son of Man has come to seek and to save the lost. (Luke 19:10)

The Prime Seeker

Before you ever sought God, God was seeking you. He is the Prime Seeker. The story of God's pursuit begins in the garden of Eden—God gave Adam and Eve a beautiful garden. Only one tree was off-limits. Adam and Eve passed over orchards of permitted fruits to eat from the forbidden one. Immediately all hell broke loose. Adam and Eve felt ashamed. They covered themselves and hid.

The Bible's first question is then asked by God: "Where are you?" (Gen. 3:9). He asked, not because He didn't know, but because He passionately pursues His fallen people. He pursued Adam and Eve even while they hid from Him. And He pursues people today.

The Relentless Seeker

When Jesus was born, God kicked His pursuit of us into high gear. God could have stayed in heaven. He could have lobbed truth bombs from a distance. Instead, He got into our world to go after us.

Jesus told a parable about a host who threw a huge party and invited his friends. His friends, however, couldn't come; they all made excuses. So the host sent his servants to gather all the hungry street people they could find. After that, there was still room. The master said, "Go out into the highways and lanes and make them come in, so that my house may be filled" (Luke 14:23). God relentlessly pursues His people. He's passionate about us.

Bottom Line

He pursued you when you didn't want Him, didn't know Him, and didn't love Him.

The People God Pursues

"As for Me, if I am lifted up from the earth I will draw all people to Myself." (John 12:32)

All Kinds of Excuses

Jesus came for every kind of person. He crossed every barrier—religious, moral, tribal, and racial—and died for every demographic group. Unfortunately the culture He was born into had narrowed the way to God. The Jews restricted salvation to Jews—or to those who behaved like Jews. Within Judaism some tribes felt superior to other tribes (see Phil. 3:5), and all the tribes felt superior to Gentiles who weren't part of God's chosen people.

This superiority led the religious faithful to separate from the unclean masses. Jesus shattered these taboos when He visited with a Samaritan woman (see John 4:3–42) and healed a Samaritan leper (see Luke 17:17–18). Every follower of Christ needs to share the Master's passion to pursue all people.

Every Kind of Person

God wrote four kinds of people into the story of the Savior's birth. (1) *The high.* The wise men represent those who are educated, connected, and rich. (2) *The low.* The shepherds represent society's blue-collar workers, the lower rungs of the social ladder. (3) *The resistant.* King Herod stands for anyone who sees himself as too powerful or self-sufficient for God. (4) *The receptive.* Mary, Joseph, and Simeon represent hearts open and ready for God's grace. Jesus stretched His hands as wide as the world and purchased salvation for everyone who wants it. Heaven will be a diverse place.

Bottom Line

No one falls beyond the reach of God's redeeming love. There are no special qualifications. There is no earning. It's pure grace.

Rejoice Always

Rejoice in the Lord always. I will say it again: Rejoice! (Phil. 4:4)

Why?

Problems and pain are everywhere. But that's not the whole story. Problems and pain for the Christian, while real and serious, are ultimately incidental, not the truest thing. The truest thing is that God *is* and that He *loves* us! The truest thing is that our biggest problem—sin—has been dealt with once and for all through the cross of Christ.

So there is reason to rejoice no matter what. Yes, it can be incredibly hard to rejoice sometimes. We don't always *feel* like rejoicing. We often feel like complaining instead. And God understands that. The psalms, in fact, are full of that kind of thing. Yet they're also filled with tenacious faith that clings to the belief that God is good no matter what things look like on the outside. So because God is who He is—completely faithful, good, and loving—there is ample reason to rejoice no matter what.

When?

The time to rejoice in God is always now. You don't have to wait. The way faith works is that we don't generally feel our way into acting, but rather we believe and act our way into feeling. So if you want to be happy in God, now's the time to start rejoicing. Now's the time to recite who He is, what He's done, and how He feels about you. Let nothing stop you. Think about it: if you can't be happy in God, who or what can make you happy? Rejoice. Always.

Bottom Line

No, not everything in your life is how you would like it to be. Rejoice anyway! Rejoicing will ultimately bring you the most happiness.

Graciousness

*Let your graciousness be known to everyone.
The Lord is near. (Phil. 4:5)*

Let It Be Known

After encouraging the practice of constant rejoicing, Paul continues this remarkable chapter with the simple instruction to be known as a gracious person. Why does he slip this in here? Because a conflict needed to be resolved between two women in the church. Nothing chases joy away quite like conflict. And there's nothing quite like conflict for ruining our peace and hurting the work and witness of the church. So Paul felt it necessary to remind these women to settle their differences for the sake of the gospel.

Francis Schaeffer famously wrote that the mark of the Christian is love, and that love between Christians is our greatest witness to a watching world. Judging from today's verse, Paul would no doubt agree. In order for our "graciousness to be known to everyone," it must be shown to everyone. That means Christians need to love one another and work through conflict. Joy and peace and a powerful witness will surely follow.

The Lord Is Near

Our lives are lived out before God. He is *near*. He is present. He is at hand. And He is coming again to judge the world—even Christians. Though we are forgiven, how we live still matters. It greatly impacts our witness. Maintaining a holy reverence for God helps us love one another better. And that's what makes unbelievers take notice.

Bottom Line

Acting graciously toward others brings unity, joy, peace, and a powerful witness. Let your graciousness be shown and known for the sake of the gospel.

Worry-free Living

Don't worry about anything, but in everything,
through prayer and petition with thanksgiving,
let your requests be made known to God. (Phil. 4:6)

Needless Worry

Worrying comes so naturally to many of us, we can easily justify it despite the misery it causes. And it does cause misery. Lots of misery. The truth is, worry shrinks our world, steals our energy, and quenches our hope. On the other side of the ledger, there really are no benefits to worry. Yes, we do need to be concerned about things and take appropriate action when necessary. And, yes, we will need to overcome our fears—faith is not the absence of fear—but worry is still useless. It's still pointless. It still doesn't make things better.

The Solution

Philippians 4:6 is one of the most useful verses in the Bible. It tells us straight up: "Don't worry about anything!" No exceptions. Things may be falling apart everywhere around you, but don't worry!

Leave it to our faithful God, however, not to remove the negative without replacing it with a positive. (Worry naturally fills the void.) We're told the solution to worry: "prayer and petition with thanksgiving." Every time we catch ourselves beginning to worry, we know it's time to start praying, ask Him for help, and thank Him for being who He is and for being fully capable of supplying what we need. This isn't always easy. Worry actually seems more practical sometimes, but it isn't. Give God's advice a try.

Bottom Line

Worry will do you in if you let it. So don't. Choose by faith and exercise your God-empowered will to pray instead of worry.

The Miracle of Peace

The peace of God, which surpasses every thought, will guard your hearts and your minds in Christ Jesus. (Phil. 4:7)

Surpassing Every Thought

Today's verse is remarkable. Part of what makes it so remarkable is that we can't fully understand how it works; we just know that it does. The promise is this: when we pray, God gives us His peace, and this peace is more powerful than the onslaught of worrying thoughts. This peace has the power to guard our hearts and minds, which truly need guarding because spiritual warfare is ongoing and fierce. A lot of what drifts into our minds doesn't originate there. We have an enemy, the devil. And daily we must contend with the sinful world system. On top of that, we are tempted (despite the indwelling of the Spirit) to revert to fleshly (godless) thinking. A battle rages for our minds and for our peace.

Experiencing the Miracle

Have you experienced what today's verse promises? Have you ever been so totally burdened that even the thought of prayer seems not only impractical but nearly impossible? Have you ever forced yourself to start praying and had trouble shutting down the racing thoughts inside, doomsday scenarios concocted by an overly active imagination that's been listening to the lies of the devil? Not easy to pray under those conditions. Yet when we persevere in prayer, the miracle of peace comes. Nothing has changed on the outside, but everything has changed on the inside.

Bottom Line

Peace is possible in every situation because God is present in every situation. We need faith to believe the promise, but if we do, the miracle comes.

Dwell on These Things

Whatever is true, whatever is honorable, whatever is just,
whatever is pure, whatever is lovely, whatever
is commendable—if there is any moral excellence
and if there is any praise—dwell on these things. (Phil. 4:8)

Glory Hunters

How is your eyesight these days? Are you making a concerted effort to see the world clearly, which is to say, as God sees it? Be assured, if you're not intentionally letting in plenty of God-light through exposure to His Word, you're bound to be stumbling around in the dark, and that's no way to live.

Philippians 4:8 is a prescription for godly thinking and for happiness. Basically it says to look for what's good in the world. In other words, be a full-time glory hunter! Yes, it's true, this world is terribly broken, and ugliness surrounds us. But that's not the whole story. There are also traces of God's goodness everywhere. And here's the thing: we can choose what we focus on! That simple truth, that simple practice, has the power to revolutionize your life.

My, How You've Grown

This "dwell on these things" lifestyle is such a simple concept, we probably don't appreciate it enough. But what we focus on will grow. Think how it is when you're in the market for a certain car. You start to notice them everywhere. What if you were in the market for God's goodness, glory, and grace? You'd start to see it everywhere!

Bottom Line

By God's grace, you can control what you think about. Why not think the best things? Why not dwell on the best things?

Generosity's Gain

*One person gives freely, yet gains more; another withholds
what is right, only to become poor. (Prov. 11:24)*

The Paradox

Question: Do you think the less you give away, the more
you will have? A lot of people live that way, and consequently
they never experience God's financial blessings. It's one of those
divine paradoxes that defies conventional wisdom: we become
richer by being generous. The more we give, the more God
supplies so we can give even more away. That's why financial
security and generosity are inseparable. God wants us to be generous with what He's given us because if we are, He will give us
more. This isn't some "health and wealth" principle we can use
to manipulate God. It's just that God is generous to those who
are generous.

The Reasons

Here are three reasons to give. First, it's a statement of *gratitude*. We realize all that we have comes from God. Second, it's
a statement of *priority*. We acknowledge that God is first in our
life. And third, it's a statement of *faith*. We trust that God will
take care of us in the future as we faithfully give.

Many people think we should give to God after all the bills
are paid. But the Bible commands us to give our first and our
best to God so we can see Him accomplish amazing things in
our lives. We give not because God wants something *from* us
but because He wants something *for* us. Make giving a lifelong
practice, and watch God work.

Bottom Line

Giving pays in the long run. God rewards those who give
generously. So plan to give, and watch God work in your life.

Me? A Teacher?

*What you have heard from me in the presence
of many witnesses, commit to faithful men who will
be able to teach others also. (2 Tim. 2:2)*

First Caring

The Bible cites many instances in which brothers fought—
Cain killed Abel; Jacob usurped Esau's position; Joseph's brothers sold him into slavery. Moses interrupted a fight between two of his Israelite kinsmen, saying, "You are brothers. Why are you mistreating each other?" (Acts 7:26).

But fighting between brothers is just one example of our difficulty in doing what God most wants us to do: "love one another" (John 15:17). In Christ you have a whole bunch of brothers, and one of the best ways you can love them is to invest in them. In particular Paul's challenge to men in 2 Timothy is for us to be proactive in training younger or immature brothers in the faith. He's calling us to care about our brothers, not fuss with them.

Then Sharing

Joe White is one man who cares. The director of Kanakuk Kamps for youth since 1976, he founded Men at the Cross in 2008, a ministry designed to teach men to disciple other men.

White says that if a man wants to be a discipler of men, he must make five specific responses to the gospel: (1) to radically commit his life to Christ, (2) to learn how to disciple others, (3) to see his wife as his first ministry, (4) to understand he is created in Christ for good works, and (5) to cultivate his relationship with Christ as he disciples others. How well do these responses describe you?

Bottom Line

In your church or other men's ministries, find a way to begin learning how to disciple younger brothers in Christ.

Dangerous Hope

Happy is the one whose help is the God of Jacob,
whose hope is in the LORD his God. (Ps. 146:5)

Hopeless or Hopeful?

The movie *Shawshank Redemption* is a story about two men who become friends in prison. Red is serving a life sentence for a murder he committed. Andy is serving two life sentences for murders he did not commit. One day they are talking and the conversation turns to hope. Red says, "Let me tell you something, my friend. Hope is a dangerous thing. Hope can drive a man insane." Later in the movie Andy writes in a letter to Red, "Hope is a good thing, maybe the best of things. And no good thing ever dies."

Hope's Object

So which is it? Is hope a dangerous thing, or is hope a good thing? The psalmist might say that it all depends. It depends on where our hope lies. Placing our hope in people, events, or circumstances is a dangerous thing because we can't rely on those things. They provide no guarantees, no warranties, no control, and no power to back up the promises they make. But if we place our hope in God, we will not be disappointed (though we will often have to wait, and we will sometimes be confused while we're waiting). God stands behind His promises. He backs up His Word. He has proven Himself faithful over and over again. He is a God you can count on. He is a God we can place our hope in.

Bottom Line

Where is your hope? If it's not in God but in something else, you will eventually be disappointed.

How You Begin

*Yahweh, the God of heaven, the great and awe-inspiring
God who keeps His gracious covenant with those who
love Him and keep His commands, let Your eyes be open and
Your ears be attentive to hear Your servant's prayer. (Neh. 1:5–6)*

Why Wait?

Scripture is filled with stories of men who acted impulsively to solve a problem. We think of Peter's ear chop, Moses' sand-burial move, and Uzzah's rescue of the ark of the covenant. Each ended in disaster. Nehemiah, however, was different. While he was bothered by the condition of Jerusalem, he began his plan of action where every man should begin a work of God—on his knees. In fact, he waited a good six months before harnessing the courage to approach the king and ask permission to lead the rebuilding effort.

Six months? Why wait? Because Nehemiah understood the power of prayer in the life of a leader.

How to Pray

Nehemiah began his prayer with humility, recognizing the people's sin and pleading for God's mercy. He didn't see himself as the great savior of the Jewish people. He didn't possess an overinflated assessment of his skills. He didn't make demands of God. He just humbly prayed.

Leaders have a tendency to act first and pray later. They're action oriented by nature. But this is where they often sow the seeds of failure. Every man, whether leading a Fortune 500 company or a small family, must prioritize prayer. That's where Nehemiah really got it right. His prayer life more than his hard work or organizational skills led to success. He understood, as we also must, that no success can be achieved apart from God.

Bottom Line

Prayer is the leader's most powerful weapon.

Powerful Praise

The LORD gives, and the LORD takes away.
Praise the name of Yahweh. (Job 1:21)

When It's Tough

Praising God is our natural response to His glory and goodness. But what about when things are terrible, as they were for Job? Somehow Job was able to rise above his circumstances (at least some of the time) and praise God despite his pain.

Elsewhere, we're commanded to "rejoice always!" (1 Thess. 5:16). And James says to "consider it a great joy, my brothers, whenever you experience various trials" (James 1:2). Pain does not preclude praise. In the dark times praise truly becomes a sacrifice—a defiant act of faith against the enemy and all he throws at us. Praise recognizes that our good God is still in control and worthy of worship no matter what.

Praise Always Helps

Praising God may sometimes feel like a sacrifice, but it is always hugely beneficial for us. Praise takes our minds off our problems and focuses our minds on God. It gives God the right to rule and to reign in our lives however He sees fit. It acknowledges that God knows more about what He is doing than we do. It believes that God can take all the bad stuff of life and make something good out of it (see Rom. 8:28). Commit to praising God no matter what is going on in your life and watch your faith grow. That kind of praise brings glory to God and inspires others.

Bottom Line

Difficult as it may be sometimes, we're called to praise God in all circumstances. It is the ultimate act of trust, and it brings great glory to God.

Nonstop Rejoicing

Rejoice always! (1 Thess. 5:16)

Mission Impossible?

Let's face it, a lot of things are wrong in the world and in our own lives. Joy stealers abound—mounting bills, disappointing jobs, illnesses, relational tensions, never-ending to-do lists, and on and on it goes. Rather than feeling joyful, we often feel more like the prophet Jeremiah when he said, "My joy has flown away; grief has settled on me. My heart is sick" (Jer. 8:18).

So how can Paul, with a straight face, tell us to "rejoice always"? How can he say elsewhere, "I am confident about all of you that my joy will also be yours" (2 Cor. 2:3)? And Paul wasn't the only one who said things like this. Jesus said to His disciples, "I have spoken these things to you so that My joy may be in you and your joy may be complete" (John 15:11).

An Inside Job

The reason Paul and Jesus could lay down an expectation for continual joy is because they knew that the source of joy is ever present and inexhaustible—the Holy Spirit living inside of us, reminding us of the grace of God in Jesus Christ. Joy does not depend on our circumstances. It comes from the inside, not the outside.

Many of us have heard this truth before, but we have a hard time believing it. It seems too simplistic. It doesn't seem to account for *our* really bad situation. Well, it may be simple, but it's true, and it applies to every one of us. It's a matter of faith.

Bottom Line

Believers always have reason to rejoice because God is always present. The more we learn to rejoice in Him, the easier it all becomes.

Work Smart

Unless the LORD builds a house, its builders labor over it in vain; unless the LORD watches over a city, the watchman stays alert in vain. (Ps. 127:1)

Hardly Working

Fewer than 20 percent of people feel they have jobs that use their strengths, which means most people barely tap into their potential in the workplace. This often creates frustrated employees who feel underused and end up watching others get promoted ahead of themselves.

Some men try to overcome this situation by working harder. But longer hours and more sweat do not always lead to greater success. As Psalm 127:1 says, "Unless the LORD builds a house, its builders labor over it in vain." Our jobs are primarily opportunities to serve God and honor Him.

Career Builder

Working for God—and not an earthly boss—changes our attitude about the workplace. We're less likely to complain or grumble when we're assigned tasks that fall outside our areas of expertise. We're better able to focus on the people we work with and the eternal significance of what we're doing rather than how we're being treated.

Studies show that the average man will have more than ten jobs during his lifetime. Some jobs will play to our passions; others will be personally deflating. But what might be God's purposes for you, even in a disappointing job? What could He teach and accomplish through you here that would probably not happen anywhere else? God calls us to represent Him wherever we are.

Bottom Line

God wants to help you in your work no matter what you do. If you look to serve Him in your job, even a tough situation becomes bearable.

Anger Issues

A fool gives full vent to his anger,
but a wise man holds it in check. (Prov. 29:11)

The Exploding Bomb

Some of the bombs dropped on England by the Germans during World War II are still killing people. Sometimes they are set off, blowing up at construction sites, in fishing nets, or on beaches, even this many decades after the war. In fact, undetected bombs become more dangerous with time because corrosion can expose the detonator.

The writer of Proverbs knew that one's temper is like a bomb. When it goes off, it can cause a great deal of damage.

The Defused Bomb

The same danger found in the unexploded bombs of a long-ago war is found also in people who have not dealt with their anger. Buried anger explodes when we least expect it. And when anger detonates, it severs relationships. It causes ulcers. It leads to murder. When anger is turned inward, it leads to depression. When it is turned outward, it leads to aggression. It can't just be buried.

Anger is like a splinter in your finger. If you leave it there, it gets infected and never stops hurting. But if you remove it, the sore heals and you feel better. Take a moment and confess any unresolved anger to God. Defuse the bomb that is ticking inside you. Give it up and move on. You'll be glad you did. And all the people around you will be thankful too.

Bottom Line

If you can't control your anger, it will control you.

Asked and Answered

LORD, why do You stand so far away?
Why do You hide in times of trouble? (Ps. 10:1)

Where's God When You Need Him?

The men who wrote the psalms showed the broad range of human emotion, and they often asked the same agonized questions we all sometimes ask—like in today's verse, as if feeling stranded by God on a deserted island right as a hurricane is barreling down on us.

The psalms give us permission to voice our worst fears to God—even our fears about Him. It is OK to tell God what you are feeling, even if it is flat-out wrong. He already knows what you're thinking anyway, so pray those thoughts to Him. He can take it.

Holding On to Promises

But while it is OK and even important to voice our feelings, it is even more critical to voice back to God His promises. Because the truth is that God does not leave us, has never left us, and will never leave us. The Bible says this in many ways and in multiple places. Hebrews 13:5 assures us, "He Himself has said, 'I will never leave you or forsake you.'"

Our faith must rest on the unshakable promises of God, not on the fickleness of our feelings or the limitations of our understanding. When we hold on to God's promises and let His Word trump our fears, we are developing the kind of faith that makes angels stand up and cheer, the kind that gives us a freedom and confidence from out of this world.

Bottom Line

When your emotions tell you God has abandoned you, it's time to quote back to God His promise never to forsake you. That is faith in action.

Understanding the Past

If anyone is in Christ, he is a new creation; old things have passed away, and look, new things have come. (2 Cor. 5:17)

The New Has Come

When a baby is born, we assume some things. Under normal circumstances if the baby is healthy, then with enough time and nutrition he or she will one day become a mature adult.

But some babies don't seem to grow for various reasons. The child's body may be unable to process nutrition and to strengthen itself. The child may have a defective gene or faulty metabolism. For these infants doctors often diagnose them with FTT—Failure to Thrive. So why would there be any Christians labeled FTT? At the moment of our salvation, aren't all things made new?

The Old Is Still Here

Yes, our sins have been forgiven. But our past can continue to influence us. Chances are, your family patterns of loving and relating to one another came from your parents. And where did they get them? From their parents, of course. Gender roles, how anger and conflict are handled, sexuality, spirituality—the blessings and sins of our ancestors continue to shape who we are today. Ignoring this reality doesn't make it go away.

What unhealthy ways of living did you learn from your parents? You may be a member of the family of God, but you have learned a lot from your earthly family. And at some point every follower of Jesus needs to put off the sin traps of the past and be "morphed" into the family of God. The only other option is FTT.

Bottom Line

To follow Jesus, take a step backward so you can go forward.

Dealing with Anxiety

*How long will I store up anxious concerns within me,
agony in my mind every day? (Ps. 13:2)*

The Pressure Is On

King David endured an onslaught of attacks from both inside and outside his kingdom. His enemies were many, their plots numerous, and it took a toll on this man of God. In today's verse he asks God how long he must endure "agony in my mind every day?"

You may not have an enemy literally trying to kill you, but you have a spiritual opponent who wages repeated attacks on you. Have you ever felt that you were under siege? A swirl of dilemmas beyond your control may be ramping up your anxiety level. Maybe you are waiting for the hammer to fall at work— or it has already fallen. Or your kid is acting out, and nothing you do seems to help. Your marriage seems strained. Fill in the blank for your own life. Whatever it is, it is consuming you with anxiety.

Resting in God's Character

Trust is the primary remedy. Leaning into God, going back to Him again and again, and casting your burdened mind on Him are the first steps to peace. Even if the situation does not improve, even if God does not answer your prayer the way you wish, you can gain a tremendous sense of peace by simply trusting that your Father in heaven knows what you are going through and is working "all things" together for your good (Rom. 8:28). Remember, you always have the choice to trust God rather than give in to worry.

Bottom Line

God is working out His plan in your life even if you do not understand why He allows all the heartache.

Friends of God

I do not call you slaves anymore, because a slave doesn't know what his master is doing. I have called you friends, because I have made known to you everything I have heard from My Father. (John 15:15)

Who Are Your Friends?

I am a friend of God! Now that's a line worth saying three times in a row—especially when you realize it's the words of Jesus, talking about you! But friendship has several levels. You've probably got some guys at work who will talk March Madness with you. And a couple of guys in your Bible study class have become close friends. And your old college roommate is a special friend even though he lives across the country now. But to be friends with God? Doesn't that require something extra?

Well, Jesus did everything necessary for you to have a relationship with the Father. And you can't add anything to your salvation. But it *is* a relationship, which means it's a two-way street with regard to communication.

Levels of Friendship

One level is simply talking to God through prayer. And this is important. But your other friends would soon leave if you always did all the talking. A second level of friendship is *listening* to God. This requires slowing down and giving Him and His Word your full attention. But the deepest level of friendship is simply *being* with God. You know you're with your best friend when you're both comfortable with the silence and you don't have to do anything to be content with each other. That's possible with God too.

Bottom Line

Ask God to deepen your friendship with Him. That's a prayer He absolutely delights to answer.

Soul Therapy

Yahweh, if You considered sins, Lord, who could stand? But with You there is forgiveness, so that You may be revered. (Ps. 130:3–4)

The Drowning Victim

We are often like Raymond in the movie *Rain Man*. Every time someone offended him, he would record the infraction in his spiral notebook. What an unhappy practice! Aren't you glad God is not like that? We commit some horrible offenses. We hurt others with our words; we sting others with our actions. If God kept a record of all our sins, we would be like a drowning victim on the open ocean without any hope of rescue. We'd be goners for sure.

The Powerful Rescuer

But instead God offers forgiveness, a pardon for our sin and release from our guilt. In fact, God makes a habit of forgiving sin. Forgiveness of sins is nothing less than the embrace of a loving God around sinful man. Here's the picture: We are drowning in the despair of our sin, knowing we will perish if help doesn't come. But God, in His love and mercy, reaches out to us, offering forgiveness. His grip saves us and His mercy pardons us from the penalty of sin.

Are you in the depths of despair due to your transgressions? You can't continue to keep breaking the rules without reaping some serious consequences. But whenever you are ready to come clean, the Lord is waiting to forgive you and restore you. He is an expert rescuer with His amazing grace.

Bottom Line

It's never easy to confess your sins, but if you do, pardon is waiting. Don't pretend; come clean and be free. Do you need to confess anything right now?

God Cares for You

Even if my father and mother abandon me,
the LORD cares for me. (Ps. 27:10)

Fear of Abandonment

A lot of men feel as if they have to do life on their own. They may have many reasons, but one primary reason is that their family of origin has often communicated this message in subtle or not-so-subtle ways. We can hear a lot about the need to work hard, be independent, and figure things out for ourselves. Some of that is good, but maybe some of it isn't so good.

While we may not have actually been abandoned by our family, we can feel a sense of abandonment if they weren't there for us during crucial times of development and decision-making. Just sit in any men's group for a little while and you'll discover how many men feel as though everything is up to them. That's a lonely place to be, and it's not what God intends for His adopted sons.

Part of a New Family

As a member of God's family, you are never alone. We're promised in Psalm 27:10 that even if our parents abandon us, God never will. He cares about us. He's always with us. He wants to guide us and help us. He loves us! And because He loves us, He graciously puts people in our lives who will stick with us—imperfectly, yes, but faithfully nonetheless. As we learn to trust other people and rely on them for help, we learn to trust God a little bit more too. That's by design. God is creating a close-knit family.

Bottom Line

Going through life feeling all alone is an awful burden. Ask God to supply faithful friends and reach out to others too.

Pass Down the Blessing

May Yahweh bless you and protect you . . . may Yahweh look with favor on you and give you peace. (Num. 6:24, 26)

Mountaintop Connection

Dan and Caleb agreed to go on a father-son getaway in the Rocky Mountains, which is how you could describe their relationship—rocky. After a week of encouraging each other in rock climbing, studying the Bible together, and talking about dreams, they started seeing each other in a new way. On the final night dads were asked to stand up and say some words to their sons in front of the group.

Dan got up and looked his son in the eyes. "Caleb," he said. But that's the only word he could get out as he gripped his son in a bear hug and the two cried in each other's arms. Several minutes passed before Dan got himself together to say, "Caleb, the Lord bless you and protect you."

Bless Your Children

In the Old Testament, God instructed the priests to bless the Israelites. Many cultures contain ceremonies that allow parents to bless their children. Sadly many Christian fathers miss out on this important rite of passage. Our kids long for our blessing. They desire to hear the words "I love you" and to know their fathers are proud of who they are, not for what they can accomplish.

The Bible records numerous times when fathers blessed their sons. Make sure to pass on the blessing to your children. It will have an immeasurable impact on their confidence in your love for them and even in their confidence in their heavenly Father's love.

Bottom Line

Create a plan to have a time of blessing for your teenage children.

The Goodness of God

The LORD God is a sun and shield.
The LORD gives grace and glory; He does not withhold
the good from those who live with integrity. (Ps. 84:11)

A Foundational Truth

Praying to God for things we need and want is so much easier when we have a clear understanding of His character, how good and generous He is. The reason God "does not withhold the good" from us is because He *is* good—infinitely good, completely good, always good. When we "live with integrity," seeking first the kingdom of God and His righteousness (see Matt. 6:33), we will more readily see that God doesn't withhold good from His children.

But God doesn't always *seem* good to us because not everything that happens to us seems good. Living in a fallen world such as ours, we experience pain, injustice, confusion, and frustration. But this does not mean God is not good. The cross settled that question once and for all.

The Fight to Believe

A Christian who doubts God's goodness is in trouble. We simply won't trust someone we don't believe has our best interests in mind. And if we don't trust God, we won't grow. Simple as that.

Know that Satan's number-one strategy is to cast doubt in your mind about God's goodness. He will tell you that God hasn't really forgiven you. He will make God out to be a cruel taskmaster. Don't believe him for a second. God is 100 percent good, 100 percent of the time.

Bottom Line

Every time you're tempted to doubt God's goodness, remind yourself of the cross. He has proven His love for you there.

Time for Trusting

Lord, You have been our refuge in every generation. Before the mountains were born, before You gave birth to the earth and the world, from eternity to eternity, You are God. (Ps. 90:1–2)

The Eternality of God

Augustine, like countless other philosophers, wrestled with the nature of time. Aristotle related time to motion, like the sun moving across the sky. Einstein placed space, matter, energy, and time on an interconnected continuum.

Scripture doesn't philosophize about time. It simply teaches that God created the sun and moon, in part to mark the passing of days. It also teaches that God is bigger than time. He transcends space and time because He created them. He holds them in the palm of His hand. We finite humans experience time as a succession of events, like floats passing by in a parade. But to an infinite God, the beginning, middle, and end are seen in a single moment—like He's watching from a helicopter. God exists above and beyond time. He is eternal.

The Lord of Time

Because God is eternal, He is "our refuge in every generation." The passing of time has no effect on God. We often live in emergency mode. The shortness of time makes us feel rushed. But not God. He never hurries. He never grows old or forgetful. He never runs out of time. He can even stop time if He wants (see Josh. 10:12–13).

God wants His children to shed their limited, temporal view and try to see life from the standpoint of eternity. Even when life's problems fill your vision, they are still only temporary.

Bottom Line

Your eternal God has given you eternal life and invites you to live with an eternal perspective.

Magnificent Patience

If Abraham was justified by works, he has something to brag about—but not before God. For what does the Scripture say? Abraham believed God, and it was credited to him for righteousness. (Rom. 4:2–3)

God's Acceptance

Abraham is a key figure in the biblical story as he illustrates God's acceptance of us. But he also illustrates the patience of God and the lengths God is willing to go to in order to preserve His people.

Abraham illustrates that our acceptance by God is based on faith, not works. Christianity is not a "merit based" religion; it is grace based. We are justified by the works of Christ, not our own, and our responsibility is to trust in the sufficiency of those works. This is how Abraham becomes a great example to us.

God's Patience

On the other hand, if you read through the story of Abraham, you often see some inexplicable lapses in trust. In Genesis 12 and 20, Abraham fails to trust God to preserve his life, and he lies to powerful rulers about his relationship with Sarah. In Genesis 16, he fails to consult God, choosing to go along with his wife's plan for giving him a son by sleeping with her handmaiden Hagar. Yet at the end of each of these events, Abraham is preserved in spite of his sin. God shows His tremendous patience, reaffirming that His acceptance of us is based on His grace and purposes, not our good deeds and performance.

How about you? Have you seen God's mercy overcome even your biggest blunders? There's reason to live faithfully for Him but no reason to despair.

Bottom Line

If you are in Christ, take comfort. God is far more faithful to you than you are to Him.

God's Knowledge

*Oh, the depth of the riches both of the wisdom
and the knowledge of God! How unsearchable
His judgments and untraceable His ways! (Rom. 11:33)*

God Knows

God knows all that is knowable. There is no limit to His knowledge; He is *omniscient*. He doesn't get smarter with age because He is already infinitely smart. Nobody needs to teach Him, inform Him, or guide Him. He doesn't worry about falling behind in knowledge. He's not the least bit befuddled by the latest developments in technology. God knows all that happens, all that could happen, and all that would have happened. If you were to change a single variable in history, God would already know how that single change would ripple forward to the end of time. Nothing can ever surprise God; all knowledge—both potential and actual—is known to Him.

You Can Trust Him

From the motions of the smallest subatomic particle to the most massive structures of outer space, to the deepest longings of your heart, God knows. You can entrust your life to your infinitely wise heavenly Father. Your trials do not surprise Him. And because He knows, He also supplies all you need to rise above adversity. In His wisdom He weaves together the perfect amount of blessing and trials into your life. Even the hard stuff in your life, seen from God's perspective, creates huge blessing, reward, and beauty for you. You never need to worry or fear. God has not forgotten you and He has not misplaced you. You are always under His loving, watchful eye.

Bottom Line

If God is able to keep track of the hairs on your head, He certainly knows what you need today and He is certainly able to provide it.

Providence

You planned evil against me; God planned it for good to bring about the present result—the survival of many people. (Gen. 50:20)

The Providence of God

Many ancient Greeks believed that life was determined by the Fates, three cold, unfeeling goddesses who spun each life's thread and cut it off at whim. According to Norse mythology, the trickster god, Loki, toyed with mortals like a cat with a mouse. His name comes into English as Lucky—though it would be unlucky if he actually existed. Others believe life is governed by soulless forces like karma or the alignment of the stars. Not exactly encouraging.

But Christians believe differently. The course of the universe and our lives is not determined by impersonal forces but by our caring and powerful God. He shepherds all things in space, time, and history toward His staggeringly beautiful objectives. Theologians call this His *providence*.

Nobody's Victim

Because of God's providence, you are nobody's victim—not in an ultimate sense, anyway. Joseph's life shows how God can bring good out of evil (see Gen. 50:19–21). And Christ's cross provides the greatest example of God's amazing ability to turn the worst event into the best (see Acts 2:23).

God is leading you. Sometimes you rejoice on the mountaintops; other times you suffer in dark valleys. But God always has His goals in mind. In His incredible grace He couples His highest glory with your highest good (see Eph. 1:3–6). Never give in to fear; God is on the throne, and He is good.

Bottom Line

You are not a victim of bad luck or bad horoscopes. God Almighty is the caring and powerful ruler of your life and the world. You can rest in His hands.

He Understands

He knows what we are made of,
remembering that we are dust. (Ps. 103:14)

Bunch of Nonsense

When it comes to the spiritual life, most of us feel inadequate. And rightly so! Jesus exhorted us to be perfect, but the closest we usually come is making our lives a perfect mess.

Such feelings of inadequacy are more or less inevitable; the question is how we respond. It's easy to get discouraged and slip into believing that God is constantly disappointed and angry with us. But that is just a bunch of nonsense planted by the enemy.

Stumbling toward Joy

We are double-minded creatures, far from the holiness God is calling us to. However, today's passage reminds us that God deals tenderly with our weakness. He is not exasperated with us; He is not ready to snuff us out. (Prune, perhaps; snuff out, no.) Nor has He resigned Himself to merely tolerating us.

No, God takes positive joy in His children and in the growing little bits of grace we exhibit. He encourages our stumbling, bumbling efforts to walk, as any father does with his children. Of course, God cannot be mocked. Whoever uses God's patience as license to sin will find trouble in the end. Yet for those who truly know Him, His patience is the linchpin of our security and salvation. Let His countenance of love be the transforming power in your life.

Bottom Line

Satan is ever whispering words of condemnation in our ears, but we must combat this with the knowledge that God is patient and kind.

The Master's Example

*Husbands, love your wives, just as Christ
loved the church and gave Himself for her. (Eph. 5:25)*

The Love of the Lord

Once there was a Great High God. He was Lord Eternal, Sustainer of all, and Creator of all. He was the Lord God Almighty. He was all-knowing, all-powerful, and undefeatable. His justice, righteousness, and perfection were without end, as was His love for the man and woman He had created.

But then, tragically, the Lord's beloved fell. The first man and woman chose to disobey God and wander away from the only secure source of love they had ever known. Their fall from innocence set the path the rest of humanity would follow. Disobedience and perpetual chasing after false gods became the norm. But thankfully, that's not the end of the story. God wouldn't give up on His people. He would send a rescuer, His own Son.

The Example of the King

This Messiah, this Rescuer King, this Husband of the bride, is our example in all things. The Bible doesn't provide a lot of specific instructions for husbands, but it does tell us the most important thing: love your wife as Christ loves you.

How can you possibly do this? On your own, it's impossible, "but with God all things are possible" (Matt. 19:26). Start by praying for your wife daily. Be sure to forgive quickly and seek forgiveness even quicker. Ask the Lord to help you be patient and understanding. Look for ways to serve and support her. Jesus will help every step of the way.

Bottom Line

The only way you can love your wife well is if you're experiencing Christ's love for you. He is the source.

Guaranteed Victory

The LORD is the stronghold of my life—
of whom should I be afraid? (Ps. 27:1)

Triumph

If the world does its worst to you, you still win because the Lord is the stronghold of your life. The worst the world can do to a Christian is kill him, and death only assures the believer an even more epic reward when he is welcomed into heaven. The Bible is filled with stories of men of faith who sometimes had great victories (David trounced Goliath) but who also "lost" by human standards (John the Baptist was beheaded). Hebrews 11 summarizes a lot of these stories. In all these accounts of faith, the men who placed their trust in God triumphed even if they "lost" in the faith-deprived eyes of the world.

War Zone

The Bible makes it clear that the human race is caught up in a cosmic battle between good and evil. There is no neutral territory. It should therefore not surprise us when we take fire from those who oppose God. Many of the apostles died for the faith, and many of our fellow believers around the world suffer severe persecution for the "crime" of following Jesus. Even if you are not physically attacked, the devil is waging a war against your faith. God does not promise us smooth sailing or victory by earthly standards, but we are assured of being "more than victorious" (Rom. 8:37) when God calls us home to our reward. So hang in there and keep fighting. You're fighting from victory toward victory.

Bottom Line

We are in an intense spiritual battle, but our ultimate victory has already been won by Jesus. In the stuff that really matters, you cannot possibly lose.

Man on the Run

Jonah got up to flee to Tarshish from the LORD's presence.
He went down to Joppa and found a ship going to Tarshish.
He paid the fare and went down into it to go with them to
Tarshish, from the LORD's presence. (Jon. 1:3)

A Fugitive

Have you ever run away from home? Some children try it until they get hungry, and some even do it for real. Adults run away, too, seeking to change circumstances while abandoning responsibilities. The thing is, it's possible to run away and still live in the same town, be married to the same person, and even continue working in the same job—to run away privately, spiritually, emotionally.

Jonah ran away. Jonah was a Hebrew prophet, a spokesman for God. His orders came from on high. Perhaps in the past he had been faithful and obedient to follow God's call. But now, well, things were different. He was a man on the run.

An Impossibility

Maybe Jonah imagined that God's presence was kind of like a radio signal—the farther you go from the tower, the weaker the signal gets. Maybe he figured if he went far enough, he could get all the way off God's map where there would be no annoying God-signal at all.

Running from God is a logical impossibility. It's like drawing a round square—can't be done. God is omnipresent—everywhere—and you can't escape from Someone who is everywhere. Jonah tried and failed. We often try it ourselves and fail. A rebellious streak in us that doesn't know what's good for us. Don't try to run.

Bottom Line

God is everywhere. This thought will either scare you or comfort you. Which does it do for you?

Stages of Faith

Encourage with great patience and teaching. (2 Tim. 4:2)

What They Believe

"Because I said so" might get you by for a while when you're telling your child not to stick a knife into an electrical socket. But fast-forward to the teenage years, and this phrase doesn't carry the weight it once did. Sooner or later kids begin to explore the universe and choose their own worldview. They pull their faith out of their chest cavity, reflect on it, and ask the critical question, "Why do I believe? Because my parents/pastor/peer group said so? Or do I believe because I've examined the evidence for myself?"

Why They Believe

Your kids need to go through this phase so their faith can become their own. It can be painful as you watch your older teen strip away some of what you hold as sacred. He or she is realizing that the world isn't always black-and-white, and God can't be contained in a neat little box and explained with pat answers.

When your teen moves into this phase of faith, don't panic. Let him see some of your own doubts and struggles. Admit that some hard questions puzzle theologians to this day. And assure him God is big enough to handle any question. In fact, He doesn't turn us away when we come sincerely seeking truth. As He did with doubting Thomas, Jesus simply invites us to step toward Him and examine Him closer. If your kids do that, they will not be disappointed. Their faith will become their own.

Bottom Line

Encourage your children as they forge their own faith in Christ.

Incomprehensible Love

I pray that you, being rooted and firmly established in love, may be able to comprehend with all the saints what is the length and width, height and depth of God's love, and to know the Messiah's love that surpasses knowledge. (Eph. 3:17–19)

Rooted and Established

A plant with deep roots doesn't get washed away during a storm. Similarly, a person with deep roots in God's love doesn't get washed away during a storm either. And as we all know, this life includes lots of storms. We need to be sturdy people who aren't going anywhere when the winds of life blow against us.

Every Christian is "rooted" in God's love by virtue of conversion. We are also "established" in His love. We don't have to build up to it. We don't need to achieve anything, qualify for anything, or be a Christian for a certain length of time to be firmly established in His love.

The Need to Grow

Yet while we are "rooted and firmly established in love" as soon as we become Christians, we continually need to grow in our knowledge of God's love. His love is so strong and unchanging and out of this world, we can't fully understand it. It "surpasses knowledge." Yet in the rest of Ephesians 3:19, Paul urges believers to remain focused on Christ's love "so you may be filled with all the fullness of God." More every day. When our roots are deep and established, there's no end to the watering and strength we can receive from His incomprehensible love.

Bottom Line

God's love is not at all like normal human love—fickle, finite, failing. It's an inexhaustible fountain of goodness and blessing. Pray for more understanding.

Safe to the End

*I have written these things to you who believe in the name
of the Son of God, so that you may know that you have eternal life.*
(1 John 5:13)

Eternal or Temporary?

Most of the time you never question it, but every once in awhile you have a nagging suspicion that maybe you just *think* you're saved. Is salvation a game of Russian roulette with eternal consequences?

First of all, God doesn't want you to have to play a guessing game for the rest of your life. Evidently, early Christians struggled with the same questions, so John tried to answer their fears and nagging doubts about salvation. "The one who has the Son has life," wrote the apostle (1 John 5:12).

In His Hands

Second, Jesus didn't come to give you week long life; He came to give you eternal life. If it could be taken from you, it wouldn't be eternal, would it? Third, if the status of your salvation was based on your performance, none of us could ever be sure. But just as you were saved by grace, you are kept safe by grace. Your security does not depend on you!

Consider this: All of your sins were in the future when Jesus gave His life at Calvary. So if you've got Jesus, you've got all the life you'll ever need! You are secure in His hands. He will never leave you or forsake you (see Heb. 13:5). You can rest knowing that you're His.

Bottom Line

Your heavenly Father will never disown you. If you struggle to believe that, ask Him to increase your faith. He wants you to rest secure in Him.

What Will You Risk?

*I was overwhelmed with fear and replied to the king,
"May the king live forever! Why should I not be sad
when the city where my ancestors are buried lies in ruins
and its gates have been destroyed by fire?" (Neh. 2:2–3)*

Nehemiah's Risk

Nehemiah felt the burden of his people. He sought the Lord's face continually. But then he took a decisive step. What was Nehemiah willing to risk to ensure that God's work would be done among God's people?

First, he gave up a secure and lucrative position in the king's palace. Second, he risked his carefully cultivated respect in the kingdom by casting his lot with a ragtag refugee group in Israel. Third, he risked the ire of the competing interests in and around Jerusalem who would fight to keep the walls from being rebuilt. Fourth, he gave up the comfort of his home and familiar surroundings.

It's Going to Cost You Something

While many see the problems of a world in need, and some even pray for God to bring about a solution, few are willing to consider making sacrifices themselves. Surely God will send others to the mission field, others into the homes of disadvantaged kids, others to volunteer for the homeless. That's how we think.

But what if God is asking *you* to do something? Are you willing to give up the comfortable? Are you willing to risk life and reputation? Are you willing to throw yourself on the mercy of the Almighty? God is calling people in our day just as He called Nehemiah in his day. Will you answer that call? Will you willingly sacrifice yourself for others?

Bottom Line

What are you willing to risk to answer the call of God?

When You're Dissed

A person's insight gives him patience,
and his virtue is to overlook an offense. (Prov. 19:11)

Get Even?

It happens without warning. A driver cuts you off on the freeway. A joke is made at work at your expense. A buddy disses your car, somebody from church judges you without really knowing you, and even your kids make fun of your favorite team. Feel like you're the Old Testament version of sackcloth, ashes, and boils? Well, you could get even.

But getting even never really evens the score, does it? In fact, revenge is a bitter poison that affects the vessel it's carried in. That's why God says, "Vengeance belongs to Me; I will repay," (Rom. 12:19). It's easy to get caught up as judge and jury, so next time you're insulted or offended, remember Proverbs 19:11, and you'll find a much better way to deal with your anger than seeking revenge.

No, Get Wise

Consider the source of the criticism. Often you'll find that the one dissing you is full of pain and hurt, and the only way he knows to relate to others is through hurtful words and actions. When you begin to see that person as one who needs God's grace to help him change, you begin to acquire patience in dealing with him. God even gives you the strength to overlook his offense.

Even Jesus had to endure insults, but He chose not to retaliate (see 1 Pet. 2:23). Instead, He gave Himself over to the only One capable of judging correctly. May God give you the wisdom to do the same.

Bottom Line

Learn to overlook insults by putting yourself in God's hands and letting go of the offense.

You Talkin' to Me?

The LORD came, stood there, and called as before,
"Samuel, Samuel!" Samuel responded, "Speak,
for Your servant is listening." (1 Sam. 3:10)

Is That You, Lord?

Lily Tomlin once said, "Why is it that when we speak to God, we're said to be praying, but when God speaks to us, we're said to be schizophrenic?" The world assumes that if you hear God speak, you're at best a misguided fool and at worst a psychotic killer. Some theologians don't even believe that God speaks anymore.

God chose not to speak to Eli, the high priest, but to Samuel, an innocent, humble little boy. If God really speaks, how can you increase the chance that He'll say something to you?

I'm All Ears

For starters, point your satellite in the right direction. You won't glean God's wisdom from talk-show hosts and the latest magazine at the checkout counter. God's written Word is the final word. And the more disciplines you practice in your life, the more conduits to heaven you will have. The Word, prayer, submission, fasting, worship, giving—think of these as channels through which you can hear God speak.

Then make sure there's nothing between the dish of your heart and the signal. It's easy for sin to grow up between you and God. Ruthlessly examine your heart, and confess and repent. The adventure awaits—real life doesn't begin until you hear God speak to you.

Bottom Line

Put yourself in a position to hear God speak each day. Any good relationship is based on good communication.

Old Faithful

He remains faithful forever. (Ps. 146:6)

Who Is the Greatest?

Geysers are plentiful in Yellowstone National Park, but the most famous is named Old Faithful. Other geysers shoot the water higher, others are more spectacular, but Old Faithful is the most visited. Why? Because it is faithful. It erupts every hour. You can count on it.

Such is God. He is faithful. God, eternal and unlimited, stands in stark contrast to humans, temporal and limited. The psalmist knows of God's consistency, that the Lord "remains faithful forever" (Ps. 146:6). In contrast to humans who tend not to keep their word, God always keeps His word. He always fulfills His promises. We can always count on Him.

Whom Will You Trust?

We all have to face the question—where do I put my trust? We have two alternatives, either to trust people (including ourselves) or to trust God. Most of us, if we're honest, would admit we spend most of our time trusting other people: financial planners with our money, government officials for our laws, professors with our education, doctors with our health. And sometimes these people fail us because they are flawed just as we are.

If everything fell apart in your life, who would you turn to first? Would you turn to family and friends, or would you turn to God? Look first to your heavenly Father.

Bottom Line

Trusting in God is the only way to live because He is the only One who is completely trustworthy.

Give It Your All

Don't work only while being watched, in order to please men, but work wholeheartedly, fearing the Lord. (Col. 3:22)

The Goal

Why do you go to work? To provide an income? To fulfill a calling? To pursue a dream? To keep busy? Whatever your reasons, you most likely have days when you lack the energy and motivation to work hard. This may be especially true if your work environment presents stresses like a heavy workload, mistreatment from management and peers, or the uncertainty of job continuity (or all of the above).

Yet Scripture tells us our motivation for working shouldn't come from our feelings or fears about the job but rather from our commitment to obey God (see Col. 3:22), to be a witness to others (see 2 Thess. 3:7), and to store up treasures in heaven (see Matt. 6:20).

Working Hard

When your job weighs you down and you find yourself daydreaming about your favorite hobby, purpose to show God a thankful spirit by working hard with integrity for your employer. Instead of drudging through another day, ask God to open your eyes to opportunities to be salt and light in your work environment. And save the personal e-mail and sports updates for your lunch break.

Proverbs 18:9 warns that slacking off at work is a destructive path. Work to impress your heavenly boss because your real paycheck is waiting on you in heaven, and you will not be underpaid there!

Bottom Line

Jesus didn't like every part of His earthly job either, but He submitted to God and carried out His work faithfully and with integrity. You can do the same.

Source of Provision

*Our Father in heaven . . . give us
today our daily bread. (Matt. 6:9, 11)*

Doing Your Best

Every day we hear or read about our struggling economy.
Even for those secure in their jobs with a stable source of income,
there's an air of uncertainty about what lies ahead. Certainly
keeping (or finding) a job is necessary if we are to provide for
our families. And we accept that we may have to make some
sacrifices and trade-offs to do it well, like personal relaxation or
time to spend on outside activities—even good activities. But
we must be careful to avoid letting this noble pursuit be what
defines us and drives us.

Seeking God's Best

Scripture gives many examples of those who push beyond
their worries and circumstances to find God. A common factor in each story is a conversation of some sort between God
and man. Dedicated, intentional time in the Word and prayer is
essential if we truly want to know God and receive the peace and
provision He promises.

So don't let your time with God today end with this devotional. Spend some time in prayer telling God exactly what's on
your heart. He already knows, of course, but a lot of times *you*
don't really know until you start praying! Remember, God wants
you to ask for His help. He wants you to engage with Him. Let
Him speak to you through His Word.

Bottom Line

Blessing follows obedience, and obeying God requires
hearing His direction. Cultivate your prayer life and learn to
discern God's voice.

Wife for Life

Enjoy life with the wife you love
all the days of your fleeting life. (Eccles. 9:9)

Empty Nesting

Any father with teenagers in the house knows the joys, heartaches, and excitement of these years. High school sporting events, musicals, dances—it's as if your child's social calendar becomes your own. So when kids head off to college, you feel a gaping hole in the home, and often in the marriage relationship.

Marriage experts and speakers Drs. Les and Leslie Parrott have been shocked to see the rise in divorce among empty nesters. The fastest growing spike of divorce is among this particular age group and demographic, the Parrotts point out, leaving many couples to miss out on the second-half stretch of their marriages when satisfaction is actually the most possible and available.

The Good Life

The Parrotts encourage couples to follow the Bible's advice to "enjoy life with the wife you love all the days of your fleeting life" (Eccles. 9:9). If marriage satisfaction could be charted, the Parrotts say it would start high during the newlywed years. Once children enter the picture, it drops a little. It tends to hit the low point during the teen years when busy schedules make it difficult for couples to connect emotionally, physically, intimately. Once the relationship hits the bottom, however, couples who stay together and work to reconnect will often find a togetherness that far exceeds anything they've previously experienced in their marriage.

Bottom Line

Trusting in God is the only way to live because He is the only One who is completely trustworthy.

Manliness Defined

If I, your Lord and Teacher, have washed your feet, you also ought to wash one another's feet. For I have given you an example that you also should do just as I have done for you. (John 13:14–15)

The Whole Picture

Bruce Willis, John Wayne, Clint Eastwood. These guys are the epitome of manly strength according to one common cultural stereotype. What about Jesus, though? He was the perfect Man, yet how do most people in our culture view Him?

The picture hanging in many churches and homes portrays a man with brown flowing hair and sparkling eyes with light flowing around His perfectly groomed beard. He seems like a guy who knows more about styling techniques than salvation. The Gospels, however, paint a completely different picture of the Son of Man.

The Manly Example

At the close of the Last Supper (see John 13), Jesus didn't just finish off His wine in one big gulp, give each man a pat on the back, and swagger into the sunset. The manliest man of all time actually laid His robe aside, took up a towel, and tied it around Himself. He then washed His disciples' feet, the job of the lowest slave. In that moment Jesus shows more than just His humility. He also shows meekness (power under control), a servant's heart, limitless love, and ultimately, what a true man is—a servant. A man is not defined by cutting a rugged profile or filling up a movie screen but rather by serving others in humility.

Bottom Line

Let's seek to be real men. We shouldn't define manliness by our culture's definition but by the example of Jesus.

Clean Up Your Mess

Do not repay anyone evil for evil. Try to do what is honorable in everyone's eyes. (Rom. 12:17)

When the Trash Spills Out

Despite our best intentions we occasionally say and do things that hurt others, even those (sometime especially those) we love the most. Oftentimes our pride and fear—the same things that usually created the mess to begin with—keep us from properly making amends.

Pride tells us our hurtful words and actions are justified and we have nothing to apologize for. Fear tells us to protect our image or we will be disrespected, dominated, or deemed inadequate. The result of this pride and fear is a battle for control that only prolongs bad feelings and undermines the trust needed in a healthy relationship.

Take Care to Tidy Up

Being the first to apologize is not a sign of weakness, nor does it mean the other person is right. On the contrary a sincere apology displays strength of character and true concern for the feelings and dignity of the person we've offended.

Scripture clearly teaches us to be humble and not hold ourselves in higher esteem than others. And as husbands and fathers, we desire to protect our families against anything that would harm them physically, emotionally, and spiritually. The combination of these two qualities—humility and strength—is called *meekness*. Far from being weak, it's strength used for the benefit of others. It's a quality that pleases God and helps create a safe, healthy environment for everyone.

Bottom Line

Surrender your pride and apologize. It shows obedience, courage, humility, love, and strength. Does anyone come to mind?

Work: The First Ministry

The LORD God took the man and placed him in the garden of Eden to work it and watch over it. (Gen. 2:15)

Working Man

When God created man, the first task God gave him was not "religious" in character, at least in the way we typically think of religious work. His first field of service was actually a *field*, not a temple or church. His first task was more like that of a gardener or farmer than a priest or minister. This is not to minimize the fact that the highest priority for man is to worship God. But in this case man worshipped and served God through his work—his normal, everyday, nonreligious work. This was God's idea.

The True Original

Our work is no substitute for the gathered worship of the church on the Lord's Day, but it is a real ministry. All work that is done unto the Lord is true service for the Lord. Martin Luther once said, "The works of monks and priests, however holy and arduous they may be, do not differ one whit in the sight of God from the works of the rustic laborer in the field or the woman going about her household tasks, but that all works are measured before God by faith alone." Do you see your work that way? When we understand the value and dignity and holiness of all legitimate work, it takes on a whole new excitement.

Bottom Line

Your work is your ministry, and you should treat it with the same sense of accountability and responsibility to God that you would expect of your pastor.

Leading the Way

They will not hunger or thirst, the scorching heat or sun will not strike them; for their compassionate One will guide them, and lead them to springs of water. (Isa. 49:10)

Deception Is Subtle

Try as we might to prevent it, we are constantly exposed to influences and pressures that challenge what we know from Scripture. This is especially true for our kids. "Come on, just once. Nobody will ever know," whispers the father of lies (see John 8:44). Our challenge as fathers is to help our kids recognize Satan as the source of these deceptions and to help them choose truth over the false promises of whatever he's using to influence them toward bad choices.

Actions Speak Louder

The amount and quality of time we spend with our kids is critically important, but our kids spend more waking time away from us than they do with us. So we need to make the truth of God's Word an audible, visible, relatable part of their everyday life, not just on Sundays or family nights. Some ways to do that include: (1) making church attendance and involvement a priority, (2) modeling how to have a daily quiet time, (3) praying with your kids regularly, and (4) intentionally making time to talk with them, asking hard, uncomfortable questions when necessary.

We certainly can't lead the way for our kids if we don't know it ourselves. Only when we seek God's truth for our own lives can we lead our children to that same source of truth—an intimate relationship with God and His Word.

Bottom Line

It's not enough to set rules and curfews; we must teach and model how to apply God's truth to all of life's struggles and temptations.

Following Orders

God is not a God of disorder but of peace. (1 Cor. 14:33)

Out of Order

Have you ever seen a little boy put on a sweater? He puts button one in hole two, then button two in hole three, and so on until he runs out of buttons. He ends up "sidegoggling" because he began out of order. Our God is a God of order. Everything He does, He does according to order. When God's creation follows His order, the result is harmony, fulfillment of purpose, and glory to Him. Whenever we see confusion or disaster in God's creation, we know His order is not being followed.

The horrific breakdown of the home today indicates that humanity is not following God's order for the home. More than a million children run away each year. The divorce rate is around 50 percent. Many couples choose to live together and not get married: it used to be love, marriage, baby carriage—now it's love, baby carriage, and maybe marriage—not God's plan.

House in Order

The Bible gives God's order for the home in Ephesians 5:22–6:4: Christ is the head of the man, and the man heads up his wife and children in a loving, sacrificial way. Men, your leadership in the home is God ordained and should reflect Christ's loving headship of the church. In a sacrificial way the man provides, protects, and guides his wife and children. Is your home "sidegoggling," or is it working according to God's order? There's a big difference.

Bottom Line

God's plan for you is to lovingly and sacrificially lead your wife and children. That's the order of things. That's how strong, happy families are built.

The Wheelbarrow

*Carry one another's burdens; in this way you will
fulfill the law of Christ. (Gal. 6:2)*

What It Does

Some of our sins are willful; others are due to poor judgment. In Galatians 6:1–4, Paul talks about our responsibility
toward those in the latter category. The picture here is someone
overwhelmed by a heavy load.

Is someone in your world struggling with sin or the consequences of their sinful choices? We are reminded that our
response should be to help shoulder the load, and our motivation is to see them restored. Too often in our "to each his own"
culture, our response is to ignore it, excuse it, or judge the person because of it. Yet by the example of Jesus, and throughout
Scripture, we are taught to be merciful to those struggling in sin
(see Luke 6:36) while also supplying the comfort, counsel, and
help the circumstance may require. This command also comes
with a warning: be gentle and be careful. Guard against any
pride or self-righteousness seeping in.

How It Works

Helping to restore someone does not require a counseling
degree or prior experience with the subject matter. What it does
call for is a willing heart that is sensitive to the leading of the
Holy Spirit. Just as a wheelbarrow depends on its operator for
what it carries, where it goes, and when it empties, so we should
depend on God's Spirit within for the wisdom, discernment, and
timing of our help to others. He is more than able to guide us to
know how we can best help.

Bottom Line

Be a wheelbarrow. Help carry the burdens of others with
God as your operator, directing where, when, and how you help.

The Tape Measure

With the judgment you use, you will be judged, and with the measure you use, it will be measured to you. (Matt. 7:2)

What It Does

Noah was a capable craftsman, but if he were building your dream house, you'd probably prefer he use a tape measure rather than his forearm for measurement. After all, a cubit (from elbow to tip of middle finger) will be slightly different from one person to the next, whereas a tape measure is marked with common, consistent space between points, giving the same dimension for anyone who uses it. Taken in context, this consistency in measurement is what we see in Matthew 7:1–5 when Jesus cautions us about judging others.

How It Works

His message is not that we are never to judge. In fact, He tells us in verses 15–16 to be discerning and to assess others by their fruit. His warning, however, is about measuring others by one standard and ourselves by another. This teaching echoes the warnings in Amos and Micah against using dishonest scales. Our standard of measure must be biblical, not some self-imposed, self-righteous standard we come up with on our own (see 2 Cor. 10:12).

Before judging someone else's behavior, first consider these two questions: (1) Am I guilty of the same offense? and (2) Am I covering up or making excuses for sin in any area of my life? An honest answer to those two questions will often cause us to repent before judging someone else.

Bottom Line

We often see faults in others without recognizing them in ourselves. Confess your own mistakes, then extend mercy just as you have received God's mercy.

Authentic Life in Christ

I have spoken these things to you so that My joy may be in you and your joy may be complete. (John 15:11)

Real Benefits

Deep joy is found in being part of the body of Christ, His church. The man who invests his time, energy, and abilities in his local community of faith can expect to receive many personal benefits.

Several years ago Dr. K. P. Yohannan preached a sermon in Kerala, India, using John 15 as his text and the body of Christ as his subject. He began by citing some of the typical blessings we often rightly associate with being involved in the life of the church—serving each other; laughing, sharing and praying together; being honest with one another; challenging and being accountable to one another; encouraging one another. These are all good things we should be thankful for. But authentic body life involves even more than that.

Real Body Life

First, he said, a church should be Christ-centered, a characteristic we may need to work on, considering that more than twenty-eight thousand denominations currently exist in the world, not all of which are particularly Christ-centered. Second, Dr. Yohannan said that churches must acknowledge their common ground. Unity in the church around the historic, central doctrines is absolutely essential. Finally, he said love needs to be paramount. Love must be evident in word and in deed.

These things may be challenging, but they are essential for the body of Christ to thrive and grow. Are you experiencing these elements in your church? How can you contribute to a more authentic life together as believers?

Bottom Line

Invest yourself in the body of Christ, and enjoy the blessings of body life.

What Do You Want?

Do not covet your neighbor's house. Do not covet your neighbor's wife, his male or female slave, his ox or donkey, or anything that belongs to your neighbor. (Exod. 20:17)

Living Large

High-speed collisions and high-intensity games make watching sports a popular activity for men. (That is, if you can call sitting on the couch with a remote control and a bag of chips an activity.) Big-money contracts allow professional athletes to live extravagant lifestyles. Big houses. Beautiful wives. Bodacious cars. It's easy for men to become envious. But going all the way back to the Ten Commandments, God knew this wasn't a healthy way to live. That's why he told us to be careful what we wish for.

Not Always Greener

God wants us to be content with what we have. Our Creator knows us better than we know ourselves and entrusts us with exactly the right amount of "stuff" we truly need (even if it happens to be a little less than our neighbor). Plus, having more things doesn't necessarily lead to happiness. Many well-paid professional athletes would tell you that money actually becomes a problem among those without the responsibility and support to manage their huge salaries well. With family members and old friends coming out of the woodwork, always asking favors, some discover their wealth is as much of a curse as it is a blessing.

When you're tempted to get a little green with envy over a neighbor's green (or a sports star's very large amount of green), focus on all the blessings God has given you in the form of possessions and relationships. You are blessed!

Bottom Line

Look around at what you have—whether it's a lot or a little—and be thankful.

Heart Health

*Guard your heart above all else,
for it is the source of life. (Prov. 4:23)*

The Heart as a Hindrance

The heart is an amazing organ—a muscular little machine that fuels our physical existence by pumping blood through our bodies 24-7. At the same time it has been identified symbolically for centuries as the seat of love and affection, the source of feelings and emotions—both positive and negative.

The Bible warns in Jeremiah 17:9, "The heart is more deceitful than anything else." Harry Layden, director of a family counseling and evangelistic ministry in Tulsa, Oklahoma, says hindrances to the heart of a home include, among other things, blockages (blatant sin), departing hearts (turning from God), divided hearts (priorities in the wrong order), and broken hearts (family crises). The heart needs to be healthy or big problems will surely come. That's why it must be guarded so carefully.

The Heart, Our Only Hope

Layden emphasizes, however, that the heart is the source of life for the family as well. The heart of a healthy family is a man who demonstrates fear of the Lord and integrity in every area of his life, a man who seeks to serve his family unselfishly.

When your heart leads you toward sin or rebellion against God, don't give up or give in. Repent and return to a close walk with the Lord. Revive your commitment. Restore your integrity. God will strengthen your heart to do the next right thing.

Bottom Line

Check your heart condition today. Resolve to turn away from any sin or wrong attitudes and return to a right relationship with the Father.

Worth the Wait

The body is not for sexual immorality but for the Lord, and the Lord for the body. (1 Cor. 6:13)

Honor the Bond

Our secular culture has cheap substitutes for marriage and flippant disregard for the value of sexual purity. God, however, desires that we hold this foundational relationship in the same high esteem that He does. As single men who are approaching or awaiting marriage, this demands faith in the character and wisdom of our Creator, as well as the self-control that comes from the indwelling Holy Spirit.

Biologically guys are wired for sex in a major way. We want it early and often. The drive is so strong that it can seem impossible not to act on it when the opportunity arises. Indeed, much of contemporary culture will judge you as inhibited or just plain weird if you decide to wait for sex until you say your marriage vows.

Hold Out for God's Best

But God truly has our happiness in mind when He calls us to wait for marriage. God designed marriage not as a limitation but as a wonderful and healthy freedom. Marriage includes doing what you really want to do with whom you want to do it, all in the context of honest love, full commitment, and the vulnerability of trust. Sleeping around may bring a short-term thrill, but it leaves behind no depth, no real growth, no sense of something and someone you can depend on through good times and bad. In reserving sex for marriage, God is not holding out on you. He truly wants you to be sexually fulfilled, and this happens only on God's terms—in marriage.

Bottom Line

If you have trusted God for your salvation, trust Him also with your sexuality.

Going with the Flow?

Do not be conformed to this age, but be transformed by the renewing of your mind, so that you may discern what is the good, pleasing, and perfect will of God. (Rom. 12:2)

Conform or Transform?

Today's verse is a familiar challenge for us to let Christ change our lives as we renew our minds. *Conform* and *transform* are pivotal words that contrast the concepts Paul teaches in this verse, and there's quite a difference between the two.

Conforming to something, like to worldly values, is something that more or less happens to us without much effort. The word *conform* comes from the Latin *conformare*, meaning "to fashion of the same form." It basically means to "go with the flow." The prefix *trans* also has its roots in Latin, but it means "across, beyond, or through." We cannot transform ourselves—it is *beyond* us—only the power of God can transform us.

Saul or Paul?

Paul's life provides an example of moving from being conformed to being transformed. As Saul, he conformed to the pharisaical tradition of his people. He says of himself: "I persecuted God's church to an extreme degree and tried to destroy it. . . . I was extremely zealous for the traditions of my ancestors" (Gal. 1:13–14). That was the old Saul.

Everything changed for Paul, however, after encountering God in his Damascus Road experience (see Acts 22:6–21). That was the beginning of a radical transformation that would reshape his identity and his mission. God wants to transform us too.

Bottom Line

Don't conform to the things of the world, but allow God to transform your life to His will. What's one area of your life that really needs transformation?

Be a Warrior

The Angel of the LORD appeared to him and said: "The LORD is with you, mighty warrior." (Judg. 6:12)

Unlikely Warrior

"Gideon, you're a mighty warrior." That message may have provoked laughter from Gideon as he stared in disbelief at the angel of the Lord who suddenly appeared to him outside his home. Gideon knew he was anything but a mighty warrior. He said, "Lord, how can I deliver Israel? . . . I am the youngest in my father's house" (Judg. 6:15).

But what the Lord was telling Gideon is not that he was already a mighty warrior but that it was time for him to become a mighty warrior since the Lord promised to be with him. And so it is for every man of God who dares to follow God's call on his life. We are mighty because God is with us.

Reluctant Warrior

What's particularly noteworthy is that God met Gideon in the midst of his brokenness. Gideon was like most men—he'd just as soon stay away from conflict, taking a passive approach to life. But the time had come for action, and God was calling Gideon to step up and live with courage.

God purposely calls men like Gideon to the front lines where His strength can be put on full display. God outlines the battle plans, empowers the troops, and delivers the victories. God is still in the business of turning cowards into champions, Gideons into warriors. And we live in a world that's desperate for this kind of strong leadership. Will you join the battle? Will you step up and fight?

Bottom Line

God calls every Christian man to fight for what's right and to fight it in His strength.

Security Measures

The one who lives under the protection of the Most High dwells in the shadow of the Almighty. (Ps. 91:1)

When You're Scared

Have you noticed that the more emphasis we place on security, the less secure we feel? Not only do we feel insecure on a national scope with terrorism and crime, but we also feel insecure on a personal level. Falling stock market. Threat of job loss. Assault on personal safety.

The psalmist writes, "The one who lives under the protection of the Most High dwells in the shadow of the Almighty" (Ps. 91:1). The writer invites you to come close, to feel the warmth of the One he is writing about, and to share in the protection He offers, to find safety in His truths, and to rest secure in the peace He provides. For people troubled by the news of the day and the conditions in our personal living space, this is just the kind of invitation we need to hear.

Who Protects You

The term *dwells* implies that you live in conscious, daily fellowship with God—your defense shield, your alarm system, your protective coating. He is everything you need to feel secure in an insecure world.

This verse really does have a security blanket feel to it. Not an actual blanket, of course, but a Person. In the same way that many children will not let their security blanket out of their grasp, so believers are meant to be constantly in touch with their Source of security. We're meant to live constantly under the shadow of the Almighty . . . where we are safe.

Bottom Line

Real security is not found in things—job, stock market, fat bank account, alarm systems but—in the Person of Jesus Christ.

Two Powerful Words

Jesus wept. (John 11:35)

God with Tear Ducts

John's words, written to a primarily Greek audience, must have come as a bit of a shock. Jesus wept? The gods weren't supposed to show this kind of emotion toward their subjects. They were usually thought of as austere, unmoved, unattached.

Just picture for an instant the Son of God with tears running down His face. What an image of a loving, compassionate Savior. But why would Jesus weep if He was about to raise Lazarus from the dead? Jesus wept because His friends Mary and Martha were grieving over the untimely loss of their brother Lazarus. Jesus wept at the results of sin. In that grave were the gritty realities of the fall—death, separation, decay, and pain.

Loving Sinners, Hating Sin

There is another aspect to Jesus' emotion that day. John earlier writes that Jesus was inwardly moved—angry—when He first came upon the mourners. Combine that with John 11:35, and you have a Jesus who is angry at sin but weeps with its victims. It's easy to get this backward—ignoring sin but hating sinners.

Jesus was a model of compassion. Still today He weeps when one of His children experiences loss. He weeps when they lose a job. He weeps at funerals. He weeps in divorce court. He weeps in prison. This is our God. He's not detached from our problems. He's a God who suffers with us. And He strengthens us to bear the pain.

Bottom Line

Jesus is a God who weeps with sinners. Do you show compassion to others who are suffering? Ask God to give you His heart for those who are hurting.

From Head to Heart

We have come to know and to believe the love that God has for us. God is love, and the one who remains in love remains in God, and God remains in him. (1 John 4:16)

Our Common Struggle

Knowing the attributes of God can provide great comfort, and no attribute is more comforting than knowing that God is love. We were made to experience this. We sense it in our deepest being.

Yet while we know the Bible says God loves us—today's verse is a great example of that—we often have a tough time believing it in a way that transforms our lives. While we may know it in our heads, we may not always believe it in our hearts. It can seem too good to be true, almost like wishful thinking.

Persistence Pays Off

How can we experience the love of God—or any of His attributes—in a greater way? The first and most important thing we can do is ask the Holy Spirit to help us experience what the Bible says is true. James 4:2 says, "You do not have because you do not ask." Luke 11:13 adds, "If you then, who are evil, know how to give good gifts to your children, how much more will the heavenly Father give the Holy Spirit to those who ask Him?" And then Romans 5:5 declares: "God's love has been poured out in our hearts through the Holy Spirit who was given to us." We receive God's love through the Spirit's work inside of us. Keep asking Him for more!

Bottom Line

The love of God is inexhaustible. He's not rationing it out. But if we want to experience more of it, we will need to ask repeatedly and expectantly.

Sainthood

To all the saints in Christ Jesus. (Phil. 1:1)

Really?

If you are a Christian, you are a saint. Really. It's true. Did you know that? In both your heart and your experience? According to God (the One whose opinion matters most), you are set apart and holy. Your identity is that of a saint. Sure, you will continue to struggle against sin this side of heaven, but being a sinner is not your primary identity anymore. That changed the instant you came to faith.

Many of us find this hard to believe because we spend so much time looking at our own imperfect performance and so little time looking at Jesus' perfect performance on our behalf. There's a reason we tend to focus on the wrong thing, though, and it may not be what you think.

Pride Is the Problem

Many of us are still sort of shocked by the fact that we struggle with sin to the degree we do. We wrongly believe the cross and grace were important when we first got saved, but now it's up to us to maintain our end of the bargain. Then when we fail to perform up to our standards (let alone God's), we get down on ourselves.

So we try harder. And fail again—until pretty soon the idea of being a saint can seem like nothing more than a work of fiction to us. But that's pride speaking. God wants us to confess our sins and then go forth as saints because that's who He says we are.

Bottom Line

A large part of the Christian life consists in believing what God says despite our feelings or current experience. Embrace your sainthood!

Perspective

He lets me lie down in green pastures;
He leads me beside quiet waters. He renews my life;
He leads me along the right paths. (Ps. 23:2–3)

Overly Busy

The spiritual life is not frantic or distracted or overly busy. Those are not "fruit of the Spirit." Patience and kindness are, however. And those Spirit-produced qualities are quick to be lost in the overly busy person's life. Who has time to be kind or love, to experience joy or enjoy peace? Certainly not the person who's always on the run. And that means the average Christian in our culture doesn't have time . . . or doesn't make time.

There is a better way, though. Jesus invites us into a life that results in wholeness and purpose rather than disintegration and chaos. But we must be willing to accept His invitation. We need faith and courage to be willing to swim against the current of our culture.

Gotta Get Away

The order of verses 2 and 3 in Psalm 23 is instructive. First, God leads us to rest and reflection, and this rest and reflection results in a renewed life that walks the right paths. In other words, slowing down allows for intimate communion with God, and this produces peace, perspective, and purpose. God is not the author of confusion but of clarity. Getting away, even in the form of a daily quiet time, helps center a person in God and in His perfectly paced will. Make sure you're taking enough rest so you can gain His perspective. It's an absolute necessity.

Bottom Line

Experiencing the peace of God and enjoying His perspective is largely a matter of how we organize our lives. We must make time to hear from Him.

Daily Encouragement

*Encourage each other daily, while it is still called today,
so that none of you is hardened by sin's deception. (Heb. 3:13)*

Assume Everyone Needs It

If you assume everybody needs encouragement to pursue God every single day, you'll be right every single time. That's because the deceitfulness of sin is always there, threatening to lure us away from God's truth and righteousness. The devil doesn't take any days off, so we can't either.

But our vigilance against the devil's deceptions is not a solo effort. We all have blind spots that only others can help us see. And we all have weaknesses that only others can help us overcome. Rather than attempt to live as lone-ranger Christians, we're meant to be a band of brothers who stick together and fight for the advancement of God's kingdom in our own lives, the lives of our families, and in a lost and hurting world. That's God's battle plan for us. And one of His best tactical weapons is the simple power of encouragement, one brother to another.

How Encouragement Works

Encouraging one another often begins with asking good questions, trying to dig in to what's really going on in a friend's heart. The goal is not to condemn but rather to bring any darkness into the light so it can be forgiven, letting truth and righteousness regain the ascendancy. Sometimes it will just be pointing out how you see God working in a friend's life and urging him to keep going. Make sure you're encouraging your brothers daily. It's crucial.

Bottom Line

Encouragement is not optional. We need to receive it, and we need to give it. Make sure encouragement is a big part of your life.

Investing in Others

Don't neglect to do what is good and to share,
for God is pleased with such sacrifices. (Heb. 13:16)

Too Poor to Invest

Investing our time in others is as life-giving for us as it is helpful for someone else. Yet we can come up with a dozen good reasons why we shouldn't or can't spend time with someone:

- I'm too busy at work to have a personal lunch.
- I'm too exhausted to take on something new.
- I've got too many problems of my own.
- My priority is spending quality time with my family.
- I'm not qualified to help someone else.

If you can identify with any of these, it's probably because they're all valid reasons. Some are even biblically correct, like prioritizing your family. Yet the imperative to invest in others is given over and over in Scripture. It's a must.

Serious Investing

You don't need a counseling degree or a problem-free life to walk alongside someone and encourage them in their spiritual journey. In fact, it's often our scars and heartaches that help others relate to us. The key is being obedient to what God has called you to do. If God has laid someone on your heart or has shown you a way to use the gifts He's given you, pray about how best to invest your time and talent so you can help. Then don't be surprised when He multiplies what you give to others in your service to Him.

Bottom Line

God doesn't call the qualified; He qualifies the called. Allow God to use you to help others.

Walking with God

Lord God of Israel, there is no God like You in heaven or on earth, keeping His gracious covenant with Your servants who walk before You with their whole heart. (2 Chron. 6:14)

The Goal

The Christian life is a relationship with God more than anything else. It's not primarily a set of helpful life principles. It can't be confined to a systematic theology textbook. And it certainly isn't just the accumulation of various emotionally charged religious experiences, as wonderful as those often are. Again, at its heart, it's about relating to God in a moment-by-moment, real relationship with all its ups and downs (due to our ups and downs), and with real communication back and forth.

As obvious as this description, it's often just obvious enough to be overlooked. If we're not careful, we can assume the obvious while it recedes farther and farther into the background of our thoughts and experience.

No Tightrope Walk

God is holy, and our relationship with Him will necessarily involve our transformation to be more like Him. (Thankfully, He rubs off on us and not vice versa.) This happens in us and to us as we obey the Holy Spirit's promptings, which are in line with the Word He has inspired. But we don't listen perfectly all the time. We stumble and fall. Thankfully, we're not walking a tightrope with no net below. It's more like we're journeying with our Best Friend who offers us grace, forgiveness, and hope.

Bottom Line

Walking with God is life's greatest joy. It's also a great adventure. Our job is to trust and obey. God will take care of the rest.

Unbreakable Love

I am persuaded that not even death or life, angels or rulers, things present or things to come, hostile powers . . . or any other created thing will have the power to separate us from the love of God that is in Christ Jesus our Lord! (Rom. 8:38–39)

Stuck Together

To illustrate the unbreakable nature of God's love, a pastor took two boards—each about a half inch deep, maybe three feet long, and half a foot wide—and said that one board represents us and the other board represents God's love. He then held the boards far apart and said that when we sin, we feel like God's love is far from us. Or when life comes crashing down around us due to the sins of others or just living in a fallen world, we feel like God's love is far from us.

That's not the case, though. To illustrate this, he glued the boards together with "stronger than wood" wood glue, then screwed them together, then nailed them together, then wrapped duct tape around them. We got the point! Nothing was going to break that bond!

Can You Believe It?

Your feelings will often lie to you. And your perception of reality is often skewed. So if you want to be a stable, joyful, courageous Christian, you need to believe God loves you *no matter what* based on the clear and reliable promises of His Word. This is the test of faith, and great reward comes with belief.

Bottom Line

The battle to continue to believe in God's love *no matter what* is where the rubber really hits the road in the Christian life. Ask God for faith to believe!

God's Dwelling Place

*The whole building, being put together by Him,
grows into a holy sanctuary in the Lord. You also are being built
together for God's dwelling in the Spirit. (Eph. 2:21–22)*

Power

The church consists of ordinary people indwelt by an extraordinary God. So while we may be "clay jars" (2 Cor. 4:7), our contents are extraordinary—the living God Himself! We need to know this reality and experience it. Our expectations for the Christian life are often way too low considering the staggering claims the Bible makes about our position in Christ and His position in us. He has taken up residence in us through the person of the Holy Spirit. Just think of it, Almighty God lives in you! Anything is possible now.

Check this out: 2 Corinthians 5:17 says, "if anyone is in Christ, he is a new creation; old things have passed away, and look, new things have come." Yet we easily forget to look for and expect the newness of life that God has worked in us, beginning with conversion but never diminishing afterward. We have real power to change because God lives inside of us.

Presence

A man who knows in an experiential way that he is indwelt by God's Spirit is a powerful presence in the world. God is able to work through him as a conduit of grace. This is especially true when it comes to evangelism. We can be sure that a Spirit-filled Christian has eyes for the lost because God has eyes for the lost. God's presence fuels our mission.

Bottom Line

It's one thing to talk about the doctrine of the indwelling Christ; it's another to believe it and experience it. We have God's power and His presence!

With All Your Strength

Be doers of the word and not hearers only,
deceiving yourselves. (James 1:22)

The Missing Ingredient

Author Paul Coughlin believes there is a significant and disturbing lack of courage in many Christian men today. He argues that an overemphasis on the mind and heart while largely ignoring the will has left us with a lot of passive men waiting around for God to do something. That's not how the life of faith is designed to work.

Faith *does* things. It doesn't *earn* things, of course, but it does *do* things. We men sense this, and we know it by experience. We know that we come alive when we're out there sacrificing for others and making our little corner of the earth look a little bit more like the kingdom of God. And while we must overcome some fears if we're going to act courageously, we were made to do just that. God designed us to crave a redemptive adventure that costs us something. Otherwise, we go through life half dead, and the world and our families suffer.

Strength of Will

While we can do nothing spiritually significant apart from Christ, God probably won't do anything spiritually significant through us apart from us—that is, apart from our cooperation. Seems obvious, right? Mark 12:30 says we're to love God with all of *our* strength, *not* God's strength. Granted, He gives us whatever strength we have, but He also calls us to use it to love Him and others. The time to act is now.

Bottom Line

God has given us a will as well as the strength to exercise it. Let's stop waiting around and start taking action.

No Fear

He will not fear bad news; his heart is confident,
trusting in the LORD. His heart is assured; he will not fear.
In the end he will look in triumph on his foes. (Ps. 112:7–8)

Happy Man

Psalm 112 starts off with a bang (and an important biblical truth): "Hallelujah! Happy is the man who fears the LORD, taking great delight in His commands" (Ps. 112:1). Almost the whole psalm is a celebration of that fact. Usually we don't associate fear with happiness. And certainly a lot of people are *afraid* of God and are not the least bit happy. The difference, of course, is whether you know God as your loving heavenly Father who inspires reverential awe (what the Bible means by the "fear" of God), or whether you see God as your judge who's out to get you. The former delights in God's commands and benefits from obeying them, while the latter despises them and suffers the consequences (see Ps. 112:10).

Who? Me?

According to verse 7, this happy fellow is not afraid of bad news. Rather, he's "confident, trusting in the LORD." He knows that whatever difficulties come his way, he will triumph in the end. So he doesn't bother fearing anything or anyone but God. He simply does what is good and reaps the blessings of obedience. "Light shines in the darkness for the upright. . . . Good will come to a man who lends generously and conducts his business fairly" (Ps. 112:4–5). How about you? Has your fear of God dissolved all your other fears?

Bottom Line

Fight fear with fear—the fear of God. Then you'll be happy and free and a blessing to others.

Marriage Fight

Show some courage and be men. . . .
Be men and fight! (1 Sam. 4:9)

A Fight Worth Having

Normally the words *fight* and *marriage* don't go together well when it comes to defining a Christ-honoring relationship. But while most men need no encouragement to fight *with* their wives, virtually all men need encouragement to fight *for* them.

If we really believe marriage is a sacred institution given by God and representing the love of God for His church, then we ought to be warriors for the one who happens to live under our own roof. Too often, though, we're passive bystanders, allowing the enemies of busyness, selfishness, and pride to win battles God has equipped us to win.

How to Be Victorious

Know that the weapons you employ in this fight are different from those wielded by the world. You fight with humility, selflessness, and love. A man of God who models Christlike sacrifice and service will win the heart of his wife. When he offers a listening ear, when he leads in the home, when he treasures his wife's desires, he invests in the long-term success of his marriage. Their relationship becomes untouchable to the enemy. That man is doing things God's way.

How does a husband begin the march to marital victory? He begins by engaging the battle, by examining his priorities, and asking himself a singular, probing question: *Am I willing to fight for what I love?*

Bottom Line

God has called every man to engage in the fight for a great marriage. Are you fighting for yours?

Suffering and Joy

Is anyone among you suffering?
He should pray. Is anyone cheerful?
He should sing praises. (James 5:13)

Prayer

Ask any moderately sized group of Christians, and the answer to James's question about suffering will always be yes. We suffer often. There's no escaping suffering in a fallen, broken, sinful world. If you're not currently suffering, you will be sooner or later. That's just the way it is.

But there is help. According to James the suffering person should pray. A lot of times we do this instinctively. We're desperate. We know we need God's help. We turn to Him in prayer, begging Him to relieve the pain and change the situation. But sometimes it seems like we would rather just sit and stew, complain and worry. It's almost like we're in shock over the situation and unwilling to accept reality. We believe that by thinking about the problem over and over again, we're somehow going to solve it. What works, however, is turning to God in prayer.

Praise

Of course, there will be times when everything is going great in our life and we're downright cheerful about it. In those times James says we should sing for joy. We should praise God unreservedly. Again, a lot of times this happens naturally, but sometimes we can hold back a little because we know the good times won't last forever. That's no way to live, though, always waiting for the other shoe to drop. So sing for joy while you can. It will strengthen you for later.

Bottom Line

Life has its ups and downs. When you're suffering, pray. And when things are going great, praise. In both cases you'll be turning your attention to God.

Bond Servant of Christ, Part 1

*Paul, a slave of Christ Jesus, called as an apostle
and singled out for God's good news. (Rom. 1:1)*

Bond Servant of Old

Paul was an apostle of Christ, and this established his authority with the church. But he was also a *slave* of Christ, which established his heart for God and for the church. Yet instead of thinking of slavery as we're accustomed to—wholly oppressive—we ought to think of it as the greatest opportunity any of us could have.

As a first-century bond servant of Christ, you would understand that your life is not your own. At every point your will would be lined up with your Master's will. Your sole purpose would be to do His will, not your own. And yet His will would not be burdensome (see Matt. 11:29).

Bond Servant of Today

The spirit of America is an independent, rugged, self-reliant, roll-up-your-sleeves, "you can do it" kind of attitude. We place great value on this kind of person in our country, and we take great pride in being that kind of country.

But the kingdom of God does not function by that spirit. Instead, the kingdom is built on the willing service of "slaves"— those who have traded their captivity to sin for a liberating dependence on Christ. Like a wild horse that needs to be broken to be of any use, God wants to break us of our foolish, imaginary independence. And so the bond servant of Christ has happily signed away his rights to himself and become a liberated slave of the one true Master.

Bottom Line

Are you holding on to some of your own rights as you try to serve Christ?

Bond Servant of Christ, Part 4

Spotlight Seekers

A fourth characteristic of a bond servant is this: your position is in the background, and your master's position is in the forefront. Humility is a hallmark of the bond servant. He never forgets who the master is and who the servant is. Jesus Himself warned His disciples to avoid becoming like those teachers of the law who loved the place of honor at banquets (see Matt. 23:1–6). That's not a servant's attitude. The servant isn't concerned with what others think and doesn't have designs on getting the credit, the limelight, the promotion.

Hiding behind the Cross

If anyone had a right to the spotlight, it would have been the apostle Paul. Yet in 1 Corinthians 2:2 he shunned the spotlight, remarking, "I didn't think it was a good idea to know anything among you except Jesus Christ and Him crucified."

There is also the matter of jealousy between bond servants. If God chooses to honor another and not us, that's none of our business. The bond servant doesn't compare his service or reward with another's. Everything already belongs to Christ. There is nothing left to sacrifice. Instead, the words of a bond servant are simple: "We are good-for-nothing slaves; we've only done our duty" (Luke 17:10).

Bottom Line

Jesus died so people could break free from their chains of sin and become bond servants of the King of kings—for life and eternity!

A World of Hope

I have a hope in God, which these men themselves also accept, that there is going to be a resurrection. (Acts 24:15)

Hostile Territory

As God's children we live in a world that rejects our faith and rejects us also. For although this is God's world, He has chosen in His sovereignty to allow Satan—the great usurper, both God's enemy and ours—to wield inordinate influence in the affairs of men, to make things uncomfortable for Christians. As a result, we cannot and are actually commanded not to grow too comfortable here. Although God gives us many blessings in this life, that doesn't mean our outward circumstances are always pleasant. Sometimes they are painful and difficult.

A Hopeful Truth

But He does give us hope. And this hope is a greater blessing than the greatest of earthly circumstances. We are promised an eternal life in paradise that will make the trials of this life seem "momentary" and "light" when viewed in ultimate perspective (see 2 Cor. 4:17).

This is not an empty promise. God has guaranteed our resurrection and our eternity by the resurrection of Christ. As Jesus is now, so we will be. His bodily resurrection guarantees ours. All the real disappointments we experience on this earth will be redeemed in the resurrection. As C. S. Lewis described in *The Chronicles of Narnia*, a day will come when death will work backward, when all that is wrong in this world will be made right forever. That is our sure hope.

Bottom Line

Life on this earth will not always be easy, but we can handle it because of our unshakable hope in the resurrection.

Stick with It

*The one who looks intently into the perfect law
of freedom and perseveres in it, and is not a forgetful
hearer but one who does good works—this person
will be blessed in what he does. (James 1:25)*

Passion and Purpose

Any man who's had a job he loved—one he couldn't wait to get to every day—knows the difference that comes from being passionate about one's work. If our job maximizes our gifts and skills, we wake up excited to see the morning start.

A second major element of a fulfilling job is being able to recognize a purpose in it. Even if we don't particularly like what we're doing, we can do it with integrity and commitment because we know it's putting food on the table, providing clothes and educational expenses for our kids. The purpose makes it bearable.

Perseverance

Sometimes, however, we find ourselves doing work that elicits neither passion nor purpose. A situation like that requires every ounce of stick-to-itiveness we can muster up. All we can do, if we desire to stay faithful, is to persevere, stay true to the course, employing the spiritual strengths of discipline and self-control.

In the movie *Standing Firm*, writer/producer Kyle Prohaska created a character named Steven, a young man who prays for and witnesses to his father for a long time before seeing any hope of positive results. He stays disciplined and focused; he perseveres. We, too, must often keep giving our best even when our work draws nothing out of us. It's a matter of faith, patience, and trust.

Bottom Line

When you feel no passion and see no purpose, demonstrate discipline by prayerfully persevering in the situations that challenge you.

Open Mouth, Insert Brain

My dearly loved brothers, understand this: Everyone must be quick to hear, slow to speak, and slow to anger, for man's anger does not accomplish God's righteousness. (James 1:19–20)

Patience Required

"Quick to hear, slow to speak, slow to anger." Those words sound good as they roll off the pages of the Bible. But as a lifestyle this patient approach to relationships requires extreme sacrifice and the willingness to be hurt and humbled for the one person God has called you to love the most (other than Himself)—your wife.

A husband's willingness to believe in the good will of his wife and to prayerfully think through his responses before answering goes a long way toward building a strong marriage.

Wise Words

James's words were not originally spoken as good marriage counsel specifically. They were shared with the early church, a group of people suddenly thrust together in community—a people who hailed from diverse cultures, backgrounds, and religious systems, which meant there were bound to be disagreements among them. Nevertheless, his words are perfect medicine for troubled marriages.

Husbands are called to lay down their lives for the woman they married. In practical terms this includes laying down our egos and our desire to "win" arguments. It's a matter of choosing by God's grace to love unconditionally. Reacting with patience and grace is not the natural reaction, but it's the right reaction. So choose to stop, listen, and respond with grace. When you do that, you become part of the solution.

Bottom Line

God calls men to respond to their wives with humility and grace.

Anger

A hot-tempered man stirs up conflict,
but a man slow to anger calms strife. (Prov. 15:18)

Unhealthy Anger

The Bible warns against being a hot-tempered man. Healthy anger can actually be a good thing, helping you fight hard for worthwhile causes—for the people you love, for the defenseless, for truth. But unfortunately, anger is more often used as an instrument of evil, harming relationships or exploiting the weak.

A hot-tempered man stirs up conflict. Do you bark at your wife or kids? Throw temper tantrums? Do you seethe with bitterness or seek revenge? Do you leave conflict in your wake? Instead of letting anger motivate noble deeds, it can easily degenerate into violence, destructiveness, and abuse. A hot-tempered man turns his home into a battlefield, imposing his outbursts on his wife and children, leaving them his primary victims. He fills his workplace with stress and can even turn fun pastimes—like a church softball game—into inappropriate expressions of misplaced rage.

Healthy Anger

Jesus stands ready to change you into a man who is "slow to anger." That doesn't mean you'll never get angry; it just means your anger can be transformed for righteous purposes. You can become angry yet still respect people and honor their boundaries. You can use anger to preserve relationships instead of destroying them. You can passionately shield the weak and stand for truth even at great cost. Instead of a dangerous emotion that springs from sinful pride, your Christlike anger can become a holy energy that motivates virtue.

Bottom Line

By God's grace you can transform your anger from destructive to life-giving.

Always Be Prepared

*The kingdom of heaven will be like 10 virgins who took
their lamps and went out to meet the groom. Five of them were
foolish and five were sensible. When the foolish took their lamps,
they didn't take olive oil with them. (Matt. 25:1–3)*

Oil in My Lamp

A song often introduced to kids in Sunday school or VBS
a generation ago included the lyrics, "Give me oil in my lamp,
keep me burning," based on Jesus' story of the wise and foolish
virgins in Matthew 25. A wise man will take every step to be
prepared for whatever situation he expects to face. It may be
your wife's honey-do list: before you paint the walls, cover the
old paint with a good coat of primer. It may be your own spring
tasks: before you crank up the lawn mower, be sure to change the
oil and sharpen the blade. Good preparation is a must in many
areas of life.

Ready in My Life

The principle of the Boy Scout motto—"Be prepared"—
serves us well as grown men. And some of our best preparation
comes from being spiritually sharp to face whatever curveballs
could be coming across your plate.

Strive to spend some time in God's Word every day. Pray
about the needs in your life, your family, your church, and your
workplace, taking your concerns to Him and receiving His
calming perspective. Seek to cultivate relationships that encourage you to grow in your faith. Faithfully doing these things can
strengthen you for the tough challenges that will come sooner
or later.

Bottom Line

Start applying the disciplines that will help you be spiritually prepared for whatever life brings your way.

Coming Clean

*Your iniquities have built barriers between
you and your God, and your sins have made Him hide
His face from you so that He does not listen. (Isa. 59:2)*

When We're Hiding

Does God seem distant to you today? Have you prayed but felt nothing? Have you read the Bible but heard nothing? The fact is, we can engage in all kinds of spiritual disciplines and still be convinced that God has removed Himself from our problems, unaware of our desires and deaf to our pleas. Is something wrong with Him?

The prophet Isaiah asserted that the problem is not with God but often with us. The sins you haven't dealt with—whether from going too fast to notice them or wanting too badly to hold on to them—build "barriers between you and your God," causing Him to "hide His face from you so that He does not listen." God is not hiding from *us*; we are hiding from *Him*, not wanting Him to have access to every part of us, only the parts we feel comfortable with Him knowing about.

When We're the Problem

In the movie *Apollo 13*, Commander Jim Lovell (Tom Hanks) uttered the words, "Houston, we have a problem." We, too, have a problem. We harbor sinful habits, words, actions, and attitudes that we try to conceal. Rather than admitting our sin, we hope that praying, Bible reading, and church attendance will cancel it out. It won't.

Communion with God is preceded by confession before God. To fully experience His presence, we must come out of hiding and acknowledge our ongoing struggle. Abundant forgiveness is available, but first we must admit that we need it.

Bottom Line

God doesn't expect perfection, but He does expect honesty.

Honey and Vinegar

Masters, treat your slaves the same way, without threatening them, because you know that both their Master and yours is in heaven, and there is no favoritism with Him. (Eph. 6:9)

Bad News Bears

For most of the season, the young baseball team lost every game by a fairly sizable margin. They swung their bats and missed. They dropped pop-ups and let ground balls go through their legs. Pitchers would throw ten feet over the batter's head one time, then bounce the ball ten feet in front of the plate the next.

The coaches, however, didn't yell and scream to embarrass the players. They did everything they could think of to encourage the youngsters. The team worked on the fundamentals over and over again, trying to get better. And finally, all the hard work eventually paid off with a late-season victory . . . then another.

In the Long Run

Remember the old adage, "It's easier to draw flies to honey than to vinegar"? The coaches could easily have gone the "bad cop" route and turned baseball games and practices into boot camp, but they didn't. As a result every single kid still loved the game at the end of the season, and the coaches weren't filled with regrets.

It was certainly frustrating at times to lose so often and so badly, but what will the kids remember years from now? In the long run, it wasn't all that important that little Billy made an error. It was far more important for him to see Jesus in his coaches. Keep a sense of perspective, guys.

Bottom Line

Both harsh criticism and sincere encouragement can impact a kid for a long time. Which will you choose to provide?

Ernie Harwell

*Even when I am old and gray, God, do not abandon me.
Then I will proclaim Your power to another generation,
Your strength to all who are to come. (Ps. 71:18)*

That Rich, Deep Voice

For more than forty years, Ernie Harwell was the voice of the Detroit Tigers baseball team. Across the Midwest, Harwell's rich, deep voice became a cultural icon as he described the exploits of Al Kaline, Denny McLain, Mark Fidrych, and Kirk Gibson. In 1981, the famed broadcaster was honored by induction into the Major League Baseball Hall of Fame.

In September 2009, Harwell was diagnosed with terminal cancer. At ninety-two, he faced the end of his life with a dignity that was truly incredible to behold. He expressed no fear and no regrets during a touching interview with Bob Costas shown on MLB Network. Harwell died on May 4, 2010. All of baseball grieved his passing.

Praise the Lord

When Harwell entered the Hall of Fame, he honored Christ during his acceptance speech. "I praise the Lord here today," he said. "I know that all my talent and all my ability comes from Him, and without Him, I'm nothing. I thank Him for His great blessing."

Even after being diagnosed with cancer, Harwell continued to express a deep and abiding faith in Jesus. He never flinched, never wavered. He was a great ambassador of the game and a witness for Jesus right until the end. Ernie Harwell was certainly not a perfect man—none of us are—but he was a fine example of grace and humility. Rest in peace, Ernie.

Bottom Line

Ernie Harwell's life and career were a great testament to his faith. How will others see Jesus in you today?

True Love

*Husbands, love your wives and don't
be bitter against them. (Col. 3:19)*

Do unto Others

When you are angry with your wife, you don't typically feel like romancing her in that moment. But emotional love is not the kind of love Paul talks about in Colossians 3:19. The Greek word he uses is *agape*, which describes a love based on a decision or choice of the will rather than a feeling. While both emotional and physical love certainly play vital roles in a healthy marriage, men must cultivate a committed, unconditional, sacrificial love that stands firm even when we're angry. That's how Christ loved the church, and that's how husbands are charged to love their wives. *Agape* love does not depend on the receiver's actions; it looks to the highest good of the other, even if at your own expense (see 1 Cor. 13:4–7).

God's Kind of Love

Our natural bent is to become bitter or angry when we feel wronged. Others might even tell us we have the right to be upset or take revenge. But Paul reminds us that even when a wife wrongs her husband, the husband never has permission to act unloving toward his wife.

God's Word also tells us to forgive just as we have been forgiven by Christ (see Col. 3:13), and to "love because He first loved us" (1 John 4:19). Consider that the next time you feel like lashing out or getting even.

Bottom Line

Ask God today to give you the supernatural ability to see your wife through His eyes and to love her with His love.

So Thankful, It Hurts

The earth and everything in it, the world and its inhabitants,
belong to the Lord. (Ps. 24:1)

What We Receive

We are often reminded in the Bible to be thankful for the many ways God has blessed us. But for those experiencing financial pressures, job loss, health issues, marital strife, and other trials, gratitude may not come so easily.

Still we are reminded not to let these trials keep us from showing thankfulness for God's mercy and His gift of salvation. Whether we are comfortable in life or struggling under a weight of adversity, God has given us an opportunity to know Him and serve Him.

What We Give Back

In our key verse today, we see that everything belongs to Him. And oddly enough, this even includes the hardships we struggle with. Yes, God wants us to offer up our struggles to Him with a grateful heart, asking Him to accomplish His purposes in us no matter where we are or what we're going through. In fact, it's usually the circumstances beyond our choosing that help us find out and prove what real faith looks like—what it means to trust God no matter what.

The thanks God wants from us is more than an emotion; it's a dedication of what we have and where we are, even when our faith and courage seem insufficient. In the midst of trials, choosing to be grateful will allow God to transform us, helping us go against our feelings to discover the blessing of His presence.

Bottom Line

Scripture teaches that God inhabits the praises of His people. So if you're hurting, all the more reason to praise!

Be Still

You will be delivered by returning and resting;
your strength will lie in quiet confidence. (Isa. 30:15)

Contrasting Reputations

When disaster comes, do you want to be the superhero? Do you want to feel unstoppable like the Jason Bourne character in the Bourne movies? That'd be great, right? Yet this world, with its self-centered values, is utterly backward. Hence, the otherworldly shock that God's thoughts and ways are not our thoughts and ways (see Isa. 55:8). Contrast the Jason Bourne-like character with Hezekiah, king of Judah from the time he was twenty-five years old. "Hezekiah trusted in the LORD God of Israel. . . . He remained faithful to Yahweh and did not turn from following Him" (2 Kings 18:5–6). His confidence was not in himself and his ingenuity.

Contrasting Styles

Jason Bourne is self-reliant, quick to act, and nearly superhuman. Hezekiah, conversely, was God-reliant, quick to seek the Lord, and unspectacular. When he received a threatening letter from the all-devouring Assyrians, he did not respond with a flurry of activity and desperate battle plans. Rather, he "read it, then went up to the Lord's temple, and spread it out before the Lord" (2 Kings 19:14). Hezekiah acknowledged and praised the Lord, requested His help, and asked that the Lord would be glorified.

Hezekiah believed that the Lord is sovereign over the greatest threats on earth. In response to his faith, the angel of the Lord struck the Assyrians, who left Jerusalem without ever shooting an arrow.

Bottom Line

When troubles arise, bring your problem straight to the Lord. Acknowledge and praise Him, and pray that He be glorified.

Duly Dependent

He gives greater grace. Therefore He says: God resists the proud, but gives grace to the humble. (James 4:6)

Receiving Gifts

It's one thing to be thankful for a gift you might otherwise have bought for yourself, like a DVD your brother-in-law gives you for your birthday. Those gifts are thoughtful and sometimes sentimental, but they don't elicit the kind of thankfulness you feel when you get something entirely outside your power to obtain on your own. That kind of thanksgiving springs from a recognition of your own limitations and the goodness of the giver.

Receiving Grace

At the beginning of His Sermon on the Mount, Jesus said, "The poor in spirit are blessed, for the kingdom of heaven is theirs" (Matt. 5:3). He calls us blessed (approved, favored) when we confess our total dependence on Him. Moreover, when we acknowledge our inability to satisfy our own needs, He tells us that all the resources of heaven are available to supply them.

Abraham Lincoln had the right idea when in his Thanksgiving Proclamation, delivered on October 3, 1863, he urged the country to give God thanks with "humble penitence." Before going on to encourage prayer for the divided nation and the victims of the Civil War, he correctly reminded the people to stop pursuing personal agendas, living as if they controlled their own destinies. Instead, he called them to prostrate themselves before God and give thanks for His provision and promises.

We are undeserving recipients of His grace. We have every reason to be thankful.

Bottom Line

Humility is mandatory to true thanksgiving. Without it we have pride and self-sufficiency, neither of which leave any room for God.

Stewardship vs. Ownership

She proceeded to do according to the word of Elijah. Then the woman, Elijah, and her household ate for many days. (1 Kings 17:15)

First Things First

In 1943, psychologist Abraham Maslow proposed a theory that has since become famous as his Hierarchy of Needs. The theory holds that physiological needs such as food, water, air, shelter, and sleep are most important. Next are the needs for security, which include health and income. All other needs, he contended—such as love, esteem, and self-actualization—become important only after the physiological and security needs have been met.

Believing without Seeing

If Maslow's theory has any merit—and most psychologists agree that it does—then the outrageously generous actions of the widow in 1 Kings 17 defy normal reason. But look at the result! Her oil and flour never ran out because she first gave what she had to the Lord's service. God's principles far surpass the limits of human understanding.

Everything we have belongs to the Lord (see Ps. 24:1). And whether we have plenty or not enough, we are stewards of what He has given us. Before we seek to meet our own needs—however we define *need*—we should first consider what God wants us to do with our resources. Even when we have good cause for not giving above and beyond what is normal for us, God may from time to time, want us to ignore our own reasoning and rely on His. It's a matter of faith.

Bottom Line

There's a balance between prudence and generosity. The key is recognizing what we have as gifts from God and seeing ourselves as stewards.

That's the Ticket

There is salvation in no one else, for there is no other name under heaven given to people, and we must be saved by it. (Acts 4:12)

Great Seats

Ben and his dad had great tickets to a minor league baseball game. They were so close to the action, one of the players tossed them a ball during the game. That's not all. Ben was even chosen from the small crowd to announce, "Play ball!" just before the first pitch. And if that wasn't enough, young Ben also had the chance to race the team mascot around the bases between innings. Ben's dad thought surely that if such special treatment kept up, his son would have had the chance to play third base by the end of the night.

But none of it would've been possible without that ticket.

Truly Priceless

As fun as the baseball game was for Ben and his dad, it pales in comparison to what heaven will be like. Consider the peace and contentment of an eternity spent in Christ's presence. Revelation 21:4 says, "He will wipe away every tear from their eyes. Death will no longer exist; grief, crying, and pain will exist no longer, because the previous things have passed away." Peace and joy forever. Wow!

That's humbling, isn't it? What's most incredible, however, is that there's no cost to you for such complete and utter joy. Your cost of admission has already been picked up by Christ's death, burial, and resurrection. There's no need to camp out or line up around the block. The ticket is yours for the asking!

Bottom Line

Your entry into heaven has already been bought and paid for by Jesus Christ. Take some time to thank Him for that today.

Big Praying

*Do not say: "I am only a youth," for you will go to everyone
I send you to and speak whatever I tell you. (Jer. 1:7)*

The Shrinking Prayer

If you have a son or daughter who has become a prodigal, who has wandered far from both family and faith, your praying may gravitate toward basic appeals. You're just asking God to minimize the fallout—praying that she won't get pregnant outside of marriage, that he will avoid further trouble with the law, that they will get over their addictions, that they will stop wrecking their lives.

But our kids deserve bigger, better prayers than that—prayers that God delights in answering, prayers that go beyond damage control.

Ask Outlandishly

Jeremiah was young when God called him as a prophet. Daniel was a youth, and Samuel was just a boy. God can do amazing things with and through teens—more than just keeping them out of trouble. So pray big. Pray that God overwhelms their rebel heart with a powerful revelation of His grace and love. Pray that God will use your kid—even if he is in total rebellion right now—to touch the lives of countless people with the message of redemption, forgiveness, and a God who specializes in giving fresh starts.

Some of the deepest, most committed Christians in your church likely had a period of wasted years in their past; yet God's love got through to them. So ask Him to do it again. Pray large and audacious prayers for your kids, knowing that you have a large and audacious God.

Bottom Line

No matter how far they wander, the hope remains of God working a profound and deep change in your kids. Keep praying for that.

Leading Roles

The Most High is ruler over the kingdom of men,
and He gives it to anyone He wants. (Dan. 4:25)

The Test of Leadership

The Bible makes it clear that God places rulers in their positions. This does not mean they are all good leaders; some are profoundly evil. And when they stand before God in judgment, they will have much to answer for.

When God allows someone great authority, it is a test of leadership. In the passage surrounding today's verse, King Nebuchadnezzar of Babylon failed the test miserably. Many leaders likewise fail. Israel had some awful rulers, too, but some (like David and Joseph) had a heart for God and for the good of the people. Whether good or bad, however, these leaders have their positions by the providence of God, and they hold their authority only as long as He allows it. So keep a sense of perspective whether your candidate wins or loses during election season.

The Leader in You

You may not hold an elected office, but God has nevertheless placed you in a sphere of leadership and influence. If you are married, you are the leader of your family. If you are single, you have friends, coworkers, and fellow Christians who are continually influenced by your leadership. Like it or not, you are a leader. Take that seriously as you interact with those God has placed in your life. You have an incredible capacity to influence people for good, but you will only be a good leader if you submit to the leadership of the Lord in your own life.

Bottom Line

To varying degrees, God has entrusted all men with a leadership role. He will richly reward those who lead well.

Total You Makeover

*To all who did receive Him, He gave them the right
to be children of God, to those who believe in His name,
who were born, not of blood, or of the will of the flesh,
or of the will of man, but of God. (John 1:12–13)*

No Equals

We live in a pluralistic world where any and all beliefs, life-styles, philosophies, and religious and political systems are held to be of equal value and must be tolerated and accepted. Further, it is common for individuals to hold different and sometimes widely divergent religious positions. There are those who will attend a Christian church on a Sunday morning, then some other religious service during the week, and may engage in all kinds of religious practices derived from Eastern and New Age religions. Such people will claim to hold Jesus in high regard but treat Him as one religious option among many.

All of Us

Over against the pluralism, religious syncretism, and wide-spread moral and spiritual confusion of our culture stands the clarity and authority of Jesus Christ, the Son of God, the only way to the Father (see John 14:6). Jesus creates a whole new spiritual race comprised of every people group on the planet. He's not out to add one more religious option to the mix.

The radical nature of His mission is described in 2 Corinthians 5:17, where His people are said to be a "new creation"—that is, in Christ we become something we weren't before. "You are a chosen race, a royal priesthood, a holy nation, a people for His possession" (1 Pet. 2:9). That's a pretty thorough overhaul of the old you.

Bottom Line

Walk in the newness of life that Christ alone brings.

Thrown to the Lions

They brought Daniel and threw him into the lions' den. (Dan. 6:16)

When Bad Things Happen

From everything we understand about Daniel, he was doing everything right, was utterly pleasing to God, and yet was thrown to the lions nevertheless. Every man who loves and serves God can learn a lesson from Daniel. Too many guys assume God is punishing them or has abandoned them when the storms of life hit. We rail at God or simply withdraw from Him in pain and confusion. We so easily forget we have an enemy who is out to "steal and to kill and to destroy" us (John 10:10). We forget we live in a fallen world where bad things do happen to "good" people. We forget that most of life is waged on a battlefield, not wasted in a man cave.

Faith Builders

God wants to build a muscular faith in us, and He often does it by allowing us to be thrust into dire straits. He is not toying with us or punishing us. He is making us deeper and better and stronger, and we need to stop resenting Him because of it.

Ever have a coach work you really hard to improve you? Ever have a drill sergeant push you to the limit to turn you into a competent soldier? That's what God is up to on a far larger and more important scale. Believe that He loves you and has your best interests at heart when He puts you through spiritual boot camp. If we trusted our coach, we can certainly trust our God.

Bottom Line

You gain spiritual strength when your faith is given a workout through life's trials.

God-blessed Finances

When will I also do something for my own family? (Gen. 30:30)

Jacob's Concern

Every man is concerned about his family and fortune. In Genesis 30–31, the patriarch Jacob had grown a sizable family for which he was responsible. To accomplish his desires and dreams, Jacob needed to make money. So he made a seemingly impossible financial arrangement with his father-in-law (see Gen. 30:31–33), and yet God blessed Jacob so that he was able to provide for his family (v. 43).

In frightening economic days many men are concerned about their finances and their ability to take care of their families. And while wise financial planning is crucial, the most important element in financial success is the blessing of God.

Jacob's Secret

Jacob serves as an excellent example to men who are concerned about their finances. First, he was willing to begin with nothing plus God—"You don't need to give me anything" (Gen. 30:31). Is God your main resource? Second, he was willing to work—"You know how hard I have worked for you" (30:26). Are you a hard worker? God blesses diligence. Third, he was honest—"my honesty will testify for me" (30:33). Are you willing for your integrity to answer for you? Fourth, Jacob honored God in the tithe—as a young man starting out, he made a vow to put God first in his finances (28:22). The ingredients for Jacob's financial success were dependence on God, hard work, and honesty, wrapped in an opportunity.

Bottom Line

Depend on God for guidance with your finances.

Honor Your Wife

Husbands are to love their wives as their own bodies.
He who loves his wife loves himself. (Eph. 5:28)

Priceless Treasure

What priceless treasure do you have in your possession? A first edition of Melville's *Moby Dick*? A Ming Dynasty porcelain vase? A reconditioned '67 Mustang convertible? Whatever it may be, you treat your prized possessions with tender care and great respect.

On your wedding day you pledged your vows of love, commitment, honor, and faithfulness to your wife. To honor your wife is to make a decision to place high value and importance on her. Love involves putting that decision into action. By treating her as a priceless gift, you grant her a position worthy of great respect and a high place of honor in your life.

Persistent Care

As the marriage continues, this value of honor must forever be guarded and extended. Never take your wife for granted. Recognize the intrinsic worth she brings to the relationship. Recall the sacrifices and contributions she has made to your well-being and to your growth and development as a person. Has she done more than you have given her credit for? You continually extend honor to her by recognizing her accomplishments, speaking about her with respect, extending common courtesies, praying for her, supporting her new ventures, and overlooking her shortcomings. And the best part is that your wife will love you all the more as you honor her.

Bottom Line

Marriage is for better and for worse. The better part of marriage comes by extending this virtue of honor. Make it a hallmark of your marriage.

Job Hunt

The one who hires a fool or who hires those passing by is like an archer who wounds everyone. (Prov. 26:10)

Will to Work

If you have never been unemployed, you probably know somebody who has been—or is. As you look at your own career or try to help a friend get his on track, remember that God created us to work. He gifts each person with skills that can be used in the workplace and for His glory. Developing those skills so they fit into the current job market is a challenge, yes, but we must never give up. Even in the hardest, most discouraging, and desperate of times, God is still crafting us for usefulness.

On the Mark

Having faith in God and in the talents He's given you can help you through a lengthy job search or during other difficult times in life. The financial constraints we feel during a season of uncertainty can cause us to lose sight of these basic truths, and the time constraints we place on God's ability to act can twist our perspectives. But if we know we're working to improve our skills, if we know we're praying for God's direction, if we know we're willing to follow Him wherever He takes us, He can cause this ordeal to become preparation time for fulfilling His dreams for our lives.

While companies and employers are busy making their hiring decisions, trying to be smart with who they add to their payroll (as the verse above from Proverbs attests), we can be sure that when they hire us, they are taking on a person grown wiser for what he's been through.

Bottom Line

Look to God for guidance in your career and when you're helping others who are searching for work.

Screen Glare

*The LORD spoke with Moses face to face, just as a man
speaks with his friend. (Exod. 33:11)*

Face Out

Late-night talk-show host Conan O'Brien once joked that
Facebook, Twitter, and YouTube were joining forces to cre-
ate one huge time-wasting website. The new site was called:
YouTwitFace.

While O'Brien's joke is obviously funny, the amount of
time teens spend in front of a computer, cell phone, or tablet
screen is no laughing matter. Oxford University neuroscientist
Susan Greenfield believes it can be harmful. She says repeated
exposure to social networking can actually damage children's
brains. Her research suggests that sites such as Facebook can
decrease attention spans, encourage instant gratification, and
foster self-centeredness.

Face-to-Face

As fathers we must set limits for our children, especially
when it comes to potentially detrimental behaviors. While the
computer can make homework and research easier, too much
screen time hinders our children's social abilities. Personal relationships and communication skills are best formed face-to-face.
As the verse above reminds us, "The LORD spoke with Moses
face to face, just as a man speaks with his friend." God is a personal God. He spoke to Moses personally, and He wants us to
build relationships the same way. When our children make real-
world friends, they're better equipped to succeed in the future.
Encourage your children to spend more face-to-face time with
friends.

Bottom Line

Do your children spend too much time on the computer?
Set limits and enforce the rules so they'll learn better friendship
skills.

A Little Compassion

As a father has compassion on his children, so the LORD has compassion on those who fear Him. (Ps. 103:13)

Fork in the Road

Grace is kind and compassionate, while the law is harsh and demanding. Too many Christian dads believe in grace on a theological and intellectual level but practice law when it comes to parenting. This is especially true for guys who were not raised in a grace-enriched home. Without really thinking about it, we can default to whatever dysfunction we grew up with.

"Laying down the law" seems to work—for awhile. But fear gets old with time, and it breeds the rebellion dads are hoping to prevent. Grace does not mean being a pushover, or not having standards. Instead, grace builds on love and relationship. A child will do for love and relationship what he would never do out of mere fear and duty.

The Path of Grace

Remember what it was like to be in your kids' shoes? School can be a place of bullies, peer pressure, fear of failure, raging hormones, petty gossip, and getting picked last for the game. You may have had a hard day at work, but your kid may also have had a hard day at school. Grace calls us to listen and engage, to be kind, thoughtful, and empathetic toward them, helping our children learn to do the right things for the right reasons. Only parenting with grace can meet that challenge.

Bottom Line

Your heavenly Father relates to you with love, grace, and forgiveness, and He wants you to do likewise with your kids.

Isn't She Lovely?

You are absolutely beautiful, my darling. (Song of Songs 4:7)

Say the Words

"You are beautiful." At every stage of her life, your wife needs to hear those words from you. Just as you easily commented on her beauty when your love was new, she needs you to affirm it in the decades of raising kids. And when you are both retired and wrinkled, she still needs to hear how lovely you find her to be.

Aging can be hard on anyone, but in a culture that almost worships youthfulness, it can be especially hard on a woman as she sees the difference between herself and the airbrushed models that are held out as the standard for beauty. She may struggle to feel she's measuring up—that she's still beautiful. You can help!

Words of Blessing

A woman is reassured when she hears her husband say she is beautiful. Beauty involves so much more than mere appearance. Tell her all of the wonderful, ageless characteristics you find so appealing about her. And as you age, remind each other often that we look forward to a future when God will give us new, glorious, eternal bodies. The years will take a toll on all of us, but God will more than reverse it. We are God's church, His bride, and while He sees us as beautiful right now, He will makes us so glorious in the not-too-distant future that even the angels will be struck with awe.

Bottom Line

Your wife needs to hear you say the words, "You are absolutely beautiful to me." Say it today, and say it often.

Perfect Peace

*You will keep the mind that is dependent on You in perfect peace,
for it is trusting in You. (Isa. 26:3)*

Peace Is Possible

The alarm goes off and the race begins. You rush to get ready for work, maybe scarfing down a quick breakfast if you can, your mind already thinking of all the things you need to get done today. Then you enter the rush of traffic. Why you're competing with other drivers, you don't know. But by the time you arrive at work, you're already a little revved up, maybe even a little agitated too. At least the adrenaline pumping through your veins will help you get stuff done, because you have a lot to do.

Obviously this scenario is not a recipe for living the day with a peaceful heart. When we live at breakneck speed all the time, experiencing the peace of God is all but impossible.

The Better Way

Most of us know we're out of balance in this regard, but honestly, it can almost seem easier than slowing down and fixing our thoughts on God. Of course, that kind of thinking is practical atheism—living as if God doesn't exist and can't help us!

It's time to change our thinking and living so we can experience the peace of God our hearts truly long for. How this happens for each of us will vary depending on circumstances. Ask God to show you some specific ways to help you change your pattern of living. Trust Him to help you.

Bottom Line

God's peace is available to every Christian. It's a matter of fixing our thoughts on Him and depending on Him in all things.

A Successful Career

*The LORD was with Joseph, and he became
a successful man. (Gen. 39:2)*

What Constitutes Success?

A recent survey of 27,500 randomly selected people representing 198 occupations found that the most satisfying careers
are those involving caring for, teaching, and protecting others.
The world speaks of success as being the ability to have whatever
you want whenever you want it. However, this jaded concept
of life does not correlate with true happiness and success in a
career. Success consists in achieving God-given goals that help
people. There's deep satisfaction in that.

Joseph's Success

The Scripture says that Joseph, the Old Testament son of
Jacob, "became a successful man." How? Why? Because "the
LORD was with Joseph." Early in life Joseph had dreams that
God had great things planned for him (see Gen. 37:5–11). And
yet he was thrown in a pit (37:24), sold into slavery (37:36), and
falsely imprisoned (39:6–20). Life is not easy, and careers are
often endangered by unfortunate events, but if we maintain our
faith, the opportunity for true success is always within reach.

Joseph's success was the result of pleasing God. Making
money was not his focus. Even though tough times came, he
held on to his integrity and his involvement with others (39:5;
39:21–23). No wonder he was exalted in his career (41:39–45).
What do you want out of life? Know that God wants you to
succeed, but success will always be on His terms, as He defines it.

Bottom Line

Life at its best must be a life of unselfish service, a life willing to share with others, a life that witnesses for Christ, a life of
love and faithfulness.

Is God a Prude?

*God created man in His own image; He created him in the image
of God; He created them male and female. (Gen. 1:27)*

The Big Surprise

A greeting card had the word *sex* in big letters on the outside. When opened, it read, "Now that I've got your attention, Happy Birthday!" Perhaps nothing grabs our minds, our emotions, and our actions like sex. It causes the blood pressure to rise; it causes us to squirm.

Many people think that when it comes to sex, God is the ultimate killjoy. This may surprise you, but God invented the idea and the act of sex. From the beginning, God created humankind as male and female. What it means to be man, what it means to be woman—emotionally, intellectually, physically—that difference comes from God Himself. Men and women are different by God's design.

The Startling Truth

If sex is God's idea, then it must be good and not bad; it's OK to talk about it, and it's OK to enjoy it. In fact, we would not be here if it were not for sex. God made us different so that our differences would attract us to each other. Celebrate those differences. Thank God for your wife. Enjoy your love. Remember that sex is a beautiful expression of devotion and affection between husband and wife. God knew what He was doing when He created men and women differently, and He knew what He was doing when He created sex. He's no prude, and neither should we be. So don't be ashamed of your sexuality. It's good.

Bottom Line

Sex is God's gift to you and your wife.

Pursuing the Prize

*I pursue as my goal the prize promised
by God's heavenly call in Christ Jesus. (Phil. 3:14)*

The Best Life

If a life of regret is a miserable existence, the best kind of life is a life of purpose. Our hearts desperately want to pursue something worthwhile. In a way you can look at the whole sorry history of the human race and trace every problem back to a lack of purpose or a failure to pursue the right purpose. In fact, that's what idolatry is—a failure to value and pursue that which is most valuable, namely, God.

Every Christian has been blessed with a clear and compelling purpose. And that purpose is, as Paul puts it, to "pursue as my goal the prize promised by God's heavenly call in Christ Jesus." What does that mean? Well, from the larger context of this passage and the rest of the Scriptures, it means we're called to know God through Jesus Christ. Along with that knowledge—the intimate relationship God wants with each one of us—comes our specific callings as we follow Jesus in every sphere of life.

Clearly Simpler

When we know why we're here, it makes things a whole lot simpler. It gives us the possibility of focus, effectiveness, and joy, provided we act on the knowledge we've been given. Like Paul, we need our purpose fixed firmly in our minds, and then we need to pursue it with everything in us. This is the path to an obedient, God-glorifying, joyful, fruitful life. Go hard after the prize.

Bottom Line

A life of purpose is based on God's Word. It is not something we dream up ourselves. Your purpose is to know Jesus and pursue your calling in Him.

The Death Trap

*He follows her impulsively like an ox going to the slaughter,
like a deer bounding toward a trap until an arrow
pierces its liver, like a bird darting into a snare—
he doesn't know it will cost him his life. (Prov. 7:22–23)*

The Warning

Solomon warned his young son in the verse above to beware of any woman who would lead him into sexual sin. Notice three key words in Solomon's warning: *slaughter*, *trap*, and *snare*. Have you ever visited a slaughter house? It can make the strongest people lose their lunch. Have you heard the desperate yelp of an animal caught in a trap? It will do something to your heart. Have you seen a bird ensnared, unable to free itself? It is a pitiful and tragic sight. All of these illustrations are meant to drive home the point that engaging in sexual immorality comes with painful consequences.

The Toll

There was once a man who had been a leader in a Christian organization until he fell into sexual immorality. He was asked, "What could have been done to prevent this?" He paused for a moment, then said with haunting pain and precision, "If only I had really known, really thought, what it would cost me and my family and my Lord, I honestly believe I never would have done it." Take a moment and consider the consequences of sexual immorality. The toll on your body. The grief to the Holy Spirit. The damage to your reputation. The hurt to your family. Do you really want to travel down that road?

Bottom Line

The next time you are tempted to cross the line, rehearse the possible consequences of your actions.

Mellowness of Heart

*Rest in God alone, my soul, for my hope comes
from Him. He alone is my rock and my salvation,
my stronghold; I will not be shaken. (Ps. 62:5–6)*

Busy Man

You have responsibilities and concerns and things to get
done. That's good. God designed you to carry responsibility, and
you're happiest when you're doing that well. Moreover, your
character grows as you do what you're supposed to do even when
it is difficult, inconvenient, and tiring.

There's no utopia on earth. Most of us are not living in
monasteries where we can devote hours of our day to quiet
reflection and prayer. That's the reality. And that's not what God
is calling most of us to anyway. He wants His people out in the
world being salt and light and serving others in love. But that
doesn't mean He wants His people burned out, exhausted, distracted, and discouraged.

Mellow Heart

There's a way to live a restful life amid all the stress and
busyness. One author described this as living with "mellowness
of heart." That's a good description. It's the complete opposite
of living with a distracted, striving heart. It means experiencing the "rest" God has provided us by salvation, not only in
spiritual terms but in practical living. It means learning to take
little breaks throughout the day to recalibrate. Even taking two
minutes to read some Scripture and pray can work wonders in
slowing you down and giving you some perspective on what's
important. Remember, your wisdom and strength come from
the Lord.

Bottom Line

Returning to the Lord and resting in Him is something we
can do even as we carry out our many responsibilities. We can't
afford not to.

Fire and Water

I will be with you when you pass through the waters, and when you pass through the rivers, they will not overwhelm you. You will not be scorched when you walk through the fire, and the flame will not burn you. (Isa. 43:2)

Importance of Faith

In this life a relationship with God is through faith alone. At present, we do not see Him face-to-face; that time is coming. But for now faith is our sole means of knowing Him. "The one who draws near to Him must believe that He exists and rewards those who seek Him" (Heb. 11:6).

The Lord wants us to have strong faith because in His eyes nothing is more important for us than our relationship with Him—not our health, careers, or even our families. Is it any wonder, then, that He crafts circumstances to strengthen our faith?

Strengthening Agent

Our muscles do not grow stronger through the comfort of a massage. Our muscles strengthen only through willful, effortful response to resistance. If there's no resistance, no growth. No pain, no gain. The same is true with our faith. If God only blessed us with riches, health, and success, our faith would atrophy because we'd forget that we need Him. Like muscles wasting away, our faith would become weak and ineffective.

Though trials of faith don't feel like a blessing, the result is like that of disciplined gym work. "Consider it a great joy, my brothers, whenever you experience various trials, knowing that the testing of your faith produces endurance" (James 1:2–3).

Bottom Line

All Christians face trials. Yet whether fire or water, we won't be devoured, for God is with us. And the result is a deeper, more mature faith in Him.

When You're Tempted

Run from sexual immorality! (1 Cor. 6:18)

The Response

Illicit sex is like TNT. Dangerous. Destructive. Deadly. Some people think they can play with it and not get hurt. Some people think they can walk right up to the line and have the willpower not to cross over. Venturing close to sexual temptation is a proverbial no-man's land. You are playing a personal game of Russian roulette.

When it comes to sexual temptation, the Bible is clear on the appropriate response. "Run from sexual immorality!" Don't debate it. Don't resist it. Don't see how close to the line you can get. Don't flirt with it. Don't reason. Don't rationalize. Run. Run fast. Run hard. Run away from it. Run!

The Boundaries

Therefore, avoid certain films, images, and magazines. Turn off certain television shows and late-night channels. Pass up certain Internet sites. Steer clear of certain people. Let's face it, some settings are too tempting, some touches too personal, and some liberties are too much for us to handle.

We should know our weaknesses and establish boundaries to keep us from crossing the line. By the way, these boundaries are easier to establish in your stronger moments than in your weaker ones. If you haven't already done so, why don't you take a moment and establish those boundaries now? They can be one of your keys to victory.

Bottom Line

What practical steps do you need to take to make you stronger in your battle with sexual temptation? Start taking them immediately!

Momentum

Whatever your hands find to do, do with all your strength, because there is no work, planning, knowledge, or wisdom in Sheol where you are going. (Eccles. 9:10)

Procrastination Kills

If you always wait until you feel like doing something, you won't get much done. And what's more, the rest and freedom you seek from not doing it won't give you the happiness you hoped. The truth is, life is full of resistance. There are "thorns and thistles" everywhere we must fight through (see Gen. 3:18). And because facing tedious tasks and unpleasant responsibilities isn't much fun, procrastination and avoidance are constant temptations.

As with any temptation, though, they are based on a lie—namely, the lie that we can escape pain and frustration if we pretend our obligations don't exist. But as we all know in our saner moments, living in unreality doesn't make things better; it only makes things worse. The Bible is the best reality check there is.

A Matter of Obedience

Taking care of business in our lives is not just a means to the end of greater personal effectiveness, increased happiness, and the ever elusive peace of mind we all want. It's a matter of obedience. God wants us to fulfill our responsibilities. It's all part of being enrolled in His school of character building. Speaking of school, can you remember when you were a kid and you knew you had homework to do, but you weren't doing it? It tainted your play. It's the same way for grown ups.

Bottom Line

Nike had it right: sometimes we've got to "just do it." God has given you a Spirit-empowered will that is capable of obedient action.

Seeing Clearly

The eye is the lamp of the body. If your eye is good,
your whole body will be full of light. (Matt. 6:22)

The Power of Truth

How you look at life can make all the difference. Jesus certainly taught that. In Matthew 6:19–21, He told the disciples not to pursue earthly treasures because they're so fleeting. He then went on to inform them that they can't serve both God and money. Besides, since God is their Father and He promises to take care of them, there's really no reason for them to worry about money or their life or anything else.

What Jesus is doing—both for His original listeners as well as for us—is giving us a large dose of truth that could potentially change how we see everything in life. The key is having "good eyes" with which to see the truth of His teaching and believe it.

How This Plays Out

We need truth in every area of life, but let's take a look at just one: entitlement versus gift. Sadly the natural human bent is not toward gratitude but toward ingratitude. We think we deserve certain things. And generally speaking, the more we have, the more we think we deserve what we have and more. In other words we operate with a sense of entitlement—people owe us, the world owes us, God owes us. But the truth is, everything we have is a gift—our possessions, our relationships, our lives. We need clear eyes to see that. Ask God to help you see clearly.

Bottom Line

Make sure you're seeing life the way God sees it. Make sure you're allowing the light of His Word to shine into your life.

Faith Matters

Real Faith

Dietrich Bonhoeffer got it right—belief and obedience go hand in hand. Biblical faith is a living, breathing, vibrant thing. It's believing God is really there and He's good. It's trusting God's Word implicitly. And as today's verse makes plain, we have absolutely no chance of pleasing God apart from faith.

Faith is what saves and sanctifies us. (To be more precise, the object of our faith—Jesus—is *who* saves us and sanctifies us, though faith is instrumental.) Faith is what produces obedience, which in turn grows our faith, which leads to greater obedience. To sum it up, if we're not really living by faith, we're not really living the normal Christian life as defined by the Bible.

The Nature of Faith

What else can we say about faith? Probably the closest thing to a definition of faith in the Bible occurs in Hebrews 11:1: "Faith is the reality of what is hoped for, the proof of what is not seen." The things to which our faith points are real and true, although they cannot yet be fully seen or experienced. Faith has an element of unrealized yet certain hope. And just what are we hoping for? Our full and final salvation in Jesus. It's not in any doubt—the Scriptures assure us of that—but we don't yet enjoy our full freedom as the children of God. That's coming.

Bottom Line

The Christian life is from faith to faith. It begins with setting aside our distrust of God and believing the gospel, and it proceeds with more of the same.

Biblical Optimism

Every one of God's promises is "Yes" in Him.
Therefore, the "Amen" is also spoken through
Him by us for God's glory. (2 Cor. 1:20)

More than Positive Thinking

Biblical optimism is utterly realistic. It knows that everything may not be great at the moment, but that doesn't mean things won't be great later because God is great and His promises are greatly to be trusted. This means we don't have to pretend that the bad things we experience in life are somehow good in and of themselves. They're not. They're bad. They're the result of living in a fallen world. We just need to believe that every one of God's promises is true, including this familiar one in Romans 8:28: "We know that all things work together for the good of those who love God: those who are called according to His purpose."

Living with Confidence

Practically speaking, the Christian should be of good cheer. We can be confident that God is with us no matter what. We can hold our heads high, not ceding the ground of promised blessing but living in the shadow of future glory and victory.

Our number-one enemy is the devil and his continuous stream of lies. When we listen to him, we become discouraged. We temporarily forfeit the victory that is ours in Jesus. But there's no reason for this to happen, to let him get in our heads. Not every thought that enters your mind originated with you. Just speak the truth to yourself and move on.

Bottom Line

A Christian has every reason to be optimistic because God's promises in Christ are all true. So stand firm in your confidence no matter what.

Marriage Marathon

*Endurance must do its complete work, so that you may
be mature and complete, lacking nothing. (James 1:4)*

Couples, Take Your Mark

If you're married, think back to your wedding day. As you
stood in front of your family and friends, you may have felt like a
sprinter ready to bolt down the aisle and start a new life together.
But as you've gone through a few years of married life, you've
probably discovered that marriage isn't a sprint—it's a marathon.
You've got to pace yourself.

As the world record holders for the longest marriage,
nobody knows this better than Herbert and Zelmyra Fisher. A
couple of years ago, they answered some questions on Twitter.
When asked about what they do after a bad relationship day
in their marriage, they said, "Remember, marriage is not a con-
test—never keep score. God has put the two of you together on
the same team to win."

Relational Endurance

Winning in marriage, just like winning a marathon, takes
endurance. Married life will have its share of uphill climbs. So
the next time you find yourself working hard and out of breath
in your marriage, it doesn't mean you should give up. It just
means you need to dig deep and show some endurance. James
1:4 reminds us "endurance must do its complete work." When
you're facing an uphill battle in your marriage, keep going! You'll
find that God will give you as many second winds as you need
when you continue to endure in His strength.

Bottom Line

Stay committed to finishing the "race" of your marriage.
Winning means crossing the finish line together.

Parenting Time

Be on your guard and diligently watch yourselves,
so that you don't forget the things your eyes have seen
and so that they don't slip from your mind as long as you live.
Teach them to your children and your grandchildren. (Deut. 4:9)

Making the Most of Your Time

Spending time with our children is a good thing. An Oxford University study showed that fathers today spend as much as ten times more time with their kids than dads did in 1975. But are we making the most of our time? Is the time we spend with them meaningful?

Being together can create lasting bonds, but we must be intentional. Research shows family dinners are less common. When families do eat together, the television is often on. Time spent watching movies has also increased. As fathers, we must capitalize on our time with our children, even if it isn't as much as we'd like sometimes. And as today's verse says, we need to diligently watch ourselves so we don't become spiritually lazy and fail to teach our kids how to live biblically through our example and words.

Spend It Well

Just as Moses encouraged God's people to teach their children about the things they had seen God do in their lives, we must do the same. Tell your kids how God is active and real in your life. Pass down the stories of God's goodness to your family. Discuss deep spiritual issues with them. Ask them questions about their faith. By helping to build a spiritual foundation in your children, you'll know you are spending your time well.

Bottom Line

Think of a conversation you've been wanting to have with your kids; then go have it.

You've Got Talent

*I was afraid and went off and hid your talent in the ground.
Look, you have what is yours. (Matt. 25:25)*

Use It or Lose It

During the latter part of Jesus' ministry, He told His disciples about a man going on a journey. The man called his servants together and gave the first servant five talents (a measure of currency). Another received two, while another got one. A talent was a weight of precious metal that some experts believe was worth $250,000. So even the servant with one talent had nothing to complain about.

The first two servants put the money to work and doubled it. But the last servant didn't even try to increase his talent—just buried it in the ground, then dug it back up unchanged when his boss returned. The master immediately took away the talent and gave it to the man with ten.

Investing Your Talent

Can you see yourself in this story? Which man are you? God entrusts us with many things. He expects us to be good stewards and do the best we can with His talents. Instead of being fearful during tough economic times, we need to be looking for ways to invest in God's kingdom. Hiding our money in the ground won't benefit the Master, and it won't help His investment grow. Pray for godly wisdom and always seek to use your money and resources to serve God and His kingdom. Ultimately, He has provided everything we have so we shouldn't fear losing it.

Bottom Line

While fear keeps us from using our talents, faith multiplies talent. Be faithful with what God has given you.

Listening Device

"Why were you searching for Me?" He asked them. "Didn't you know that I had to be in My Father's house?" But they did not understand what He said to them. (Luke 2:49–50)

Listen to Your Child

What's the average twelve-year-old boy like? Awkward. Gangly. Not a small boy, not a full-blown teen. Not polished in social situations or filled out with an athletic physique. Jesus was once a tweenager. Even His own parents didn't understand what He said!

But God can and does speak to believing children no matter their age. Obviously Jesus had been listening to His heavenly Father. He had hung back at His Father's house to listen to the teachers, ask questions, and come up with a few relevant answers on His own. How can we cultivate a listening spirit in our kids?

Help Them Listen to God

First, we must believe God really does speak to young believers. When a child has God's Word in his heart, the Holy Spirit can bring it to mind at the right time. And it's best for them to learn this trait young because if they ignore God's voice, it becomes harder and harder to hear Him the older they get.

So teach them the Scriptures. And while you're doing that, teach them to pray for God to make His voice clear to them. Explain to them that Jesus is the "Good Shepherd" (see John 10:1–18) and that we as His sheep can recognize His voice. Finally, remind them that God loves them so much He'll never stop speaking to them. He desires to speak with all His children.

Bottom Line

One of the greatest things you can do for your children is help them discern the voice of God.

Follow the Wise Men

*Entering the house, they saw the child with
Mary His mother, and falling to their knees, they worshiped Him.
Then they opened their treasures and presented Him with gifts:
gold, frankincense, and myrrh. (Matt. 2:11)*

Bring Him Gifts

No manger scene is complete without them. But many experts agree that the wise men didn't see Jesus until He was a toddler in Bethlehem. No matter when these robed visitors met the Christ child, we can still learn a lot from their actions. They risked their lives on a long journey to bring treasures to the new king.

And not only should we be willing to risk everything for Jesus and fall to our knees in reverence for the one true God, but we should also act like the magi when we give gifts to the king.

Be a Wise Man

Look at their gifts: gold, myrrh, and frankincense. By giving God our gold, we help fund His work. Monetary gifts to churches and ministries spread God's truth around the world. In Jesus' day, myrrh was believed to strengthen children. When we love our kids, encourage them with our words, and help them build a relationship with Jesus, we develop the next generation of Christ followers. Finally, frankincense was incense used for worship. God desires our worship not only on special holidays but throughout the year. The magi gave extravagant gifts to the king, and we should give extravagantly too.

Bottom Line

Follow the wise men's example in giving God your finances, family, and worship. Do you need to work on giving any part of your life over to God?

Known by God

If anyone loves God, he is known by Him. (1 Cor. 8:3)

Letting God In

God created us to have a relationship with Him. He wants to be close to us. Our sin is the only thing that separates us from Him, and Jesus took care of that problem once and for all by dying on the cross for us (see 1 Pet. 3:18). So the door for fellowship is wide open. We're even urged to "approach the throne of grace with boldness, so that we may receive mercy and find grace to help us at the proper time" (Heb. 4:16). But we often hold back.

We are always the limiting factor in our relationship with God. He's not cold or distant, too busy or unavailable. But we often are. We tend to reject God's overtures for intimacy. Sometimes we know our lives are displeasing to Him, and we don't want to deal with it. We feel like that's all He'll want to talk about. If we're ever going to know God deeply, though, we need to be willing to engage with Him as we are, not as we'd like to be. He can work with that. He's not expecting perfect people.

Trusting Other People

We don't often make the connection between intimacy with other people and intimacy with God, but there is an inextricable connection between the two. If we can't trust other people with ourselves, even the parts we don't like, we'll have a hard time trusting God with ourselves too. That's just how God has designed things. So we've got to be willing to risk.

Bottom Line

Allowing ourselves to be known by God and others feels risky, but it's the only way our relationships grow.

Spun Out

Even a fool is considered wise when he keeps silent, discerning, when he seals his lips. (Prov. 17:28)

Eraser Boy

The phone rang, and the caller ID said it was his son's school. Apparently, his boy had been scratching his ear with a pencil when the eraser came off and got stuck inside his ear cavity. After a mad dash to school and some amateur doctor work, the thing still wouldn't budge. It took a trip to a real doctor the next day, a specialist even, to get it removed. No, really, you can't make this stuff up!

In the end, however, it was just another "surprise" that happens every day to somebody. Yes, the eraser-in-the-ear episode was frustrating for the young man's parents, but it happened. They dealt with it and then went on about the business of being a family. If this was the worst thing they ever faced, life was indeed good.

Champ

There's more to the story, however. Less than an hour after getting the eraser stuck, the boy finished third in the school spelling bee with it still in his ear. That may not have happened had a mountain been made out of that molehill by ranting and raving about it.

Proverbs 10:19 says, "When there are many words, sin is unavoidable, but the one who controls his lips is wise." How many times have you been in a situation where the smallest things turned into a major problem because of a poor split-second reaction? Next time, think before you speak. You'll be amazed at the difference some self-control makes.

Bottom Line

Don't let life's everyday surprises spin your day—and your life—out of control.

The Waiting Game

I waited patiently for the LORD, and He turned to me and heard my cry for help. (Ps. 40:1)

Waiting Is Not Unusual

We spend a lot of our lives waiting. Waiting in traffic. Waiting at the doctor's office, the post office, or (heaven help us) the DMV. Most of this kind of waiting seems like a waste of time. It feels frustrating and fruitless to us—and it often is, although it can be an opportunity to pray for patience and for the people around us. (Tip: Always have a book with you. When you're stuck waiting somewhere, redeem the time by reading. Your stress level will go down, and your wisdom level will go up.)

No one can deny that waiting is a big part of life. And not just the trivial, inconvenient kind of waiting, but waiting for the big, important things—things we believe God desires to bring about and eventually will in His time.

Waiting Is Not Doing Nothing

As Psalm 40:1 says, we're to wait "patiently." This doesn't mean passively though. It's active waiting. It's a trusting, praying, working, believing kind of waiting that means doing everything possible to align our desires with His, knowing full well that He is ultimately in control and that His timing is perfect. As we wait patiently, we are assured that God hears our cries for help. And because we know His character—wise and good—we know He knows what He's doing and will bring about the best result at the best possible time.

Bottom Line

Waiting is difficult. It can seem like God has forgotten about us. He hasn't though. And as we learn to wait patiently, our faith and our character grow.

Good Health

Dear friend, I pray that you may prosper in every way and be in good health physically just as you are spiritually. (3 John 2)

Body and Soul

We tend to take our health for granted until we get sick or are in pain. We can't help but pay attention then. But the thing we don't often realize is just how important our bodies are to our spiritual life. You really can't separate the immaterial part of us from the material. We are both body and soul, and each affects the other.

Proverbs 17:22 says, "A joyful heart is good medicine, but a broken spirit dries up the bones." We may not completely understand the connection between emotional health and physical health, but that doesn't mean it isn't real. Our emotions affect our body profoundly. Likewise, taking care of our physical bodies can do our souls a lot of good. Paul says in 1 Timothy 4:8 that "the training of the body has a limited benefit, but godliness is beneficial in every way." Yes, training the body has its limits, but it is beneficial!

Pay Attention

We need to learn to pay attention to what's going on in our body. Are we tense? Why? What are we thinking about that is causing us to take shallow breaths? What is causing our stomach to churn? We often talk about having a "gut feeling" about something. That's more than just figurative language. That's real. That's our God-given intuition in action. Same thing with having a "broken heart." We can actually feel emotional pain in our heart; it's not just a physical organ that pumps out blood. Our bodies speak to us.

Bottom Line

If we neglect our bodies, we neglect our souls.

Ongoing Prayer

*Pray at all times in the Spirit with every prayer and request,
and stay alert in this with all perseverance
and intercession for all the saints. (Eph. 6:18)*

Constant

Ephesians 6 says a lot about spiritual warfare. It tells us our primary enemy is the devil and other evil, spiritual forces. It tells us to put on the spiritual armor of the gospel so we're protected and prepared to fight. It also tells us to "pray at all times in the Spirit."

Since the devil never takes a break, we can't afford to take one either. This means constant, alert prayer, recognizing we're in the middle of an extended, ongoing war and always in danger of taking fire. Prayer-meeting prayers are fine and good, but if that's all the praying we're doing, we're not ready for what's coming. Unless your prayer group can follow you around 24-7, you need to stay active in prayer as a matter of personal course.

Guidance

We have a desperate need to know what to do. We need to hear God's voice, and He speaks to us through the Scriptures with just the right message at just the right time. But we've got to ask. Prayer is our request to hear. It's turning to God—asking and listening. It's imploring the Holy Spirit to give us wisdom. In John 10:27, Jesus said, "My sheep hear My voice, I know them, and they follow Me." If we don't hear from God, we will wander around aimlessly, and we'll be far more vulnerable to attack. Keep praying!

Bottom Line

Prayer is the way we stay close to God, our Commander in the battle. If we don't hear His orders, we will lose the battle.

Backward and Forward

A man's heart plans his way,
but the Lord determines his steps. (Prov. 16:9)

Constant

At the end of the year we tend to look back and evaluate how we did. Did we keep our resolutions? Were we disciplined in our eating, our exercising, our devotional life? Did we consistently invest in the relationships that matter most? Did we work hard to improve ourselves professionally? This can be a dreary exercise if we feel like we came up short once again.

Perhaps we ought to try another approach. Maybe it's not the best idea for us to decide what growth looks like and then set out to do it. At some point we probably need to face reality and ask ourselves if what we're doing is really working.

Guidance

God wants us to plan and take initiative, but it is so easy to leave Him out of the process. Even if we are certain the goals we set are God honoring, this doesn't mean we won't try pursuing them in our own strength. A better approach is to ask God to direct us and help us each step of the way. We are completely dependent on Him for success and growth. We will sometimes fail, and we will need His forgiveness often. The Christian life is full of fresh starts. It is a life of continual repentance and faith. To grow spiritually is to depend on God more, not less. Our main goal should be to stay close to Him.

Bottom Line

As we focus all of our energies on staying close with God, we will accomplish far more than we could ever do on our own. Make God Himself your goal.

About Walk Thru the Bible

For more than three decades, Walk Thru the Bible has been dedicated to igniting a passion for God's Word worldwide through live events, devotional magazines, and resources designed for both small groups and individual use. Known for innovative methods and high-quality resources, we serve the whole body of Christ across denominational, cultural, and national lines.

Walk Thru the Bible communicates the truths of God's Word in a way that makes the Bible readily accessible to anyone. We are committed to developing user-friendly resources that are Bible centered, of excellent quality, life changing for individuals, and catalytic for churches, ministries, and movements; and we are committed to maintaining our global reach through strategic partnerships while adhering to the highest levels of integrity in all we do.

Walk Thru the Bible partners with the local church worldwide to fulfill its mission, helping people "walk thru" the Bible with greater clarity and understanding. Live events and small group curricula are taught in over 45 languages by more than 30,000 instructors in more than 100 countries, and more than 100 million devotionals have been packaged into daily magazines, books, and other publications that reach over 5 million people each year.

Walk Thru the Bible
www.walkthru.org
1-800-361-6131

Notes

Notes

Notes

Notes

Notes

Notes

Notes

Notes

Notes